Hybrid Play

This book explores hybrid play as a site of interdisciplinary activity—one that is capable of generating new forms of mobility, communication, subjects, and artistic expression as well as new ways of interacting with and understanding the world.

The chapters in this collection explore hybrid making, hybrid subjects, and hybrid spaces, generating interesting conversations about the past, current, and future nature of hybrid play. Together, the authors offer important insights into how place and space are co-constructed through play; how, when, and for what reasons people occupy hybrid spaces; and how cultural practices shape elements of play and vice versa.

A diverse group of scholars and practitioners provide a rich interdisciplinary perspective, which will be of great interest to those working in the areas of games studies, media studies, communication, gender studies, and media arts.

Adriana de Souza e Silva is a Professor of Communication at NC State University. Dr. de Souza e Silva works in the fields of mobile communication and internet studies, with a particular focus on how location-based technologies help us make sense of our interactions with public spaces and society.

Ragan Glover-Rijkse is a PhD student in the Communication, Rhetoric, and Digital Media program at NC State University. Her research considers the intersections between mobile media, infrastructures, and space/place.

Routledge Advances in Game Studies

For more information about this series, please visit: https://www.routledge.com

Hybrid Play

Crossing Boundaries in Game Design,
Player Identities and Play Spaces

**Edited by
Adriana de Souza e Silva and
Ragan Glover-Rijkse**

Routledge
Taylor & Francis Group

LONDON AND NEW YORK

First published 2020
by Routledge
2 Park Square, Milton Park, Abingdon, Oxon OX14 4RN

and by Routledge
605 Third Avenue, New York, NY 10017

First issued in paperback 2022

Routledge is an imprint of the Taylor & Francis Group, an informa business

Library of Congress Cataloging-in-Publication Data
A catalog record has been requested for this book

ISBN: 978-1-03-240058-7 (pbk)
ISBN: 978-0-367-42778-8 (hbk)
ISBN: 978-0-367-85505-5 (ebk)

DOI: 10.4324/9780367855055

Typeset in Sabon
by codeMantra

To Rafa, who loves games so much [Adriana]

To Ida Sue Glover and Barbara O. Glover, inspiring strong women [Ragan]

Contents

Figures

Contributors

Katreena E. Alder is a doctoral candidate in the PhD program in Communication, Rhetoric, and Digital Media at North Carolina State University with research interests in Black Film and Media Studies. During her time at NC State, she taught courses in International and Cross-Cultural Communication, Introduction to Film Studies, and Public Speaking. She is a Teaching Fellow at Augustana College during the 2019–2020 academic year.

Kristina Bell is an Assistant Professor of Game and Interactive Media Design and the Director of the Media Fellows in the Nido R. Qubein School of Communication at High Point University, where she teaches classes within interactive narrative design, multimedia storytelling, and game studies. Her PhD is from North Carolina State University in Communication, Rhetoric, and Digital Media. She specializes in ethnographic and qualitative methods, and her work focuses on the intersections of identity and video games. Her work has been published in journals such as *Game Studies, Ada: A Journal of Gender, New Media, and Technology*, and the *Journal of Interdisciplinary Feminist Thought*.

Claire Carrington is a Strategic Communications Specialist at PRA Health Sciences, where she designs visuals and content to make clinical research info more accessible to all audiences. She graduated summa cum laude from Campbell University in 2016 with dual degrees in Health Communication and Public Relations, where she was the 2016 Sullivan Award recipient. She also graduated from NC State University in 2018 summa cum laude with her MS in Communication; she was also the recipient of the NC State College of Humanities and Social Sciences Thesis Award that year with her thesis entitled "Blasting at Mastery: Math Blaster! As a Media Instrument." Her values and passions include nature, art, health research, connections, and communication. In her free time, she loves to design terrariums and sculptures, and is an avid reader and organizer.

Shira Chess (PhD 2009, Rensselaer Polytechnic Institute) is an Associate Professor of Entertainment and Media Studies in the Grady College of Journalism and Mass Communication at the University of Georgia. She is the author of *Ready Player Two: Women Gamers and Designed Identity* (University of Minnesota Press, 2017) and the forthcoming book *Play Like a Feminist* (MIT Press).

Adriana de Souza e Silva is a Professor at the Department of Communication at North Carolina State University (NCSU) and Director of the Mobile Gaming Research Lab. Dr. de Souza e Silva's research focuses on how mobile and locative interfaces shape people's interactions with public spaces and create new forms of sociability. She teaches classes on mobile technologies, location-based games, and Internet studies. Dr. de Souza e Silva is the co-editor and co-author of several books, including *Net-Locality: Why Location Matters in a Networked World* (Blackwell, 2011 with Eric Gordon), *Mobile Interfaces in Public Spaces: Control, Privacy, and Urban Sociability* (Routledge, 2012 with Jordan Frith), and *Mobility and Locative Media: Mobile Communication in Hybrid Spaces* (Routledge, 2014 with Mimi Sheller). She holds a PhD in Communication and Culture from the Federal University of Rio de Janeiro, Brazil.

Jessica Elam is an Assistant Professor of Mass Media at Baker University. Her research and teaching focuses on digital media and culture, the intersections of automation, military media technologies, and governance, new media composition and production, and the theory and practice of emerging technologies. She holds a Bachelor's degree in Biotechnology from Webster University in St. Louis, an MA in Anthropology from East Carolina University, and a PhD in Communication, Rhetoric, and Digital Media from North Carolina State University.

Sarah Evans, PhD, is an Assistant Professor of Digital Humanities and New Media at Molloy College. Her interdisciplinary research documents and interrogates inequalities in gaming and game design communities as it simultaneously seeks to disrupt, intervene in, and alleviate these inequalities. Through her work as a member of the research management team for the Refiguring Innovation in Games grant (ReFIG), Dr. Evans produced a co-authored, open-source, community-based game initiatives resource that brings together curricula, policies, and best practices of doing this type of work. She teaches classes on game design, digital production, and civic engagement through new media.

Ragan Glover-Rijkse is a doctoral student in the Communication, Rhetoric, and Digital Media (CRDM) program at NC State University (NCSU) and an affiliate of the Mobile Gaming Research Lab. At NC State, she teaches courses on mobile media and media writing in the Department of Communication. In addition to her teaching, her research focuses on the intersections between mobile media, mobilities, infrastructures, and space/place. She has attended to these intersections by considering such objects of study as mobile games, rural communities, Bluetooth beacons, RFID chips, and content delivery networks. She holds an MA from the University of South Carolina.

Larissa Hjorth, Distinguished Professor, is a socially engaged artist and digital ethnographer. Hjorth has two decades of experience working in interdisciplinary, collaborative, playful, and socially innovative digital media methods to explore intergenerational relationships in cross-cultural contexts. Hjorth has explored the socio-cultural dimensions of mobile media in many contexts such as Japan, South Korea, China, and Australia. Hjorth has published widely on the topic—recent publications include *Haunting Hands* (with Cumiskey, Oxford University Press), *Understanding Social Media* (with Hinton, 2nd Edition, Sage), *Creative Practice Ethnographies* (with Harris, Jungnickel, and Coombs, Rowman & Little), and *Ambient Play* (with Richardson, MIT Press). Much of her participatory art projects seek to provide playful critical reflection on quotidian environment and media practices from mobile games about climate change, to transforming the gallery into a Minecraft/Lego game to what happens to our data after we die (#dataofthedead). Recent exhibitions include *Model Citizen* (RMIT Gallery, February 2019). Hjorth has a strong track record in leadership from five Australian Research Council grants, co-founding the Digital Ethnography Research Centre (DERC) to university leadership roles like Deputy Dean in R&I (School of M&C) and Acting Associate Deputy Vice Chancellor. Hjorth is currently the Design & Creative Practice (DCP) Platform director at RMIT University. The Platform focuses on interdisciplinary collaboration and creative solutions to real-world problems—especially in relation to social innovation through playful, multisensorial methods. See http://dcp-ecp.com.

Cameron Kunzelman is a Lecturer for the College of Liberal Arts at Mercer University where he also works in the Office of Fellowships & Scholarships. He is completing his PhD in Moving Image Studies at Georgia State University, where he is completing a dissertation, titled Assembling the End, on how humans mediate their deaths as individuals and as a species. His research sits at the intersection of video games, visual culture, and science fiction. His academic publications have appeared in *Wide Screen Journal, Science Fiction Film & Television,* and the BioShock collected volume *Beyond the Sea.* He has worked as a video game critic and journalist across a wide range of publications including *Waypoint, Kotaku, Polygon,* and *Paste Games* where he is Editor at Large.

Ilaria Mariani, PhD in Design, is Contract Professor at School of Design, and Research Fellow at Department of Design, Politecnico di Milano.

She designs, investigates, and lectures in complex system for communication, especially games and interactive narratives as systems for communication and social innovation, between ethics and aesthetics. Her research—theoretical and practical—mainly addresses how meaningful play experiences can activate reflection, cultural and/or social impact. Covering the fields of studies of Communication Design and Game Studies (and Game Design), and to a diverse extent Sociology and Anthropology, she researches on (physical, digital, and hybrid) games and play(er) experiences. Her studies also focus on comprehending the impact of communication systems on players/users. As such, she assesses the effectiveness of artifacts in transferring meanings, combining qualitative and quantitative research, and employing interdisciplinary mixed methods. As the author of scientific essays, articles, and journal contributions, she presents her work and research at national and international conferences. She is co-author of *"Game Design"* (Pearson, 2014) and *"Location-Based Mobile Games. Design Perspectives"* (Springer, 2018).

Frans Mäyrä, PhD, is the Professor of Information Studies and Interactive Media, with specialization in digital culture and game studies at Tampere University, Finland. Since 2002, he has been heading the Tampere University Game Research Lab, and has taught and studied digital culture and games from the early 1990s. He is widely consulted as an expert in socio-cultural issues related to games, play, and playfulness. His research interests range from game cultures, meaning making through playful interaction and online social play, to borderlines, identity, as well as transmedial fantasy and science fiction. He is also the director of the Academy of Finland funded *Centre of Excellence in Game Culture Studies* (2018–2025).

Jordi Piera-Jimenez is dually trained in Computing Science Engineering by the Autonomous University of Barcelona (UAB) and in Enterprise Management and Direction also by the UAB. Further to that, he also holds MSc in Telemedicine and E-health delivered by the Open University of Catalonia (UOC) and is currently a PhD candidate on Information Society also for UOC. His PhD project entitled "Assessment of ICT-enabled innovations into the health and social care environments: the use of the cost-effectiveness analysis" is researching into the validity of different Health Technology Assessment (HTA) models for cost-effectiveness analysis for proper decision making. He started working at BSA in 2000, first as an analyst and software developer inside the ICT Department where he actively participated in the deployment and implementation of the Electronic Medical Record and in a number of research and innovation projects. Nowadays he shares his responsibilities both leading the ICT Department and the Research & Innovation Department. He is currently visiting Professor at the University of Udine (Italy) in Integrated Care and Professor Collaborator at the Open University of Catalonia (Spain) in Information Systems Strategic Planning.

Ingrid Richardson is an Associate Professor in Digital Media at Murdoch University, Western Australia. She has a broad interest in the human-technology relations and has published widely on the phenomenology of games and mobile media, digital ethnography, and the cultural and corporeal effects of wearable technologies and augmented reality. Ingrid is co-author of *Gaming in Social, Locative and Mobile Media* (Palgrave, 2014), *Ambient Play* (MIT, 2020), *Understanding Games and Game Cultures* (Sage, 2020) and *Exploring Minecraft: Ethnographies of Play and Creativity* (Palgrave, forthcoming).

Joel Schneier is a Lecturer in the Department of Writing & Rhetoric at the University of Central Florida in Orlando, Florida. He earned a PhD from the Communication, Rhetoric, & Digital Media program at North Carolina State University. His research investigates questions at the intersection of mobile communication, writing, and sociolinguistics, with a focus on process-based and computational methods for empirically studying how individuals meaningfully interface and interact with others through mobile technology. In addition to his research examining collaborative *Minecraft* play on mobile devices, his recent research has included developing keystroke-logging methods for studying synchronous writing processes on mobile devices. His research has been published in the academic journals *New Media & Society*, *Mobile Media & Communication*, and *Digital Humanities Quarterly*, as well as the edited collections *Language Variety in the New South*, and *The 5-Minute Linguist*.

Davide Spallazzo has a PhD in Design and is an Assistant Professor at the Department of Design, Politecnico di Milano. He mainly researches and lectures in the field of Interaction Design, interweaving design and technology with Communication, Product and Interior Design. Over the years, he investigated in theory and practice the role of mobile technologies in everyday life, envisioning innovative ways to employ mobile devices for learning and social purposes. His study focused in particular on the employment of mobile technologies and mobile gaming as a way to foster education and social engagement in cultural contexts. He looked at hybrid games from a design perspective, investigating them as both artifacts able to involve players in learning activities and stimulating contexts of experimentation for design students. He leads courses at the School of Design of Politecnico di Milano, including the elective course Augmented Reality and Mobile Experience. He has been involved in several national and international research projects concerning the use mobile technologies, virtual and augmented reality and gaming for museums, historic monuments, archives, and for tourism. He has authored scientific essays and articles, has presented his research in national and international contexts, and is co-author of *"Location-Based Mobile Games. Design Perspectives"* *(Springer, 2018)*.

Nick Tandavanitj has worked with Blast Theory since 1994. In this time, Nick has focused on creative approaches to computing, contributing to the group's unique mix of skills in structuring interactivity and narrative. This has led to particular skills in 3D modeling, technical design & programming for interactive installations and web-based artwork. Nick studied Art & Social Context at Dartington College of Arts from 1990 to 1993, collaborating for 2 years with Alison Cannon on a number of videos and performances. Following college, Nick became a friend and hanger on of the artists at Jamaica Street Studios in Bristol, occasionally working for Oil Experts and Stoloff & Hopkinson™ as well as working with Bristol-based artists Sophie Warren and Charlotte Crewe. In 2003, Nick became an Arts and Humanities Research Council Research Fellow at the University of Nottingham undertaking a nine-month program of research into artistic, social, and gaming applications which use mobile technology. Nick also teaches as part of Blast Theory's program of masterclasses and workshops. This work incorporates introductions to a variety of tools for prototyping and to concepts and techniques for generating interactivity. Nick has also contributed to a number of academic papers with the Mixed Reality Lab.

Stephen B. Crofts Wiley is an Associate Professor of Communication at North Carolina State University. He has conducted ethnographic research in Latin America from 1985 to the present, examining the role of media, memory, and social movements in the composition of social space. His current book project draws on participatory media ethnography among young adults in Concepción, Chile, to understand subject formation and agency in the context of transnational media fields, mobilities, and social networks. His work has appeared in the journals *Communication Theory, Cultural Studies, Media, Culture & Society,* and *Subjectivity,* among others. He is the co-editor, with Jeremy Packer, of *Communication Matters: Materialist Approaches to Media, Mobility, and Networks* (Routledge, 2013).

Acknowledgments

The seed for this book came from the CRDM Research Symposium, which takes place annually at NC State University. Every year, since 2010, a select group of faculty and students from the interdisciplinary PhD program in Communication, Rhetoric, and Digital Media (CRDM) organize a public, in-house event around themes related to the main research goals of the program, such as digital media, rhetoric, environmental communication, mobile communication, and mobilities, just to name a few. The symposium has served as an opportunity for students to interact with prominent scholars, local and from around the world. It has also created opportunities for CRDM students and faculty to present their own work to a wider audience.

In 2018, Adriana de Souza e Silva, Nick Taylor, and Ragan Glover-Rijkse organized a two-day symposium, titled Hybrid Play. The scholarship and ideas exchanged during this event inspired much of what populates this collection. Therefore, we would like to thank those who helped make this event a reality: Nick Taylor, for co-chairing the symposium with Adriana and helping to invite excellent speakers. Beyond the main organizers, we would also like to thank special event organizers: Justin Grandinetti and Eddie Lohmeyer who, together with Ragan, organized the first expo of retro mobile gaming devices and software for the Mobile Gaming Research Lab; and Eddie Lohmeyer, Jessica Elam, and Sarah Evans, who organized a critical play workshop during the event. Both of these opportunities were critical for engaging the public in a more practical way and promoting the event and the idea of hybrid play to a broader audience. Further, we would like to acknowledge auxiliary contributors: Marat Sadana for documenting the event, Nick Kotecti for the design of the promotional material and visual identity of the symposium, and Madison Beecher for serving as our public relations representative. Finally, we would like to thank our key partners: the CRDM Program Associate, Jeff Leonard, who helped us with the symposium logistics and paperwork, as well as the CRDM program, NC State's Dean's Office, CHASS Research Office, the Office for Institutional Equity and Diversity, and the

Departments of Communication and English at NC State University, who offered financial support to make this event happen.

After the symposium, we decided to create an edited book featuring the symposium's content and theme, and we would like to thank our invited speakers who agreed to contribute to our project, namely, Larissa Hjorth, Shira Chess, and Nick Tandavanitj. At the same time, we are in debt to the graduate students and NC State faculty who also presented their research at the event and worked hard to transform their presentations into chapters for this book: Katreena Alder, Kristina Bell, Claire Carrington, Sarah Evans, Cameron Kunzelman, Jessica Elam, Missy Hannah, Joel Schneier, and Steve Wiley. Finally, thanks to other very prominent game scholars who also joined this project, contributing to the breadth and internationalization of our perspectives on hybrid play: Frans Mäyrä, Davide Spallazzo, Ilaria Mariani, Ingrid Richardson, and Jordi Piera-Jimenez.

We are also grateful for the support and guidance from the editor of the Routledge Research Series, Suzanne Richardson, who believed in this project and guided us along the way.

I [Adriana] would like to thank Ragan for being extremely motivated about this book since the beginning, working tirelessly with me on editing chapters, multiple rounds of revisions, preparing the final manuscript, communicating with the authors, collecting images and permissions, and, really, organizing the whole process. I'm also grateful that Ragan is always ahead of the deadlines as well as extremely organized, two essential characteristics for the success of an edited collection production process. But most importantly, I'm thankful because working with Ragan is effortless and easy.

Finally, I would like to thank my husband, Rafael Cabezas, who loves playing games. While sometimes it's hard to talk about specific research topics with those who are outside of our research fields, it was fun to talk about the book with him—an outsider, but who could offer extremely meaningful comments and perspective on the book contents. Most importantly, thanks for the continuing support and understanding, especially since I had to work mostly on nights and weekends to complete this project.

I [Ragan] would like to thank Adriana for inviting me to co-edit this collection and guiding me through the process of writing a book proposal, editing chapters, corresponding with authors, and organizing the materials for publication. I am additionally grateful for Adriana's attention to detail, organization, and strong work ethic, which has made this process both fun and stress-free. She has been, and continues to be, an inspiring mentor who has given me countless opportunities and demonstrated how to be confident and resolute in academia. Further, if it were not for her, I would have never found my love for "play."

I would also like to thank my husband, Ray Rijkse, for his love and support throughout the process of editing this collection. Ray has been understanding while I've worked on this book in the early mornings and weekends. He's also served as an indispensable sounding board for my ideas about experiences of play and hybridity. Most of all, though, I am grateful for his daily "Poké-Walks" with me, which have given me the chance to take a break, spend quality time with him, and reflect on what it means to engage in hybrid play.

Adriana de Souza e Silva & Ragan Glover-Rijkse (September 2019)

Hybrid Play Glossary

Amiibo

Nintendo (2014)
Physical toys and objects used as parts of a video game. By connecting the object with the game, players can earn bonus in the game or save game data to the amiibo. The interaction between the physical toy and the video game occurs through a near-field communication (NFC) tag and tag reader: each toy or object is equipped with the tag, and the toy or object's tag is read by the tag reader. Over time, Nintendo has expanded the number of "NFC-tagged" objects beyond figurines to also include trading cards, which can be used in-game.

Anehdonia

Maddox Pratt (2014)
An online Twine game created by Maddox Pratt that is based off the author's own experiences with anehdonia, a symptom of depression that is an inability to feel pleasure. Pratt created the game during a panic attack and mimics the feelings/thoughts she experienced (Pratt, 2014). The game mixes images, simple animations, sounds, and text. The choices are very limited, and no good ending is possible; Pratt writes this to more accurately reflect depression (2014).

Atomic

Blast Theory (1998)
A performance designed to provoke reflection about what our choices and statements say about our identity. During the performance, the performers pushed one another to engage in transgressive acts, such as watching pornography publicly, smoking marijuana, flailing wildly, or kissing another.

A New World: An Autoethnographic Telling of Motherhood and Telltale's *The Walking Dead*

Kristina Bell (2018)

An online interactive autoethnography by Kristina Bell created in 2018. It explores her experience playing *The Walking Dead* video game series as a new mother. It includes discussions about gender norms, parenting, post-partum anxiety, and gendered technologies surrounding gaming and child-birth. It is heavily text-based, with some video, images, and sound effects.

Angry Birds

Rovio (2010)

A mobile app physics game, in which the player uses a slingshot to stra-tegically fling bird-like "bombs" to disrupt structures built by pigs. The goal of the game is for the player to cause the most destruction as possible to the pigs' structures in order to increase the player's game score. Players compete for high scores within the game.

Bee

Emily Short (2012)

An online, free-to-play, interactive fiction piece by Emily Short, created in 2012. It tells the story of a home-schooled girl as she copes with interpersonal drama/crises as she practices for a national spelling bee. Players progress through the narrative by choosing among options about how to handle each of the crises.

BioShock 2

2k Marin (2010)

This game is a sequel to the 2007 game, *BioShock*. *Bioshock 2* gameplay involves first person in the underwater city of Rapture. Gameplay addi-tionally involves collecting items in the city, which can be used for combat. *Bioshock 2* notably reverses the first game's objectivist viewpoint by mak-ing collectivism the central ideology conflict.

Bloodborne

FromSoftware (2015)

Directed by Hidetaka Miyazaki, who also directed *Dark Souls* and *Dark Souls 3*, this game takes the mechanics and narrative conceits of those games and places them into a Lovecraftian context. The player takes on the guise of a hunter who defeats various people, creatures, and nightmares on the way to fulfilling a strange prophecy.

Botfighters

It's Alive (2001)

Botfighters is considered the first location-based mobile game launched in 2001 in Stockholm, Sweden. It was designed as an urban Massively Multi-player Online Role-Playing Game (MMORPG). In the game, players take on the role of a robot warrior. The objective of the game was to locate, in the city, other player-robots and to engage in a battle to destroy them via "shooting" text-messages. A successful shot depended on the players' distance to each other and character's strength.

Candy Crush Saga

King (2012)

A match-3 mobile game where players move brightly colored pieces of candy to "match" them based on color combos. For every matched color combo, the player is able to earn points. The purpose of the game is to make as many matches as possible using a limited number of moves.

Can You See Me Now?

Blast Theory and Mixed Reality Lab (2001)

Considered one of the first hybrid reality games, *Can You See Me Now?* was played simultaneously by online players and runners on the streets of Sheffield, UK. While online players explored a 3D model of Sheffield on a computer, runners moved in the physical city using a personal digital assistant (PDA) equipped with global positioning system (GPS) and a walkie-talkie. Runners could see the location of online players on the PDA map and coordinate with each other via the walkie-talkie. The aim of online players was not to be caught or seen by runners. If an online player got caught by a "runner," they were knocked out of the game. The game has been re-enacted in many other cities in the world since then.

Chain Reactions

Samara Smith (2006)

A location-based game played in Midtown Manhattan, aimed at sensitizing players to the disappearance of independent enterprises in New York City. Each time a player encounters another person carrying a particular consumer item (e.g., a Starbucks coffee cup or a Barnes & Noble bag), they must change direction. As result, players can get lost in the city in what resembles a modern *dérive*.

Chemical Wedding

Blast Theory (1992)
A promenade performance that examined the paranoia and stigma associated with AIDS. The performance featured projected computer animations, live performers, choreography, and audience participation. The components were designed to entangle spectatorship and performance. In addition to watching actors portray a character who is sick with AIDS, the audience also had to participate in the performance. For example, at different points during the performance, audiences were asked about whether they had ever taken an HIV antibody test and, if they answered "yes," they were expected to stand under a red-light as an announcement of their sexual history.

Clash of Clans

Supercell (2012)
A "freemium" mobile game featuring invest/express strategy. During gameplay, the player designs an army and attacks other players' armies. As players effectively attack other armies, they can gain resources that can improve their defense and attack. Further, the game is multiplayer and allows up to 50 players to form teams, known as "clans," that wage wars together.

Coming Out Simulator

Nicky Case (2014)
Coming Out Simulator is a semi-autobiographical interactive fiction video game that is free and online. It was created by Nicky Case as a submission for the Nar8 Game Jam. It tells the story about a young gay Asian-Canadian teen as he struggles to come out to his homophobic family. The game, which Case describes as a cross between Telltale's *The Walking Dead (2012)* and texting, looks like a minimalistic, animated comic with text-bubbled dialogue that players can choose between.

Dark Souls

FromSoftware (2011)
Originally released for the PlayStation 3 and the Xbox 360, *Dark Souls* is a third-person action game where the player takes on the role of the Chosen Undead who must ring two Bells of Awakening and enter the city of the gods. It is characterized by an animation system that commits players totally to an action once they have pressed a button, an obscure narrative, and a rewarding respawn system. It is known for its difficult boss fights.

Dark Souls 2

FromSoftware, 2014
A sequel to *Dark Souls* that continues that game's mechanical and narrative obscurity. It is notable for having a slightly lighter fantasy tone and a wider range of areas to travel, but it has been criticized for being less conceptually coherent than its predecessor.

Dark Souls 3

FromSoftware (2016)
The final game in the *Dark Souls* trilogy, completing the narrative begun in the original game. Featuring many items, locations, and characters from the first game in a far-future form, this game is widely regarded as a more faithful sequel to *Dark Souls* than *Dark Souls 2*.

Day of the Figurines

Blast Theory (2006)
A multiplayer game, in which participants create a figurine and place it on a physical gameboard. The gameboard represents a fictional town, and the players represent townspeople. The game takes place over the course of 24 days with each day representing one hour in the game's world. To interact in the game, players can remotely send SMS to indicate what they want their figurine to do. Further, players receive SMS indicating their figurine's status as well as inviting the player to make decisions or complete tasks for the town. The purpose of the game is for players to collaborate to sustain the town's sense of community. Beyond that, the game is not built with any other express purpose, therefore allowing players to invent their own reasons for playing.

Dead Cells

Motion Twin (2018)
A 2D shooter platformer with roguelike elements. As a run-based game, it asks players both to develop their skills and to unlock specific items that will make future runs easier to complete. Troubling the idea of a distinct "souls-like" genre, *Dead Cells* borrows from many types of games and obviously transcends most labels that are applied to it.

Defender

Williams Electronics (1981)
A side-scrolling arcade game that tasks players with traveling along the surface of an alien planet and defeating the enemies who live there. Players

defeat aliens by shooting them with missiles in order to score points and advance to the next level. However, players also have to avoid being captured by aliens, which results in losing a spaceship. Players can only lose three spaceships before they lose the game. The game has been adapted to many different platforms since its initial release, and it remains a classic of the arcade genre.

Desert Rain

Blast Theory/Mixed Reality Lab (1999)
An interactive war game played on a computer. In the game, participants are asked to carry out an ostensibly fictional war mission. After the game's completion, participants learn that the mission is based on the Gulf War and that their targets were real people involved in the war. The game is meant to reflect on the realities of war given that war is increasingly carried out in a computer-mediated environment.

Diner Dash

Gamelab/Playfirst (2004)
A time management game, in which the player takes on the role of a waitress, Flo, to serve customers at the highest happiness levels in order to earn more money. If customers are satisfied, then Flo earns enough money to progress to the next level.

Detroit: Becoming Human

Quantic Dream (2018)
An interactive narrative video game dealing with the topic of what it means to be human in a world populated by humanoid androids. Revolving around three android characters, the game presents their stories and questions the relationship between human and sentient androids inspecting different perspectives. Coping with quick-time, challenging events, the player is asked to make interesting choices that drastically impact the evolution of the story. Throughout the gameplay, multiple playable characters can die and the story branches out progressing without them.

Depression Quest

Zoë Quinm (2013)
A free-to-play, online interactive fiction game created by Zoë Quinn on Twine. It walks players through a character's experience of depression. Players may make choices that range from whether to eat out or cook at home to how much they disclose to their loved ones about their depression.

The choices a player makes influences their ability to make future choices, as some choices become crossed off as a symptom of depression.

Detritus

Mary Hamilton (2013)
A short, online game made by Mary Hamilton in Twine. *Detritus* is a character study about someone who has moved away and is starting a new life. Players choose what to unpack and what to keep, as actions trigger specific memories and reflections on their past life and future choices.

Drop.it

Francesca Bonfim Bandeira, Sara Marcon, Chiara Namias, and Marco Paris (2016)
Drop.it is a location-based mobile game designed in the course Augmented Reality & Mobile Experience in the School of Design at Politecnico di Milano. The aim of the game is to raise players' awareness of environmental issues. In a dystopic future characterized by overbuilding and lack of water, players, in the role of heroes, must go back in time to our present moment to change the habits of the population and raise awareness of the importance of nature and water itself. To reach this aim, players must complete quests on their mobile device while collect ampoules filled of water that are displayed in various point of interest.

FarmVille

Zynga (2009)
A multiplatform invest/express game asking the player to tend to various farm activities, allowing them to design their farmland. Players must complete farm-related tasks to earn XP (experience points), which allows them to level up. Further, upon leveling up, players can earn in-game currency, which allows them to purchase items, such as cattle and crops, to improve their game play.

Florence

Annapurna Interactive (2018)
A short narrative mobile game that allows the player to experience a story of first love and loss. The game follows the narrative of 25-year-old Florence Yeoh, as she goes through her daily life. Gameplay is divided across 20 levels, which involves players completing small tasks in order to progress the narrative.

Karen

Blast Theory (2015)
An interactive performance piece in which participants agree to correspond via mobile app with Karen, a life coach. In actuality, Karen is not a real person, but rather an automated software system that corresponds with the participants. Initially, Karen asks participants general questions about their life. However, over time, Karen becomes increasingly invasive of participants' lives. She begins messaging at inopportune moments, like the middle of the night. She also collects participants' data. At the end of the experience, users receive a report of the data collected about them. The piece is meant to provoke reflection about the role of technology and data collection in our personal lives.

Kidnap

Blast Theory (1998)
A performance piece in which participants purchased a £10 lottery ticket in order to be kidnapped. Two lottery winners were chosen and kidnapped on a specified day at a non-specified time. The winners were taken to an undisclosed location, and their kidnapping was broadcast live via the internet. The piece was intended to provoke critical reflection about consenting to harmful activities, and it was developed in response to the Spanner Trials in the United Kingdom, in which homosexual men were prosecuted for taking part in consensual sadomasochist sexual activities.

Kim Kardashian Hollywood (KK:H)

Glu Mobile (2014)
An invest/express mobile game, where the player roleplays as celebrity Kim Kardashian and works their way up from the E-List to A-List while designing the life of their young star.

Geocaching

Dave Ulmer (2000)
A location-based treasure hunt game, in which players seek out hidden "caches," using clues and GPS coordinates. Caches are hidden by other players and often contain small objects, like tokens or notes, for players to find. Players can take objects from the cache, under the expectation that they leave something equally valuable. The GPS coordinates, and clues are often posted on the Geocaching website. The location of caches can vary from public locations to tunnels to underground sewage pipes. Geocaching is played with a GPS device so that players can find the approximate location of the cache.

Guitar Hero

RedOctane/Activision (2005)

One- and two-player multiplatform video game in which players use a "guitar-shaped" controller to perform songs. The guitar-shaped controller features five input buttons that function as frets and a strumming key that moves up and down. Players can choose among a number of popular songs to perform. Performing a song involves pressing the correct fret keys (which are displayed on the game screen) and strumming the controller based on the beat of the song. The purpose of the game is to record high scores by performing the song well.

Harry Potter: Wizards Unite

Niantic (2019)

Harry Potter: Wizards Unite is a location-based augmented reality mobile game inspired by J.K. Rowling's Wizarding World and the Harry Potter franchise. Country after country, the game is expanding worldwide, allowing its players to experience magic in the real world, visiting iconic locations in the wizarding world by accessing AR-powered Portkeys. The game allows players to walk around the physical world, using GPS to locate players and make them interact with the characters of the saga. In the gameplay, they face Wizarding Challenges, collecting clues for solving the mystery, also taking advantage of being multiplayer. Without revealing the existence of the magical world, the goal is to restore balance between the two worlds.

Hellblade: Senua's Sacrifice

Ninja (2017)

An action-adventure dark fantasy game developed by Ninja Theory, available on PC, PS4, XBox ONe, and Nintendo Switch and offers VR support. The game follows a warrior who struggles with psychosis as she seeks to rescue her dead lover's soul from a goddess. Gameplay consists of fighting and puzzle solving, and incorporates motion captured live action performances within its cutscenes.

Infinity Series

Disney (2013)

A toys-to-life video game, in which physical toys, from the Disney Franchise, are used as a part of a video game. The interaction between the physical toy and the video game occurs through a near-field communication (NFC) tag and tag reader: each Disney toy is equipped with the tag, and the toy's tag is read by the tag reader. Gameplay varies based on the Disney character that the toy represents.

Ingress

Niantic (2012)
A location-based Massively Multiplayer Online Game available for Android and iOS, and translated over time in 16 languages. Players divided into two opposing factions—Enlightened and Resistance—must roam the city to capture portals in places of recognized cultural relevance in order to create virtual triangles and control the field.

King's Field

FromSoftware (1994)
Released for the PlayStation, *King's Field* is a first-person fantasy game that shares many of the characteristics of *Dark Souls*, including an obscure plot, a darker tone, and mechanics that are not immediately clear to the player. In the game, players take on the role of a character named Hauser Forrester. Gameplay involves completing tasks and battling.

Lego Dimensions

Traveller's Tales/Warner Brothers (2015)
A multiplatform toys-to-life video game, in which physical toys are used as a part of a video game. The interaction between the physical toy and the video game occurs through an NFC tag and tag reader: each toy is equipped with the tag, and the toy's tag is read by the tag reader. Gameplay involves completing puzzles and meeting in-game objectives to progress through the levels. Importantly, the external hardware of the game is customizable because it is built from Legos, which allow for assembling, disassembling, and re-assembling.

Letterboxing

James Perrott (1854)
A scavenger hunt game, in which players hide letterboxes for other players to find. Each letterbox contains either a letter or a postcard. More recent iterations of the game include a "stamp" so that players can stamp their logbook/diary which includes a list of letterboxes they have visited; further, the letterboxes contain a log, in which players can record their visit to the letterbox for other players to view. While in early iterations of this game, letterboxes were found spontaneously or by communal knowledge, in more recent iterations, letterboxes can also be found based on information posted on the internet.

Lords of the Fallen

CI Games (2014)
Set in a fantasy world modeled on Norse aesthetics, *Lords of the Fallen* follows *Dark Souls* in its mechanical and spatial architectures. Featuring

slow, methodical combat and a nonlinear world with many possible paths, it is a notable game within the souls-like or soulsborne genres.

Mangia

Nina Freeman (2014)
An online, free-to-play, interactive narrative built on Twine by Nina Freeman. It centers around her personal experience being diagnosed and coming to terms with eosinophilic esophagitis, a chronic illness that causes severe pain after eating small amounts. The narrative also discusses issues pertaining to her body-image and relationships with her family.

Math Blaster!

Knowledge Adventure Company (1983)
An educational game for the Apple II computer launched in 1983, intended for an elementary school audience. It was the first game in the Blaster Learning System series. *Math Blaster!* contains drill-and-skill math problems, requiring players to complete math puzzles at an increasingly rapid rate. The original version was circus-themed and featured a man launched from a cannon and seals bouncing balls. It later featured an outer space theme and a space-faring protagonist named Blasternaut; this version also required teachers to manually pre-program problem sets for students to complete within the game.

Metal Gear Solid

Konami (1998)
An action/adventure stealth game only available on consoles. Gameplay involves navigating a maze without being detected by the enemy. A player is detected by the enemy when they move within the enemy's line of sight. If a player is detected, then multiple enemies will begin to approach the player. The player's goal is, then, to evade the enemy. The player's goal is also to find and defeat bosses.

Minecraft

Mojang (2011)
A game by Mojang, that involves players surviving and creating in a procedurally-generated, block-like game world. Through either Survival or Creative mode, players can use their avatars to explore seemingly infinite and procedurally-generated ecologies, mine for resources, craft tools and weapons, build complex structures, and even fight off monsters and starvation. User-maintained servers and mods, as well as countless enthusiastic sub-communities and celebrity players mean that *Minecraft* is as much a game as it is a social media network or platform with seemingly infinite

permutations of play—all within the seemingly low-resolution confines of this blocky, LEGO-like world. Purchased by Microsoft in 2015, *Minecraft* can be played on PC, gaming consoles, and mobile devices as *Minecraft Pocket Edition*.

My Father's Long, Long Legs

Michael Lutz (2013)
A free-to-play online interactive fiction horror game, created by Michael Lutz. It tells a story that focuses on a man's experiences with his father, who spends all his time digging a hole in his basement for an unknown reason. The game uses sound effects of digging, a flashlight lighting effect, and a drawing interwoven with the text.

Nineteen

Elizabeth Sampat (2013)
Nineteen is a free-to-play interactive narrative on Twine by Elizabeth Sampat. On her website, she writes that she was inspired to write it after hearing of Aaron Swartz's death and based it off her own experience with depression. The title, Nineteen, is significant because it had been 19 years since she had tried to kill herself.

Nioh

Team Ninja (2017)
Often considered a part of the souls-like or soulsborne genre, *Nioh* is a third-person action game that takes place in a fictionalized version of the year 1600. Iterating on the design of games like *Dark Souls*, it features a complex stance system, but also maintains a focus on boss battles and player skill in a mode reminiscent of FromSoftware's games.

Operation Black Antler

Blast Theory (2016)
A performance piece, in which participants adopt the role of an undercover police officer and are given a mission to surveil a group of people in a pub. In completing this mission, the participants have to justify their surveillance of the group of people. The piece was developed to provoke reflection about undercover police surveillance. It was developed primarily in response to the Special Demonstrations Squad, which was a surveillance program in the United Kingdom that involved long-term surveillance of people.

Papa & Yo

Minority Media Inc. (2012)
An adventure game by Minority Media Inc. and available on PS3, PC, OS X, and Linux. It tells the story of a young Brazilian boy who discovers an alternative reality as he hides from his abusive father in one of the favelas. Gameplay consists of solving puzzles (such as moving building) to explore and navigate through the environment.

Papers, Please

Lucas Pope, 3990 (2013)
An indie videogame that set players into the shoes of an immigration inspector in charge of controlling the people who are trying to enter the Arstotzkan side of Grestin from Kolechia. These people can be immigrants or visitors, but also smugglers, spies, and even terrorists. Relying on sets of provided documents, the player has to inspect, search, and then decide who can enter Arstotzka, who will be refused, and who will be arrested. By playing this game, the player has a glance of how the immigration system works (on the "control" side). The game touches on some of the heartbreaking stories and situations that characterize such a job.

Polar Pop Mania

Storm8 Studios (2015)
A physics game where the player shoots bubbles to release small baby seals that are trapped within the bubbles. By shooting the bubbles, this saves the baby seals on behalf of a mother seal; it additionally earns the player points. The purpose of the game is to gain high scores by popping as many bubbles as possible.

Pokémon Go

Niantic (2016)
A location-based mobile game that allows augmented reality play, if enabled by the player. The purpose of the game is multifaceted: to catch virtual creatures, known as Pokémon; to gain XP (experience points); and to earn badges, as a display of accomplishment within the game. As a part of gameplay, players must visit locations to spin virtual objects, known as Pokéstops, which gives them items that can be used in the game. Further, players can visit gyms, which allow them to participate in battles; to earn in-game currency; and to Raid, which is an often multiplayer activity of battling with a powerful Pokémon.

Queers in Love at the End of the World

Anna Anthropy (2013)
A short, online, free-to-play Twine interactive fiction game. The game, which utilizes a time mechanic, gives players 10 seconds to react to the end of the world. They may kiss their partner, hold her hand, take her, or tell her. The player's choices unlock subsequent choices until the 10 seconds is up and the world is wiped away.

Rewind

Giulia Gubbiani, Marina Rico-Sanchez, Eloisa Ronchi, Anita Rosti, and Ilaria Tabasso (2014)
A location-based mobile game designed in the course Augmented Reality & Mobile Experience in the School of Design at Politecnico di Milano. In the game, the Earth was hit by a powerful spell, cast by Mother Nature who decided to give a lesson to the crowds in the waiting rooms of plastic surgeons, who are terrified by a wrinkle on their forehead. The spell reversed the course of their lives. Suddenly, everybody is aged, and the player's aim is to dissolve the curse within a certain timeframe and to restore life to its natural flow.

Riderspoke

Blast Theory/Mixed Reality Lab (2007)
An interactive piece in which participants ride bicycles equipped with a handheld computer mounted on the handlebars. As participants ride throughout the city, they are asked to answer a question, record their answer, and assign their answer to a specific location by digitally embedding it on a map. Players can also ride around the city and listen to other participants' answers in specific locations.

Rockband

Harmonix (2007)
Multiplayer and multiplatform video game in which players can either sing or play a variety of instruments, including drums, guitar, bass, or piano. If players sing, they are scored based on how well they match the notes. If players play an instrument, they are graded based on their ability to keep rhythm and press they right keys. The purpose of the game is to record high scores by performing the song well.

Scarfmemory

Michael Brough (2013)
A free-to-play text-based interactive narrative built on Twine. It is a simple story about a scarf that the character makes and then loses. The narrative

features stream-of-consciousness style narrative. Players interact with the narrative by clicking on text modules that expand. Each text module offers a memory or detail about the lost scarf.

September 12th

Gonzalo Frasca, Newsgaming (2003)
The player performs the role of a sniper who instead of firing bullets, throws missiles. The rule is very simple: the player can shoot or not. In the first case, however, players do not just kill the terrorists but also civilians. When civilians die, other civilians become terrorists, and in a short time span, everybody turns into terrorists. However, by refusing to shoot, the player gets shot. This is a game in which winning is not allowed, and it is intended to trigger discussion among young players about the War on Terror.

Skylanders

Activision (2011)
A toys-to-life video game, in which physical toys are used as a part of a video game. The interaction between the physical toy and the video game occurs through a near-field communication (NFC) tag and tag reader: each toy is equipped with the tag, and the toy's tag is read by the tag reader. Once the NFC tag is read, a representation of the toy is displayed in the game. Gameplay involves adventuring through the game in order to destroy villains and to ultimately destroy the game's primary antagonist, Kaos.

SpaceWar!

Steve Russel (1962)
A two-player game, written for the DEC PDP-1 computer. Gameplay involves two spaceships battling with one another, using a limited number of torpedoes for attack. Gameplay additionally includes avoiding torpedoes as well as stars, which destroy the spaceship and result in losing the game.

SOS-Rescue Squad

Panza, Martina, Leonardo Pozzi, Paolo Rota, and Debora Veschi (2016)
SOS-Rescue Squad is a location-based mobile game designed in the course, Augmented Reality & Mobile Experience in the School of Design at Politecnico di Milano. The game deals with bad behavior in parks, such as the disturbance of public peace, xenophobia, and disrespect for flora and fauna. In the game, five guardians from a dystopic 2116 future—overpopulated, highly polluted, and without greenery—undertake a journey back to the present. But in the course of the journey something goes wrong; the guardians are stuck in a space-time hole and cannot finish their journeys unless someone helps them. Four players, equipped with a

mobile device and a kit, adopt different roles (the strong, the fearless, the precise, and the hound) and must help the guardians to reach our world.

Stampede

Blast Theory/Interactive Media M.A. Program at Royal College of Arts (1994)
A promenade performance designed to prompt critical reflection about legislation created to regulate and surveil crowds. In the performance, the audience was positioned as a part of the crowd and, as a part of their experience, they heard loud music, viewed live video of the crowd, and watched choreography representing police behaviors.

Stardew Valley

ConcernedApe (2016)
A roleplaying, time-management game, available on multiple different platforms. The game is about a character, who must tend to their deceased father's farm. Gameplay involves performing a variety of tasks, such as planting and harvesting crops, raising livestock, and mining for minerals, in order to earn money and expand the farm.

Tennis for Two

William Higinbothan (1958)
A tennis game, on an analog computer, which includes a line to represent the tennis court, a line to represent the net, and a circle to represent the ball. The computer receives input from the players' handheld controllers which each feature a dial for adjusting position (up or down the court) and a button for returning the ball. Gameplay involves attempting to hit the ball so that the opponent cannot return the ball.

The 10 Commandments (*I dieci comandamenti*)

Lesley Ann Culla Laura DI Filippo, Chiara Frisia, and Maia Golan (2014)
A location-based mobile game designed in the course Augmented Reality & Mobile Experience in the School of Design at Politecnico di Milano. In the game, players are equipped with a mobile device and a game kit containing dilemma cards and instructions. Players retrace the day of a girl who has to attend a casting call. The mobile device provides the players with 10 commandments they must follow in order to have a "perfect slim body," unconsciously inducing the players to follow, in the safe space of the game, harmful rules for achieving anorexia. These "rules" are derived from online blogs that offer tips about so-called "Pro-Anorexia" (Pro-Ana) behavior and present anorexia as a positive philosophy of life. By following

these rules, players lose energy, because of the eating disorder. In contrast, by disobeying the rules, they acquire a sense of guilt. The game's purpose is to immerse players in the daily life of a person struggling with anorexia.

Tic-Tac-Toe (OXO)

A.S. Douglas (1952)
A simulation of the game tic-tac-toe, on a computer terminal. This game was one of the first computer games. Gameplay involved playing against the computer and attempting to make a horizontal, vertical, or diagonal line of either three Xs or three Os on a grid with nine available entry slots before the computer was able to do so.

Titan Souls

Acid Nerve (2015)
Often lumped into the souls-like or soulsborne genres, *Titan Souls* is a 2D, third-person action game with a focus on boss battles. Inheriting equally from the mechanics of *Dark Souls* and the aesthetics of the Zelda franchise of games, it is notable for being one of the first games to adapt the *Dark Souls* sensibility to 2D. Gameplay involves defeating monsters using only a single weapon: an arrow, which has to be retrieved by the player after every "shot" that the player takes.

That Dragon, Cancer

Numinous Games (2016)
An autobiographical exploration video game by Numinous Games, available on PC, Android, iOS, Mac, and Linux platforms. It tells the story of Ryan and Amy Green's experience raising their son, Joel, who was diagnosed with cancer at the age of 12 months and died four years later. Players explore various vignettes that memorialize their experience with their son and express their feelings and experiences during their time with him and their struggle to battle the disease.

The Fellowship of the Umbrella (*La Compagnia Dell'Ombrello*)

Sara Bianchini, Laura Mor, Valerio Princigalli, and Martina Sciannamé (2014)
A location-based mobile game designed in the course Augmented Reality & Mobile Experience in the School of Design at Politecnico di Milano. The game tackles the sensitive topic of physical disabilities and related issues by creating a fictional world that is a metaphoric transposition of some of the obstacles that persons with disabilities face. Set in Middle-earth, the game

tells the story of a group of four gifted individuals—an extraordinary magician, a wise dwarf, a powerful beech, and a sharp elf—and their adventures to reach a treasure. Each character is a metaphor of a disability: the magician who cannot speak because he is "in a water world", actually is dumb, and is the only one in charge of deciphering the smartphone; the beech tree has a motor disability; the elf is visually impaired; and the dwarf is deaf.

The Lost Papyrus *(Il Papiro Perduto)*

Andrea Benedetti, Carmen Franco Conesa, Alice De Marco, and Jessica Piatti (2015)
A location-based mobile game designed in the course Augmented Reality & Mobile Experience in the School of Design at Politecnico di Milano. The game was designed to raise awareness about the impact of Alzheimer's disease on the everyday activity of sick people and of those who live with them. Four players, equipped with a mobile device and a game kit, play the role of an expert archaeologist and his brave assistants exploring a still undiscovered tomb to find a renowned papyrus. In their search for recovering valuable ancient artifacts, players are led to face more and more difficult quests that symbolize the degeneration of the illness.

The Origins of Forging *(Le Origini Della Forgiatura)*

Belloni, Elisa, Carlotta Bucalossi, Christian Mazzoleni, and Marco Menini (2016)
A location-based mobile game designed in the course Augmented Reality & Mobile Experience in the School of Design at Politecnico di Milano. In the game, the players are guided by the mobile device to take on the role of Greek Gods, and asked to re-discover their mythological roots, which are bound to contemporary works of craftsmanship. It aims at conveying the practices and values of handicraft, by inviting players to explore the surrounding and interact with several artifacts and props placed in different places of the gamespace. Such interactions and activities are part of the missions that players need to accomplish to earn their role as in-game Gods.

The Rapture

Giuditta Conti, Giulia Saracino, Anca Serbanescu, and Nicolas Valente (2015)
A location-based mobile game designed in the course Augmented Reality & Mobile Experience in the School of Design at Politecnico di Milano. The game is designed around the "revolts of black blocs." Four players are plunged into a post-apocalyptic fictional world, controlled by the totalitarian government of Soviab. The game is set in Voidville, which has a radioactive liquid leak that has been ignored by the government. As a

consequence of this leak, various monsters have been born. Gameplay requires that players, in the roles of heroes, defeat the monsters.

The Surge

Deck13 (2017)
A science fiction game that places the player in the shoes of a character who is cybernetically bonded to a mechanical exoskeleton. While the third-person action mechanics are reminiscent of *Dark Souls*, it adds several features such as suit augmentation and the ability to critically damage parts of enemies to gain benefits in combat.

The Temple of No

Crows, Crows, Crows (2016)
A free-to-play interactive fiction game built on Twine. The game incorporates satire and humor to poke fun at itself and the genre of interactive fiction made in Twine. Players can choose among three characters to follow through a narrative about an adventure to the Temple of No. Players progress through the narrative by selecting underlined words. Typically, there are one to three underlined words for the player to click in order to progress through the narrative. At the end of the narrative, the character completes their adventure and shares the wisdom learned. The wisdom takes the form of question, which asks: "Have you ever played a good game made in twine? Like, one that's actually good—not just 'good for a twine game'?"

The Terror of Thetford

Dan St. Germain (2017)
An interactive fiction game made on Twine. The game falls in the Lovecraftian horror genre, and it uses sound and graphic effects to take the player on a journey of dark madness. The narrative is told using first-person perspective. Players advance through the narrative by making choices about how to interact with other characters. However, as the player advances through the narrative, the choices become more difficult to make—for instance, the choices will be written in blurred or backward font. These effects are intended to demonstrate the gradual descent into madness.

The Treasures of Captain Torment (*I Tesori di Capitan Tormento*)

Alessia Boni, Greta Frizzi, and Silvia Taccola (2015)
A location-based mobile game designed in the course Augmented Reality & Mobile Experience in the School of Design at Politecnico di Milano. The game deals with the mental condition of depressed people and aims to raise

awareness on the plight of individuals struggling with depression, who are very often affected by feelings of inadequacy, melancholy and hopelessness, and who feel progressively marginalized by relatives, friends and acquaintances. As the title suggests, the game is structured as a treasure hunt. Four players, in the role of pirates, are guided by the mobile device in the role of the Captain himself to find his legendary treasure, by succeeding in a series of assessments masterminded by the Captain to test their valor and bravery.

The Uncle Who Works for Nintendo

Michael Lutz and Kimberly Parker (2014)
A free-to-play online horror game by designer Michael Lutz and artist Kimberly Parker. The game, which is largely text-based, incorporates background drawings and atmospheric sound effects. The game tells the story about an 11-year-old child's experience at a slumber party at his/her best friend's house. Specifically, the story centers around the anticipation and interaction with the friend's monster of an uncle who visits in the middle of the night.

The Walking Dead

Telltale/Skybound (2012–2019)
The Walking Dead is a series of episodic adventure video games by Telltale (and later completed by Skybound) available on PS, XBox, PC, Android, and iOS. It tells the story of a young girl, Clementine, as she comes to age during a zombie apocalypse in the American south. Gameplay centers around making difficult choices, branching dialogue, inventory collection and utilization to solve puzzles, and quick time events. Player's decisions shape the narrative, the playable characters, and their relationships with others. The choices players make in each game impact the next one in the series, as they are carried over in a save file. Players can compare their choices with others at the end of each episode within each game.

This War of Mine

11 Bit Studios (2014)
A survival video game, available on PC/Mac, Android, iOS, PS4, Nintendo Switch, XBox One, and Linux. It is inspired by the Siege of Sarajevo during the Bosnian War and shows how war impacts civilian survivors. Players must gather food and supplies, craft tools, and interact with other survivors. They are asked to make difficult choices such as whether to let another starving civilian join their camp and share their supplies, or whether to steal from others to feed those who are starving.

Two-Dots

Playdots, Inc. (2014)
A simple puzzle game where the player is tasked with matching adjacent colored dots in order to remove them from the gameboard. Each level of the game has a restricted number of moves with the goal of removing all of the dots within that limited number of moves. As dots are removed, the positions of other dots on the gameboard shifts, which requires strategy to ensure that they still have dots that they can match to clear the board.

XCOM: The Board Game

Fantasy Flight Games
A role-playing board game with an accompanying mobile app, which is integral to the game. The game requires one to four players, and each of the players takes on a different role as either a commander, a chief scientist, a central officer, or a squad leader. The purpose of the game is to defend humanity against an alien invasion. Alien invasions occur throughout the game, and players are notified of the invasion via the mobile app.

Introduction

Understanding hybrid play

Adriana de Souza e Silva and
Ragan Glover-Rijkse

Hybridity can refer to the blurring of spaces (online/offline), subjects (scholar/activist), bodies (machinic/organic), and networks (human/inhuman). However, hybridity involves more than just a blurring of these boundaries. It also encompasses mobility and social practices (de Souza e Silva, 2006). Hybridity occurs as individuals move simultaneously through physical and digital spaces and connect to others both physically and digitally present. In addition, Benford and Giannachi (2011) indicate that hybridity emerges when individuals occupy "multiple timeframes," "a multitude of spaces," and "various roles" (p. 41). Together, these definitions consider hybridity as both created context and the uncertainty of context. That is, while hybridity produces new temporalities, spatialities, and identities, it simultaneously destabilizes them. To experience hybridity, then, is to exist between things, in the *intermezzo*, without ever being able to settle. Understanding hybridity, therefore, demands adopting a playful disposition—one that responds to the qualities of flux, spontaneity, and unpredictability inherent to the very nature of hybridity.

We understand *hybrid play*, then, as a deliberately open-ended term, but one that connotes the potential for experimental, spontaneous, whimsical, and even critical interventions that result in, or result from, the enfolding of multiple contexts. Further, we suggest that while hybrid play has the capacity to destabilize (or shift) boundaries, engender heterogeneity, and produce new types of mobilities, this edited collection demonstrates that hybrid play can also result in reproducing boundaries, maintaining homogeneity, and exposing immobilities. Hybrid play is also a generative framework for understanding our material engagements with any manner of ludic technologies. From mouse pads to Lilypads, and Pokémon GO to LEGO, play creates hybrid bodies, networks, and spaces. And crucially, the intensified need to address long-standing inequalities in digital play calls for a further hybrid: the scholar-activist, equally at home in designing interventions as in documenting practices.

We should not forget, however, that play is intrinsically hybrid. As German philosopher Eugen Fink (1974) stated, play is part of life, and as such, an activity already intertwined with daily life activities that cannot be separated from "serious life." Why is it then necessary to create a book about hybrid play? Game studies scholarship that emerged along with the increasing pervasiveness of video (screen-based) games in daily life during the past 30 years has often focused on play as (technologically, socially, geographically) bounded. Early game studies scholarship often obscured the fact that play is messy, entangled, and nebulous—that it has always been hybrid. Play has often been viewed as restricted to a magic circle apart from other daily life activities (Caillois, 2001; Huizinga, 1970). Although this narrow application of the magic circle to digital games has been criticized (Rodriguez, 2006), early digital games scholarship still very rarely engaged with games that take place outside the computer screen. For instance, Katie Salen and Eric Zimmerman's (2006) edited collection *The Game Design Reader* included seminal works on video game history and theory, but no chapter on location-based or pervasive games. Similarly, the *First*, *Second*, and *Third Person's* trilogy (Harrigan, Wardrip-Fruin, Parkin, Cornell, & Williams, 2017; Wardrip-Fruin & Harrigan, 2004, 2007) explored different aspects of the intersection among video games, narratives, performance, and role-play, but with no specific reference to the blurring of boundaries that necessarily occur within the act of play. And although this notion of play as separate from life has been contested (de Souza e Silva & Sutko, 2008; Rodriguez, 2006), still the notion of the screen-bounded, isolated, and static video gamer prevailed.

The increasing popularity of mobile devices in the past 20 years, however, which allow us to navigate urban spaces connected to the internet and each other, led to a new wave of scholarship on location-based, hybrid reality, and pervasive games. This scholarship most often highlights the hybridity of playful spaces. In these hybrid play spaces (de Souza e Silva, 2006), mobility, communication, and collaboration occur in a combination of the physical and the digital mediated by mobile devices. But *hybrid play* is not something that emerges when we use a mobile technology to play a game. Hybrid play is a subjective experience that includes mobile identities, bodies, and mobile ways of making. As one of the first books exploring aspects of hybrid play, Friedrich Von Borries et al.'s (2007) *Space, Time, and Play* considered how the physical world and game spaces are reshaped by moving away from the stationary computer screen and into urban spaces through the use of mobile devices. Similarly, de Souza e Silva and Sutko's (2009) *Digital Cityscapes* included chapters exploring the conceptual, design, and educational nature of location-based mobile games. Specifically, the authors in that collection explored how urban spaces become playful spaces with the introduction of location-based game play. Along these same lines, Markus Montola, Jaakko Stenros, and Annika Waern's (2009) *Pervasive Games* explored games designed to be played in public spaces. Moreover, Steve Benfords and Gabriela Giannachi's (2011) *Performing Mixed Reality* defined and documented mixed reality performances with a particular focus on the art/game hybrid. Finally, in *Location-Based Gaming: Play in Public Space*, Dale Leorke (2018) offered an important contribution to understanding the history of location-based games; he also used ethnography and autoethnography to interrogate the ways in which location-based games impact both relationships to, and wayfinding within, public spaces. Most of these works, however, focus on one aspect of hybridity—the hybridity of space brought about with location-based and pervasive games.

Another set of works focus more heavily on the design and practical aspects of these types of hybrid games. For example, Davide Spallazzo and Illaria Mariani's (2018) *Location-Based Mobile Games* recommend design approaches for location-based mobile games. Additionally, in the edited collection *Social, Casual and Mobile Games: The Changing Gaming Landscape*, Tama Leaver and Michele Willson (2016) offer valued insight into the economics, design, and practices of mobile, casual, and locative gaming. Notably, they make an important contribution toward understanding the changing landscape of the games industry. These publications offer diverse approaches to the successful design and marketing of hybrid games but overlook the deeper conceptualization of hybrid play as shaping identity and defining power relationships, that is, they do not engage with the more conceptual discussions that connect mobile and screen-based games through the concept of mobility. As such, this literature very seldom is in dialogue with scholarship on mobilities and mobile communication.

An exception to this perspective is Larissa Hjorth and Ingrid Richardson's (2014) *Gaming in Social, Locative and Mobile Media*, which examines the relationship between playful practices, mobility, and space/place. Importantly, this book reframes distinctions between serious and casual gamers; it also emphasizes the permeability of play into the quotidian in the Asia-Pacific region. Hjorth and Richardson offer an important foundation for *Hybrid Play*. We, thus, extend upon their concepts to identify how hybrid play is created and to consider forms of play not limited to games or ludic spaces. For example, the authors in this collection consider whether institutionalized spaces, like classrooms (Carrington) and makerspaces (Elam and Wiley), can be sites for hybrid play. Further, they examine the possibilities for hybrid play to become intertwined with the institutional and personal objectives that extend beyond the scope of playing for the sake of play. Following this thought, this collection asks how hybrid play might allow forms of healing (Bell) or promote health (Hjorth, Richardson, Jimenez) through its affordances. Games studies scholarship, of course, has previously considered similar questions. Jane McGonigal (2007, 2015), for example, is well-known for exploring how games can be intertwined with "serious" life to improve health, education, and self-motivation. Further, Dörner, Göbel, Effelsberg, and Wiemeyer (2016) have considered serious games, that is, the use of video games to aid learning, improving health, and the like. *Hybrid Play*, however, differs from these approaches in that we are not concerned just with design or how can games can be used for improving something else. Authors in this book are exploring the hybrid nature of play itself and how it creates hybrid performances, spaces, and experiences that necessarily entangle with the quotidian and, therefore, become embedded in a variety of contexts and objectives.

Hybrid Play offers a deeper, interdisciplinary engagement with the concept of hybridity by considering how it creates differential experiences of play and contributes to a more nuanced understanding of mobile, casual, and locative gaming practices. Further, *Hybrid Play* considers a range of games—mobile games, location-based mobile games, and traditional video games—by emphasizing the hybrid nature of the play experience. The chapters in this collection, therefore, explore a variety of considersations necessary for understanding the scale and scope of hybrid play. The chapters consider hybrid play as capable of generating new forms of mobility, communication, subjects, and artistic expression as well as new ways of interacting with and understanding the world. They also explore how the design and affordances of hybrid spaces affect the experience and performance of play as well as how genre conventions and expectations influence the available forms of play. Part and parcel with the experience and performance of play, the authors interrogate how the body becomes entangled in hybrid play and, in turn, how biases and prejudices might impact which hybrid spaces certain bodies can inhabit. Finally, the authors examine how hybrid play shapes identities and, in some cases, requires assuming new identities. Collectively, the authors employ a range of approaches and methods to work toward a definition of hybrid play, while simultaneously acknowledging that any definition must be purposefully broad to encompass the range of practices, subjects, and spaces of hybrid play.

Hybrid Play features chapters from both established and emerging scholars and practitioners in the areas of games studies, media studies, communication, women and gender studies, and media art. Together, the chapters offer important insights into how identity, place, and space are co-constructed through play; how, when, and for what reasons people occupy hybrid spaces; and how cultural practices shape elements of play and vice versa.

The structure of the book

This book is divided into three sections: Hybrid Making, Hybrid Subjects, and Hybrid Spaces. It was challenging to organize the chapters into three distinct sections as, following the nature of hybrid play, the ways that authors engaged with the topic had a significant overlap. However, for the purposes of organization, Hybrid Making includes chapters that deal with practical efforts to construct hybrid play experiences, creating meaningful experiences for players and the audience. Hybrid Subjects includes chapters about how hybrid play creates new subjectivities and entangles the body in the often competing logics of work-play, serious-casual, political-educational-playful, and institutional-entrepreneurial-experimental; and, finally, Hybrid Spaces includes chapters about how hybrid play offers approaches for examining the material, social, and cultural configurations of/within play spaces.

Hybrid Making

Part I, *Hybrid Making*, starts with an interview with Nick Tandavanitj, one of the members from the UK-based art group Blast Theory. In the interview, Tandavanitj tells Ragan Glover-Rijske about Blast Theory's ideas for creating game/art works that produce hybrid play experiences for audiences. These experiences include creating works that have permeable boundaries, are pervasive, and allow a sense of presence/liveness. To demonstrate this, Tandavanitj describes the process of creating some of Blast Theory's most prominent pieces, including *Kidnap* (1998), *Can You See Me Now?* (2001), and *Operation Black Antler* (2016). He additionally reflects on the design choices that Blast Theory has to make, so that their work will achieve its goal of prompting critical reflection about social and cultural issues. For instance, Blast Theory has to determine the audience's role in a work, whether to permit or limit emergent behaviour, and how to engage audiences. By discussing hybrid play as a designed experience, Tandavanitj suggests that hybridity is not a stable phenomenon but rather one constituted by the artist, audience, and multiple enfolded contexts.

Moving from the UK to Italy, Davide Spallazo and Illaria Mariani explore hybrid games as artifacts that expand between the digital and the physical. They focus particularly on the often overlooked, but nevertheless significant, idea of threshold. They explore how thresholds can be designed, consciously integrated, and intertwined within hybrid games. Relying on Susan Leigh Star and James Griesemer's (1989) concept of "boundary objects," they examine how devices, space, objects, and people can act as thresholds, that is, switches between the ordinary and the extraordinary. Spallazo and Mariani pay specific attention to the way in which narratives can help immersion in hybrid games. To that end, they conduct a critique of narratives embedded in multiple location-based games developed during a four-year project at the School of Design, Politecnico di Milano.

In Chapter 3, Kristina Bell explores how Twine (a free text-based game-making program) and autoethnography (an approach to research writing) can be paired together to build a playable experience that is a hybrid of rigorous research and immersive storytelling. Bell starts with a discussion of how Twine and autoethnography are uniquely well-suited because they share formal similarities rooted in deeply personal, underrepresented creative nonfiction writing, and a history of resisting mainstream practices. She pulls out various themes that Twine games and autoethnography share, including the telling of personal stories, the engagement of the player through design, and the encouragement of learning through choice. Bell then discusses how she constructed a hybrid interactive autoethnography game/story about her own experience of motherhood. In describing her

Twine experience, Bell addresses four hybrid states, which emerged from the creation of the interactive autoethnography: (1) the hybridity of the researcher as a game designer/subject, (2) the hybridity of play/academic research, (3) the hybridity of highly personal writing as something to be played, and (4) the hybridity of play/the ordinary or the mundane.

Like Kristina Bell, Sarah Evans also considers Twine. In Chapter 4, Evans investigates the hybrid roles of software, environment, and social norms when students in an upper-level game studies university course are asked to design a Twine game for the first time. To frame her analysis, she uses Feminist Software Analysis as an interdisciplinary method, combining ethnography with a close reading of Twine. Evans explores several aspects of Hybrid Making: video games designed through the partnership between humans and software; the methods, a joining of divergent methodological traditions; and her overall approach, an amalgam of activism and scholarship.

Collectively, the chapters in Part I offer insights about how to design hybrid play experiences toward particular outcomes and how to embrace the affordances of tools and technologies as a part of the design process. Notably, Tandavanitj, as well as Spallazzo and Mariani offer strategies for using objects and tools to create permeability between two contexts, in order to create hybridity. Additionally, Bell and Evans discuss how Twine's simple interface for game design can both limit and prompt creativity, inviting the designer to playfully engage the interface to achieve their ends. Together, the authors in Part I contribute to an idea of hybrid play as a designed experience. In some ways, they even push back against the idea of hybridity as a destablizing experience by enacting forms of control, through their design process, that fundamentally shape how their audiences will experience hybrid play. Yet, still, in the process of creating "hybrid play" experiences, the designers, too, are enmeshed in play, often responding to the unpredictable, emergent, or unstable properties that accompany the design process.

Hybrid Subjects

While hybrid subjects are present in most, if not all, of the chapters discussed earlier, it is the second section of the book that more deeply engages with issues of identity, and how play shapes hybrid subjectivities. In Chapter 5, Frans Mäyrä discusses the hybrid agency of hybrid play. While all human agency engaged in play is arguably rather complex, the play situation in hybrid games includes additional dimensions that complicate the related agency even further. Philosopher Hans-Georg Gadamer (2004) has argued that "all playing is being-played": When we become playing beings, we are being redefined and framed by the rules and structures of the game in question. Thus, the player becomes subjected to the game, and the game "plays the player." In hybrid games such as *Pokémon GO* (a location-based game) or *Skylanders* (a physical-digital game), there are also such systemic elements (game rules, game world) that have an effect on the playing agency. Furthermore, such games also include novel technologies that combine digital and non-digital dimensions of play in a way that is different from more traditional games. There are human and multiple non-human components that constitute the game agency related to hybrid, digital-physical games. In this sense, the experience of hybrid play relates both to what happens to the player in a physical reality, and what takes place in the associated, digital version of game reality—and in the interplay of such layered play dimensions. The agency in such a game playing situation is consequently also mixed and multi-layered. In addition, Mäyrä highlights the internal tensions and potential for conflicts in how power is distributed in hybrid game play.

In Chapter 6, Shira Chess engages with the idea of hybrid bodies as casual game players. She argues that "casual game" is an industry term often used derisively or dismissively as a catch-all word meant to indicate a style of play, albeit often deployed as a genre. Casual games, in this sense, increasingly infer a discursive list of game genres, such as match-3, invest/express, hidden object, and puzzle games. Chess claims that the video game industry and dominant gaming culture often express a great deal of ambivalence toward casual games and their players—both hoping to monetize off the emerging audience, but simultaneously deploying memes like "filthy casuals" that remind players of a gamic pecking order. With this in mind, Chess explores the hybridity of casual games as being at the core of what games have the potential to become. She asserts that the world we live in, the world we play in, is a "casual" one that privileges casual temporal encounters with our mobile devices, the primary vector for these games. According to this perspective, casual gaming bodies are composed of seemingly contradictory hybrids: work/play, expansion/constriction, and freedom/captivity. Because of these hybrid modes, casual bodies can reclaim gaming as a medium for all. Thus, by pushing back against industry rhetoric that privileges the staunch structure of console gaming over the hybrid aesthetic of the casual, Chess analyzes a shift wherein more bodies can be transformed into gaming bodies.

Moving from mobile games to a traditional screen-based video game, in Chapter 7, Claire Carrington analyzes *Math Blaster!* in creating hybrid teacher roles. *Math Blaster!* was a video game released in 1983 for the Apple II computer, intended to engage and entertain elementary school students. As Carrington demonstrates, this game highlights the trajectory through which American society came to greatly value science, technology, engineering, and math (STEM) education. Occupying a newfound role as a hybrid of gaming and learning, *Math Blaster!* served as a powerful media instrument to transfer cultural ideals about STEM and computer technology to elementary classrooms. Carrington examines how teachers started to occupy a new hybrid role, positioned as both classroom managers and edutainment technology advocates for computers. She investigates the cultural prescriptions that *Math Blaster!* helped create and reinforce, highlighting the hybrid role of edutainment that this game fulfilled alongside the newfound hybrid role that teachers occupied as both learners and advocates for this new technology. Ultimately, she demonstrates how the original *Math Blaster!* game served as an instrument for instilling the values of a STEM education in the elementary school classroom in the context of the Reagan-era Cold War developments, but most importantly, how it also had significant power in shaping a genre of gaming that relied on entertainment to impart these values even today.

In Chapter 8, Jessica Elam and Stephen B. Crofts Wiley explore how University Makerspaces produce contemporary hybrid subjects. As sites of hybrid play, makerspaces operate at the intersection of multiple contradictory logics shaping the contemporary processes of subjectivation. In the makerspace, subjectivation can go many ways; depending on the combination of logics at work, certain capacities are activated, while others are suppressed. They consider university makerspaces as sites where capitalist, institutional, and State logics dominate, but where playful experimentation may also lead to the emergence of more open, active, and unruly subjectivities. As such, they put the concept of *synthetic subjectivation* (Wiley & Elam, 2018) to work in a comparative analysis of two different makerspace events: a corporate-sponsored, industry-focused "Make-A-Thon" competition organized by the library and an experimental play session carried out by Elam, in which some of the same machines, materials, and bodies were arranged to make a very different composition.

Together, the chapters in Part II: Hybrid Subjects argue that the hybrid play shapes the subject, often in service of institutional, industry, or State agendas. For instance, Mäyrä, Elam and Wiley, and Carrington contend that structuring play, for these purposes, can limit the subject's agency by framing both their identity and choices. Meanwhile, Chess, Carrington, and Elam and Wiley demonstrate how play demands adopting hybrid roles, with these roles often being in tension with or destabilizing the subject's identity. Understood collectively, these chapters further the fact that, far from being a frivolous activity, hybrid play often has social, political, and cultural stakes for the playing subject.

Hybrid Spaces

The final section of this book engages more directly with the concept of hybrid spaces, demonstrating how games promote the creation of such spaces and also emerge from them. The chapters in this last section focus primarily on the types of hybrid spaces that emerge with the play experience. In Chapter 9, Larissa Hjorth, Ingrid Richardson and Jordi Piera-Jimenez analyze hybrid play through the location-based game *Pokémon GO*. They argue that increasingly, urban environments are becoming spaces for forms of hybrid play that merge material and digital contexts. Hybridity, as they claim, is of particular relevance to the experience of games such as *Pokémon GO*, in which real-time pedestrian movement is integrated with mobile location-based functionality and network information. They analyze mobile touchscreen devices as haptic interfaces that turn our attention to the embodied and proprioceptive aspects of playful media. In this chapter, they consider the coalescence of hybrid and haptic play in location-based mobile games, and revisit notions of hybridity in relation to the concept of digital wayfaring. Their discussion draws on ethnographic work conducted in Badalona, Spain on the uptake of *Pokémon GO* by older adults and explores the benefits of hybrid-haptic play in facilitating intergenerational connection and social and physical wellbeing.

In Chapter 10, Cameron Kunzelman offers a case study of the "souls-borne" video game genre, which emerges from the *Dark Souls* franchise. The soulsborne is characterized by, among other things, an above-average difficulty in game play and opaque narratives that must be puzzled together by players. In this chapter, Kunzelman argues that Sianne Ngai's (2012) aesthetic category theory is a productive method for addressing the hybrid nature of contemporary video game spaces. Applying Ngai's categories of the zany, the cute and the interesting, Kuzelman demonstrates that the methodology is a robust way of engaging with video games and their complicated social, mechanical, and meaning-making ways of interacting with their audiences and developers. He argues that the soulsborne genre is not just a cluster of mechanics and a lack of clear storytelling, but rather the emergence of a new aesthetic category within games. In conversation with Gilles Deleuze's (1988) concept of the diagram, he claims that we can achieve a better analysis of the hybrid reality of games through a new method for engaging with these complex objects. As such, aesthetic category theory allows for the analysis of the transposable elements of a game, or what can travel on from it, and thus to better understand how subjects and spaces are formed within the hybridity that is intrinsic to video game culture.

In Chapter 11, Katreena E. Alder explores Twitter's ability, as a hybrid space, to support the contemporary African American Hush Harbors. Historically, Hush Harbors were hidden spaces where enslaved African Americans could freely express themselves and discuss important aspects of their lives they otherwise had to hide from their masters. They were semi-private or somewhat public spaces where African Americans discussed, repudiated, and, for some, escaped an oppressive hegemonic society. Alder analyzes tweets about the film *Get Out* (2017) to understand how these contemporary hybrid Hush Harbor spaces are created in Twitter. *Get Out* is about the experiences of today's black Americans in uncomfortable spaces. The hybrid nature of Twitter as both a public and private (hybrid) space allows users to create, share, critique, and communicate about their lives. In this chapter, she argues that the playful use of hashtags and memes often cultivates, shares, and represents insider knowledge from the black community, thereby allowing contemporary Hush Harbors to emerge. In exploring Twitter as a contemporary African American Hush Harbor, Alder discusses African American audiences, rhetorics, and communication practices as conveyed via memes and hashtags about the 2017 movie *Get Out*.

Finally, in Chapter 12, Joel Schneier analyzes play in the hybrid (online/offline) spaces of mobile Minecraft. *Minecraft Pocket Edition* (2011) is a mobile game in which players may continually modify a procedurally generated gameworld. Unlike the heavily researched PC and console-based versions of *Minecraft*, the under-explored mobile version offers gameplay that is unique to touchscreen interfaces since players gesticulate directly upon a screen that simultaneously displays the environment they are modifying, and play may occur across various spaces with various entangled bodies. Schneier frames mobile *Minecraft* play as *performative* (Butler, 2013), and conceptualizes mobile gaming interfaces through Karen Barad's (2003) notion of *apparatuses*. This positions the mobile touchscreen interface as a nonhuman body that comes together with human bodies through highly contingent, hybridized performances. Schneier pays attention to the spaces played, mined, and crafted as part of the cybernetic performances of these entangled and frenetic bodies. In this chapter, he analyzes three collaborative mobile *Minecraft* play sessions from a microethological study of young *Minecraft* players (Schneier & Taylor, 2018) with particular attention to play that performs and reaffirms players' co-present relationships through the digital and physical gamespaces. In doing so, he argues that *Minecraft* play—in its mobile iteration—may be seen as a focal point through which to observe the hybridization of the co-present relationships, social and technological expertises, and bodies in play spaces. In other words, mobile *Minecraft* play materializes hybrid spaces.

Across the chapters in Part III: Hybrid Spaces, the authors argue that hybrid play is an experience taking place within a multiplicity of spaces, each of which bring their own values, rules, and norms that shape a playing subject's actions and interactions. Hjorth, Richardson, and Jiminez suggest that hybrid spaces occur when digital and physical spaces converge and that such convergence can break routine mobilities and encourage new social interactions as playing subjects engage in digital wayfaring. By contrast, Schneier observes that this convergence may also encourage fixity in space and a habitual relationship to pre-existing spatial arrangements, as playing subjects attempt to find stability in the rapidly changing spaces of gameplay. Differently, Kunzelman and Alder each argue that hybrid spaces extend beyond the digital and the physical to also encompass more theoretical spaces, like the gaming industry and various cultural arenas, where individuals contest ideas and create new meanings. Each of the chapters in Part III suggests that hybrid spaces are dynamic, rather than uniform—and that such spaces may serve as a contact zone (Pratt, 1991) for competing motives, logics, definitions, and demographics. This indicates that hybrid spaces—more than simply being a context or setting where hybrid play unfolds—are central to the experience of hybrid play and are critical sites of cultural exchange.

Press start to play

In what precedes, we have offered an overview, an instructional guide (if we might), for this collection. However, we also want to encourage that this collection be read playfully, that is, by reading across sections, putting different chapters into conversation with one another, and seeing what connections emerge. The structure that we have imposed offers only one starting point, but one which we hope offers a rich understanding of hybrid play as an experience both designed and unpredictable; shaped by, and shaping of, subjects; taking place between contexts and creating new meaning within those contexts. Attending to hybrid play means recognizing that it is always already *in process*. It is to capture that process for a moment in order to examine and understand it, but to recognize that the moment is fleeting, and that we must continue our inquiries to attempt to understand both its complexity and its significance in our lives.

References

Barad, K. (2003). Posthumanist performativity: Toward an understanding of how matter comes to matter. *Journal of Women in Culture Society, 28*(3), 801–831.

Benford, S., & Giannachi, G. (2011). *Performing mixed reality*. Cambridge, MA: MIT Press.

Butler, J. (2013). *Excitable speech: A politics of the performative*. New York: Routledge.

Caillois, R. (2001). *Man, play and games*. Urbana and Chicago: University of Illinois Press.

Deleuze, G. (1988). *Foucault*. Minnesota: University of Minnesota Press.

de Souza e Silva, A. (2006). From cyber to hybrid: Mobile technologies as interfaces of hybrid spaces. *Space and Culture, 3*, 261–278.

de Souza e Silva, A., & Sutko, D. M. (2008). Playing life and living play: How hybrid reality games reframe space, play, and the ordinary. *Critical Studies in Media Communication, 25*(5), 447–465.

de Souza e Silva, A., & Sutko, D. M. (Eds.). (2009). *Digital cityscapes: Merging digital and urban playspaces*. New York: Peter Lang.

Dörner, R., Göbel, S., Effelsberg, W., & Wiemeyer, J. (2016). *Serious games: Foundations, concepts and practice*. Heidelberg: Springer.

Fink, E. (1974). The ontology of play. *Philosophy Today, 18*, 147.

Gadamer, H.-G. (2004). *Truth and method*. London & New York: Continuum International.

Harrigan, P., Wardrip-Fruin, N., Parkin, L., Cornell, P., & Williams, W. J. (2017). *Third person: Authoring and exploring vast narratives*. Cambridge, MA: MIT Press.

Hjorth, L., & Richardson, I. (2014). *Gaming in social, locative and mobile media*. Houndmills, Basingstoke, Hampshire: Palgrave Macmillan.

Huizinga, J. (1970). *Homo Ludens: A study of the play element in culture.* London: Paladin.

Leorke, D. (2018). *Location-based gaming: Play in public space.* Singapore: Palgrave.

McGonigal, J. (2007). The puppet master problem: Design for real-world, mission-based gaming. In P. Harrigan & N. Wardrip-Fruin (Eds.), *Second person: Role-playing and story in games and playable media* (pp. 251–264). Boston, MA: The MIT Press.

McGonigal, J. (2015). *SuperBetter: The power of living gamefully.* New York: Penguin.

Montola, M., Stenros, J., & Waern, A. (2009). *Pervasive games: Theory and design.* Burlington, MA: Morgan Kaufmann Publishers.

Ngai, S. (2012). *Our aesthetic categories: Zany, cute, interesting.* Cambridge, MA: Harvard University Press Cambridge.

Pratt, M. L. (1991). Arts of the contact zone. *Profession,* 33–40.

Rodriguez, H. (2006). The playful and the serious: An approximation to Huizinga's Homo Ludens. *Game Studies: The International Journal of Computer Game Research,* 6(1). Retrieved from http://gamestudies.org/0601/articles/rodriges

Salen, K., & Zimmerman, E. (2006). *The game design reader: A rules of play anthology.* Cambridge, MA: The MIT Press.

Schneier, J., & Taylor, N. (2018). Hand-crafted gameworlds: Minecraft Pocket edition and mobile gameplay. *New Media & Society, First published January, 2, 2018.* doi:10.1177/1461444817749517

Spallazzo, D., & Mariani, I. (2018). *Location-based mobile games: Design perspectives.* Heidelberg: Springer.

Star, S. L., & Griesemer, J. R. (1989). Institutional ecology,translations' and boundary objects: Amateurs and professionals in Berkeley's Museum of Vertebrate Zoology, 1907–39. *Social Studies of Science,* 19(3), 387–420.

Von Borries, F., Walz, S. P., Böttger, M., Davidson, D., Kelley, H., & Kücklich, J. (2007). *Space time play: Computer games, architecture and urbanism: The next level.* Basel: Birkhäuser.

Wardrip-Fruin, N., & Harrigan, P. (2004). *First person: New media as story, performance, and game.* Cambridge, MA: The MIT Press.

Wardrip-Fruin, N., & Harrigan, P. (2007). *Second person: Role-playing and story in games and playable media.* Cambridge, MA: MIT Press.

Wiley, S. B. C., & Elam, J. (2018). Synthetic subjectivation: Technical media and the composition of posthuman subjects. *Subjectivity,* 11(3), 203–227.

Willson, M., & Leaver, T. (2016). *Social, casual and mobile games: The changing gaming landscape.* New York/sLondon: Bloomsbury Publishing.

Part I
Hybrid making

1 You start it

A dialogue with Nick Tandavanitj from Blast Theory

Ragan Glover-Rijkse

Nick Tandavanitj is a lead member of the artist group, Blast Theory, along-side Matt Adams and Ju Row Farr. As a group, Blast Theory makes inter-active media art that blurs the boundaries between audience and subject, physical and digital, fiction and reality. This blurring produces hybridities. That is, Blast Theory's work invites the audience not only to perform hybrid roles, but also to exist in hybrid spaces and engage in hybrid encounters. Blast Theory leverages the playful disposition of their work to fruitfully engage society's important issues. They recognize that the qualities of hy-bridity open up a possibility for making new connections and forming new ideas as temporalities, spaces, and identities converge in unexpected ways. For this reason, they purposefully design hybrid play experiences to generate moments of critical inquiry. In this chapter, I interview Nick Tandavanitj about how Blast Theory does this in their games/art work. We begin by discussing the development of Blast Theory's work since its for-mation in 1991. Then, we transition to talk about the process of integrating hybrid play in their work.

In this dialogue, Nick Tandavanitj describes three interrelated character-istics that Blast Theory uses to create hybrid play experiences: (1) permeable boundaries, (2) pervasiveness, and (3) presence/liveness. The first charac-teristic, permeable boundaries, suggests that some elements of the experi-ence extend beyond their typical context and into another. For example, in some of their pieces, like *Can You See Me Now?* (2001) and *Uncle Roy All Around You* (2003), elements of the digital world intermingle with the phys-ical, thereby blurring the two or making it so that one impacts the other. The second characteristic, pervasiveness, relates to permeability insofar as it involves one element extending into another. However, pervasiveness distinctly refers to the elements of an experience becoming incorporated within everyday spaces and temporalities. An example of this occurs when a work's temporal and spatial boundaries permeate into a participant's day-to-day life (Montola, Stenros, & Waern, 2009), such that the participant might be involved in the experience during their leisure time, at work, or at school. In Blast Theory's work *Karen* (2015), for instance, participants interact with a life coach, named Karen, via a mobile app. However, as they continue to interact with Karen, she pushes against the anticipated temporal and spatial boundaries of the work by calling and texting the participant at inappropriate times, like in the middle of the night. Finally, the third characteristic, presence and liveness, refers to elements of an experience that produce a sense of being together with others, in real time, regardless of spatial or temporal contiguity. For instance, presence/liveness occurs if a game offers a way to communicate with geographically dispersed players, thereby producing a sense of co-presence despite separation. Alternatively, it occurs when individuals are brought into a space to experience something together. Several of Blast Theory's early works offer examples of presence/liveness, including *Chemical Wedding* (1992) and *Stampede* (1994). In both of these works, Blast Theory contemplates the value of bringing individuals together to share the same space and time.

Collectively, the characteristics of permeability, pervasiveness, and presence/liveness facilitate reflection about critical issues by shifting the circumstances in which individuals would normally encounter them. In the following interview, we discuss how these three characteristics produce hybrid play experiences.

RAGAN GLOVER-RIJKSE (RGR): I first learned about Blast Theory's work through scholarship considering the role of digital technologies in creating hybrid spaces (Benford & Giannachi, 2011; Crabtree & Rodden, 2008; de Souza e Silva & Hjorth, 2009). Would you say that Blast Theory's practice is driven by the playful use of technology?

NICK TANDAVANITJ (NT): When Blast Theory was formed in 1991, the group had a shared interest in politics, films, and popular culture, rather than a particular artistic practice. Blast Theory came from a range of different backgrounds: DJs, dancers, theater makers, installation artists, and sculptors. For this reason, all of the work was multi-disciplinary from the outset, and that was a consequence of the fact that there was not really an integrated practice—just a common sense of possibility and the need to make something. However, we were not led by technology. It was an era before modern mobile phones. The group had one computer when we first started out, and it did not have an internet connection. Instead, the first works were promenade performances that combined choreography, installation, music, and often a bar. The events took place at found venues, like old industrial units, shops, and empty churches. The participants had the sense of coming to a party or an evening, rather than coming to a piece of performance or art. We would bring people to those spaces and invite them to explore a series of shifting roles. For instance, in one moment, the audience could be a spectator, viewing an installation or a piece of choreography. In the next, they might be asked to step forward to perform a different role. In *Chemical Wedding* (1992), for example, the audience could drink and socialize, but then they could be asked to stand under a light and make a public declaration about their sexual history. Our impulse was about finding ways that we could invite the audience to reflect on some of the key questions that were important to us. It was also about asking them to consider the stakes of a live situation with real people, rather than just a performance. We did this by actively involving them in the project.

RGR: What led Blast Theory to engage the audience in this manner—why did Blast Theory think it was productive to encourage the audience to perform the hybrid role of both spectator and participant?

NT: In the 1990s, rave culture was significant to youth culture in the United Kingdom. We drew inspiration from this culture and believed that we could potentially harness the energy and excitement from this culture's participatory, collaborative, and celebrative nature in order to take a critical stance and deal with social issues. We recognized that this was a generation that had become politicized, after a decade of Conservative government under Margaret Thatcher. So, all of these things came together and formed us as a group to try to make works that had energy, a sense of participation, and a feeling of excitement. This notion of audience members as participants, or active in performance, has remained critical to our work since the very beginning.

RGR: That's very interesting. Could you tell me about a particular work that you think did this well? How did Blast Theory create these feelings of energy, excitement, and participation for the audience-participants?

NT: An example of this occurs in one of our first projects, *Stampede* (1994). This project was developed in response to a piece of legislation going through British government, at the time, known as the Criminal Justice Bill. The Criminal Justice Bill increased the restrictions against mass protest, but it also perversely legislated against rave culture and gatherings with amplified music. In other words, this legislation worked specifically against crowds. We took that as our starting point for the project, and so we constructed our audience as being a part of a crowd. During the performance, we had very loud music playing at different points. We had fences to cordon off the audience and choreography that reflected police behavior. We also engaged the idea of crowd surveillance by using an interactive projection system that, when triggered, would display videos of the crowd. For this component, we collaborated with the graduate students in the Interactive Media M.A. at the Royal College of Arts who had been playfully experimenting with dismantling Macintoshes. They had a Mac Quadra 660AV, which is one of the first Macintoshes to afford video input. They took apart the computer's keyboard and soldered sensor-pads into it so that the audience could trigger live video capture and sound, by stepping on the sensors, as they walked around the space. While the technology became a way of understanding both the behavior of crowds and people's context within a crowd, it was also about harnessing that energy and excitement about socializing and hopefully creating something smart to say.

RGR: What you have described so far suggests that Blast Theory's work focuses on creating social and political commentary. How has that overarching goal shaped Blast Theory's practices? How do you create moments for reflection on political and social issues?

NT: Yeah, I'll explain by example, if that's okay. Around 1998, we were researching a case in the European Court of Human Rights, colloquially known as the Spanner trial. This case prosecuted a number of gay men, who participated in a sadomasochistic party and videoed themselves. The video got into the hands of the police, and the police decided to file charges of assault against the men despite the consensual nature of the activities. We found this paradoxical—that people could participate in consensual activities, but still be prosecuted for it. So, we decided to make a performance about the pleasures of giving up control. For several months, we engaged in a devising process where, as performers, we experimented with giving up control to one another. This resulted in a short performance, called *Atomic* (1998), in which four performers tried to push one another to perform transgressive acts in front of an audience. However, we soon realized that it is not very exciting for audiences to watch people, who they know are performers, order each other around and tell each other to get undressed. So, we shifted the way that we approached our work and decided to flip things around. In doing so, we asked the audience to give power to us. What resulted was *Kidnap* (1998) (Figure 1.1). *Kidnap* invited people to nominate themselves for an abduction to take place on a pre-specified date in the summer of 1998. We decided that the event would function as an informal lottery. Potential participants would purchase tickets, and we would draw two winners to abduct and hold at a secret location for 48 hours. When the abduction took place, we aired the two participants' captivity online, and a London PR agency, Mark Borkowski, disseminated stories to the press throughout the process. Ultimately, *Kidnap* was a seminal moment in how we understood audiences in our work: we began to think of them as protagonists. Since that moment, we always start with this perspective in mind and write that into the descriptions of what we are doing when we are developing a project. For us, allowing the audience to experience something first-hand and to become the protagonist is critical to our understanding of play. In our work, the audience is the story; they are involved in the actual execution of an experience or an event.

RGR: What you're describing not only pushes back against the admittedly dated idea of the audience as a passive entity, but also invites them into the creative process of making the work. What do you think is the value of having the audience involved in both creating and experiencing the work?

NT: For us, the most successful works are the ones where the audience has actually been at the heart of the work. It creates the possibility for

Figure 1.1 Kidnap (1998). A lottery winner/participant is abducted and escorted away to be held by captors. Image by: Gregorio Pagliaro. Copyright: Blast Theory.

audiences to feel that they have something personal at stake. It also creates a sense that they may be held to account—both in the sense of taking responsibility and in the sense of having to explain what their experience is and what it might mean. For example, *Rider Spoke* (2007) (Figure 1.2) is a work in which we invited people to cycle around the city. The idea responded in part to user-created content platforms, like YouTube, that accompanied the emergence of social media. We were intrigued to see how the voices of our audience could form the center of the work, and we wanted to create a platform that encouraged different kinds of contributions and senses of community to other online spaces. To participate, riders were loaned a bicycle with a headset and a touch device on the handlebars. Over the headset, the rider heard a woman's recorded voice guiding them through the city and asking them to record details about their life. Having made their first recording, riders could then choose to look for recordings left by other cyclists in the same spaces. The project ran in 18 cities over ten years and, each time, it built a layer across the city of people's own personal accounts of their inner lives. It formed a temporary community, where those cycling could be co-present with a group of people who had previously been there.

RGR: What I find fascinating about *Rider Spoke* is that it produces a hybrid space. In other words, participants can both listen and contribute to digital narratives that been fused with the physical space. de Souza e Silva and

Figure 1.2 Rider Spoke (2007). A participant, riding her bicycle, stops to listen to a recording which will guide her through the city. Copyright: Blast Theory.

Frith (2012) describe this participatory process as reading and writing space (p. 34). We've already talked some about the role of the audience in creating a work, but what about the audience's role in the production of space? How does allowing for this shape Blast Theory's practice?

NT: Both *Rider Spoke* (2007) and *Kidnap* (1998) invited us to reflect on "space" as a key element for making a work. We had previously made work in black box studio theaters and found spaces but, from *Rider Spoke* and *Kidnap*, we had two important realizations about space. The first came from the need to make the work accessible. It occurred to us that the internet and the media provide a whole performative space, which remove from us actually being physically present as performers. This sounds naive now but, at the time, that was an important insight for us and was the start of our engagement with distributed spaces and audiences. The second realization was that, for distributed audiences, the space of the work is also, often, the space of their everyday life. As a result, audiences have the power to determine the shape of their own experiences. For instance, one person who nominated their self to participate in *Kidnap* had an experience that took place independent of anything that we actually did or anything that was in our control. On the day of the kidnapping, that person left a message for us on the free phone number that we had published for the project. This message said that they were in their house and that, from their window, they could see us waiting in a van outside to come kidnap them. We were actually not by their house at all, but they spent the day waiting for us. We found it intriguing that the piece of work might involve things that we had not planned. We realized that there might be emergent characteristics to a work.

RGR: Emergence is a term which often refers to a phenomenon that just-so-happens to occur under the right conditions (Johnson, 2001). How does Blast Theory produce conditions that invite emergence?

NT: Well, actually, not all of our works invite emergent characteristics. In some cases, we try to avoid it. But one way we invite emergence is by making works that are pervasive. That is, to make works in which the physical boundaries of the work are invisible, the lines demarcating the magic circle or play area are blurred (Montolla, Stenros, & Waern, 2009). Normally, games take place in a confined physical boundary. There is an inside of the game, in which the game exists, and an outside, in which, the game does not. However, with pervasive games, the goal is to create a permeable boundary between the two—to produce a hybrid space in which action and reflection can occur. Our pragmatic sense is that this actually becomes a form of facilitation. If you tell someone that they are about to play a game, they know that it is going to involve rules, goals, and tasks. They know that that they are going to need to do something and that they cannot just sit there and watch. However, emergence happens almost because of a lack of rules rather than producing a highly rule-based environment. It's often the result of encouraging playfulness, giving participants the time to figure out what they want to do, and creating an experience that's adaptable to the unexpected in a meaningful way.

RGR: So, if emergence creates this sense action and reflection, then why might Blast Theory choose to avoid emergence?

NT: In a lot of our more narrative-driven work, there's an emphasis on being co-present with a live event or a live performer. In those situations, we encourage the participant to focus on spectating, listening, and being present rather than inventing their own behavior. This presence and liveness allow the participant to actually feel like there is something at stake, like their participation will have a meaning or a value beyond the event. In other words, we hope for their participation to have impacts beyond the experience itself. To accomplish this, we've learned that it's sometimes best to purposefully limit or avoid emergent behavior.

RGR: The concepts of liveness and co-presence recur as significant component to Blast Theory's work. How does Blast Theory accomplish this in a structured and artificially produced setting? Of course, I do not mean "artificial" in a negative sense; I mean it to refer to the theatrics of the work.

NT: Well, there's a production or logistical level of having performers who can respond in real time to events as they occur. For instance, we did this with *Stampede* (1994), in which the performers encouraged playfulness or certain kinds of behavior. Alternatively, there's the ability to stream a work, like we did with Kidnap (1998). Live streaming gives a geographically dispersed audience a sense of co-presence and makes the event feel live before them. Finally, there's an ability to mirror the temporalities of the real world. For instance, with *Day of the Figurines* (2006) (Figure 1.3), we recognized that there is a real timeframe for text messaging and response. In this game, players create a character which they can interact with by sending text messages. However, we built delays into the system, so that when participants sent text messages to their character, the system would wait a certain number of minutes to respond. If they asked their character to travel somewhere, the system would wait a certain number of minutes or hours to text them back, based on how long it would take the character to get to that location. This delay simulated a real conversational timeframe. It produced a real sense of time and a sense of it being co-present and live. This blurred the temporalities of the game. Normally, a game has a temporal bounding of when it starts and ends. Then, within that time frame, there is a clear sense of when a person is playing and when they are not. However, with *Day of Figurines*, we wanted to push back against that. We thought that we could make the temporal bounds of the game more permeable in a fruitful way.

Figure 1.3 Day of Figurines (2006). The gameboard features a model town with silhouettes of buildings. Lines across the gameboard are a projection, which reflect the movement of players across the town. Copyright: Blast Theory.

RGR: So far, you have talked about creating permeability between the role of the audience and speaker, the digital and physical, and play and reality. This all speaks to the concept of hybridity—the idea that these boundaries become permeable and ultimately indistinguishable (de Souza e Silva, 2006, p. 265). How does Blast Theory create this permeability, though?

NT: Several things contribute to permeability. The first is the platform. For instance, mobile technologies have been really important for us. Mobile devices are in our pockets and become interweaved with the everyday world to produce a hybrid space. They bring a sense of pervasiveness—we use them to communicate with our loved ones as well as to play games. This hybrid space is really intriguing for us. It is a space where the permeability between the game world and the real world can actually take place and be quite productive. Additionally, mobile devices and mobility have really changed our day-to-day interactions—in other words, what kind of people we're connected to, how we connect with people, and how conversations are started and finished. Mobile devices also change our understandings of identity. In one moment, we are someone who is at work speaking with a colleague and, in another moment, we are receiving a text message from a family member. As a result, there is the sense that the technology has an impact on our personal lives and our activities. We kind of jump between all of those identities simultaneously. I think that is a very contemporary fate that we've become acclimatized to and that results partly as a product of technology. However, it's also to do with living in a society in which we have many parallel specialisms and living in a culture in which, instead of being a monoculture, it's a very multilayered, multi-faceted, very fragmented, and hybrid culture. As a consequence, we see the rise of a new sense of "hybridity"—one not related to technology, but rather centered on the self. We are hybrid beings, and we are hybrid social actors because we have many roles. We are also hybrid audience members because there are many layers through which we can examine and interpret cultural texts.

RGR: You mention that several things contribute to permeability, one of which is platform. What are some other things that contribute?

NT: Another way to create permeability is by creating a sense of uncertainty about the boundaries of the world. For us, this means making games and art work that take place in the city itself, so that the participant's experience is embedded within the real world. For instance, in *Can You See Me Now?* (2001) (Figure 1.4), the audience is invited to be led around a physical city by online players, who are navigating a virtual version of that same part of the city. This is one of our seminal pieces of work in terms of thinking about the production of hybridities, especially because there might be a disjunction between the layers. Some of these disjunctions are very prosaic, such as in a 3D virtual

Figure 1.4 Can You See Me Now? (2001). A participant runs across the city, using a map displayed on a PDA to navigate. The participant's goal is to "catch" the online players, who use arrow-keys on their computer to navigate a map of the city and avoid the players in the physical world. Copyright: Blast Theory.

environment. For instance, this particular work highlights the disjunction between the digital and physical spaces, and it identifies what that disjunction feels like.

RGR: How did Blast Theory actually make this disjunction something felt by the audience-participant?

Blast Theory created *Can You See Me Now?* (2001) alongside the Mixed Reality Lab, based at the University of Nottingham and led by Professor Steve Benford. During the 1990s, the Mixed Reality Lab's interest was around the way that virtual and physical spaces might merge and how those immersive 3D environments might transform the experience of physical spaces. When we collaborated to make this piece, we were still in the early days of Web 3D and 3D environments on the web. Polygon counts were in the low thousands. Collision detection and physics were extremely basic, so we could demonstrate gravity but not terrain-following. Players had an animated character that slid around at the same speed throughout, so some of the disjunction arises between the people walking on the physical street and the people experiencing a digital map of the street. The difference was that those on the physical street were physically running up-and-down hills, through

alleyways, dodging traffic, running through crowds of people, and navigating a real physical space and real urban environment. Those in the
digital space, however, only saw a large rectangle representing the side
of a building, and they were able to slide seamlessly along it. So, there's
a disjunction between the properties. An online player could hear the
person who is running down the real street, walking through a crowd
of people, or waiting for passing traffic, but these properties were not
present in the same way within the digital space. So, there is a sense
that these different types of spaces have presumptions about how the
participant moves or what the participant's experience is like.

RGR: So the prosaic disjunctions arise from the difference in experiences
of digital and physical spaces. Are there other kinds of disjunction that
merit attention?

NT: Another understanding relates to a topological disjunction. Physical
spaces are more contiguous; they're marked by boundaries that are visible, whereas digital spaces have a property of being mutable as well as
constantly transforming and changing. However, there are exceptions
to this. For instance, the second time we did *Can You See Me Now?*
(2001), it took place on the waterfront of Rotterdam, and it was on
a massive development site. So, in the two weeks that we had been
rehearsing, some of the buildings had been transformed but the digital
spaces had not reflected this change. This drew our attention to the
differences between physical and digital spaces in terms of how those
spaces progress or change over time. We also became curious about
the ecology and life of those spaces. Often, we think of digital spaces
as being able to drop-in and pierce physical spaces. In other words,
digital spaces can penetrate physical space in a way that produces some
different kind of engagement. However, I think that in the future, it's
important to consider how digital spaces might further engage with
physical topographies so that they might more fairly reflect a physically
delineated community, or they might more fairly engage with people
in physical spaces. For example, location services are becoming more
sophisticated, but it's not the same as a full engagement with physical
space; it just provides a more detailed topography. We think of digital
spaces as being entirely mutable and where anything is possible, but
digital space should try to tether things back to a referenced reality,
particularly considering issues like fake news. So, we need productive
ways of doing this—of tethering these spaces back together and back
to the physical environment.

RGR: So how does Blast Theory do this? How do you tether something
back to a referenced reality without just adding a more detailed topography? How do you make that tethering meaningful?

NT: A way we accomplish this is by blurring the distinctions between
reality and fiction in a productive way—one that asks the audience
to reflect on their choices when they think they are inconsequential.

We like to do this by using documentary materials because documentary materials are a way of crossing those boundaries. Documentary materials are an accessible kind of form for participants to latch on to ideas. One example in which we used documentary materials to cross boundaries between reality and fiction occurs in our ongoing project, *Operation Black Antler* (2016) (Figure 1.5). This project explores a real government surveillance operation called Demonstration Squad, which investigated surveillance groups in the 1960s all the way through to the early 2000s. In this project, participants are invited to take the role of an undercover police officer and make a judgment of whether they could justify a police surveillance on a group of people that they are told to investigate. The project is a response to three major historical moments. The first was the recent Investigatory Powers Bill in the UK, which gives the government the power to gather bulk electronic data about anyone's communications. The second was the Department of the Metropolitan Police, which undertook long-term surveillance over a period of about forty years in the UK. Their surveillance program, called Special Demonstrations Squad, placed undercover police in groups, such as environmental action groups, animal rights groups, and even in trade unions. In some cases, the police officers entered into relationships with people they were targeting with for surveillance and even had children with those people. The third starting point has been Brexit. We are making the work in the course of the Brexit referendum,

Figure 1.5 Operation Black Antler (2016). Participants are briefed on their undercover mission to surveil a group of people, deemed suspicious by the police. Copyright: Blast Theory.

and we actually showed the work the night of the Brexit referendum. So, combining those three things, we tried to put together an experience that placed people at the center of a problem. We wanted to present them with a dilemma and ask them to account for the decisions they make, even though the decision exists within a fictionally-constructed world. This sense of accountability derives from the fact that their decision is based on real issues in the United Kingdom, such as right-wing politics, migration, class, and disparities of experience between different parts of the UK. Although the sense of play is there, the questions that are being asked and the modes of talking about them are based on actual and factual current events, and this makes it a way of making people take account for themselves because, although it's playful activity, we're not asking them to take it lightly. The combination of those two things is important especially with *Operation Black Antler.*

RGR: We spoke earlier about how Blast Theory creates moments for social and political reflection. Do you think that the participant can fully do this when the distinction between fiction and reality becomes blurred?

NT: Well, the flip side of *Operation Black Antler* (2016) would be *Desert Rain* (1999) (Figure 1.6). In *Desert Rain*, we actually chose to withhold the fact that we were using documentary material until the very end of the work. The audience was invited to take part in an ostensibly immersive computer game. Participants were placed in a virtual environment

Figure 1.6 Desert Rain (1999). The virtual interface of the war game, which unbeknownst to participants, simulates the Gulf War. Copyright: Blast Theory.

and scenario. They were given a mission, and everything appears as a game-like experience. Only at the end did participants learn that the game related to a historic event, during the first Gulf War, and that the people, who were the fictional targets within the game, were actually real people who had significance in the Gulf War. In that instance, we used documentary material to perform a dramatic reveal. To accomplish this, we encouraged lightheartedness or playfulness in the first part of the game to give contrast to the revelation that it was actually about the real Gulf War. We did this because there's often an association with games and play that they're light, inconsequential, or frivolous. We wanted to challenge these ideas to indicate that games and play can be demonstrative for adults. We wanted to show that we can use some of the properties of play to encourage reflection and to engage new forms of knowledge and awareness. So, yes, I think that these things can invite meaningful reflection.

RGR: How does this create new forms of knowledge and awareness for the participant?

NT: I think that goes back to that idea of hybrid roles, in which people quite happily switch between different modes of thinking and performing. With both *Operation Black Antler* (2016) and *Desert Rain* (1999), things center around a theatrical level of reality. Participants are encouraged to role play; they're encouraged to improvise personalities and identities. However, we always ask participants to use their identity as a starting point and to use their own experiences for role playing. We do this because we want the participants to take the game seriously. We want them to take account for their actions by recognizing that their actions were, in part, based on their own identity. The goal is to generate a moment when people say, "the situation was not what I thought it was" or "what is it that I've just done and what have I learned?"

RGR: These are all of my questions. Do you have any additional thoughts you'd like to share?

NT: One thing that I really wanted to point out is that although we make things that often are called games and are ostensibly interactive, lots of our work is actually quite instructive and linear. We also make art that is exclusively consumed online or via apps. We also make work that sits in museums and galleries. But in essence, all our work looks at how we can nurture a place where people can talk in new ways and find a new voice that lets them understand things from a different perspective. Our goal is to place the audience in situations that allows them to find a new way to talk about and reflect on the world.

RGR: Thank you so much for taking the time to talk with me.

References

Atomic. (1998). *United Kingdom: Blast Theory*. Retrieved 30 April 2019, from https://www.blasttheory.co.uk/projects/atomic-installation/

Benford, S., & Giannachi, G. (2011). *Performing mixed reality*. Cambridge, MA: MIT Press.

Can You See Me Now? (2001). *United Kingdom: Blast Theory & the Mixed Reality Lab*. Retrieved 30 April 2019, from https://www.blasttheory.co.uk/projects/can-you-see-me-now/

Chemical Wedding. (1992). *United Kingdom: Blast Theory*. Retrieved 30 April 2019, from https://www.blasttheory.co.uk/projects/chemical-wedding/

Crabtree, A., & Rodden, T. (2008). Hybrid ecologies: Understanding cooperative interaction in emerging physical-digital environments. *Journal of Personal and Ubiquitous Computing, 12*(7), 481–493.

Desert Rain. (1999). *United Kingdom: Blast Theory & the Mixed Reality Lab*. Retrieved 30 April 2019, from https://www.blasttheory.co.uk/projects/desert-rain/

de Souza e Silva, A. (2006). From Cyber to hybrid: Mobile Technologies as interfaces of hybrid Spaces. *Space and Culture, 9*(3), 261–278.

de Souza e Silva, A., & Frith, J. (2012). From voice to location. In J. Farman (Ed.), *Mobile interfaces in public spaces: Locational privacy, control and urban sociality* (pp. 78–108). New York: Routledge.

de Souza e Silva, A., & Hjorth, L. (2009). Playful urban spaces: A historical approach to mobile games. *Simulation & Gaming, 40*(5), 602–625.

Johnson, S. (2001). *Emergence. The connected lives of ants, brains, cities, and software*. New York: Scribner.

Karen. (2015). *United Kingdom: Blast Theory*. Retrieved 19 August 2019, from https://www.blasttheory.co.uk/projects/karen/

Kidnap. (1998). *United Kingdom: Blast Theory*. Retrieved 30 April 2019, from https://www.blasttheory.co.uk/projects/kidnap/

Montola, M., Stenros, J., & Waern, A. (Eds.). (2009). *Pervasive games. Theory and design. Experiences on the boundary between life and play*. Burlington, MA: Morgan Kaufmann Publishers.

Operation Black Antler. (2016). *United Kingdom: Blast Theory*. Retrieved 30 April 2019, from https://www.blasttheory.co.uk/projects/operation-black-antler/

Rider Spoke. (2007). *United Kingdom: Blast Theory*. Retrieved 30 April 2019, from https://www.blasttheory.co.uk/projects/rider-spoke/

Stampede. (1994). *United Kingdom: Blast Theory*. Retrieved 30 April 2019, from https://www.blasttheory.co.uk/projects/stampede/

Uncle Roy All Around You. (2003). *United Kingdom: Blast Theory*. Retrieved 19 August 2019, from https://www.blasttheory.co.uk/projects/uncle-roy-all-around-you/

2 Keeping coherence across thresholds

A narrative perspective on hybrid games

Davide Spallazzo and Ilaria Mariani

Games are powerful and complex forms of entertainment. They are interactive artifacts that require interdisciplinary knowledge and know-how to be carefully and wisely designed. Game design is further complicated in games that bridge the physical and the digital to build hybrid worlds. In engaging with location-based games, users can access the hybrid-reality game experience in two ways: looking at their surroundings and watching how they are represented on their mobile devices (de Souza e Silva & Sutko, 2011). As a result, the designer is faced with advanced levels of complexity. In this chapter, we analyze hybrid games as complex ecosystems, which consist of many different and connected parts and embrace the specific perspective of the designer in charge of crafting such games as meaningful experiences (Mariani, 2016; Spallazzo & Mariani, 2018).

In 2013, we began conducting research through design aimed at understanding how games can convey meanings and how this process might be enhanced and improved. Because of our complementary backgrounds as designers and researchers in the linked fields of gaming, communication and interactive narratives, and interaction design, we chose to focus on a genre of games that pervade the surroundings in which they take place, bridging the physical and the digital (Montola, Stenros, & Waern, 2009). Hybrid-reality games (de Souza e Silva & Delacruz, 2006; de Souza e Silva & Hjorth, 2009), mixed-reality games (Flintham et al. 2003; Montola, 2011), and augmented-reality games (Jacob et al., 2012; Squire et al., 2007) are terms frequently used in literature to identify games that are played between digital and physical worlds, with digital information overlapping the player's physical world. The first two terms emphasize the process of hybridizing the physical world with the digital one, identifying games that take place simultaneously in physical and digital spaces (de Souza e Silva & Hjorth, 2009). The third refers to games that superimpose augmented-reality graphics on the physical world through a smartphone camera.

In this chapter, we analyze location-based mobile games (LBMGs henceforth) as games that exploit mobile devices' location awareness to link information to places and players to each other (de Souza e Silva & Hjorth, 2009). A well-known example of this genre is *Botfighters*. Released in 2001 by It's Alive as an urban Massively Multiplayer Online Role-Playing Game (MMORPG), *Botfighters* allowed players to locate other players in the city and engage in a battle to destroy them. In games like *Botfighters*, location is key, since the gameplay changes based on players' position, thereby mixing a device-mediated digital experience with a physical one. LBMGs, in this sense, are games that take advantage of mobile devices' location awareness to provide players with a contextual, situated game experience—a topic which is also explored by designers and artists who have created interactive, distributed, and live performances (Benford & Giannachi, 2011).

We approached this issue by analyzing and working on the overall process of designing games in the educational context of the School of Design, Politecnico di Milano. This was a four-year-long research project involving 240 BSc design students with mixed competencies that enriched our knowledge much more than we expected. Every year, about 60 students, divided into groups of four/five, designed and tested LBMGs as working prototypes and conducted a final assessment of the course. At the conclusion of project, a total of 57 LBMGs were designed and studied.

First, the investigation focused on what it means to design games that have the paramount features of requiring players to continuously swing back and forth between two realities while playing. Moreover, by occurring in the everyday space, these games also required players to engage in sense- and meaning-making of both their surroundings and the objects involved in the activity (or their representation), and above all, the interactions activated through the game (Spallazzo & Mariani, 2017). In addition, the very features of these games, as hybridizing the physical and digital spheres, make them more interconnected and dynamic than others, thus requiring that they are carefully designed as complex systems of interaction and communication (Mariani, 2016).

There is a significant body of research investigating games from multiple perspectives, such as how games play with different aspects of our culture (Caillois, 1958; Flanagan, 2009; Kaufman & Flanagan, 2015), and how to design game mechanics and dynamics (Ermi & Mäyrä, 2005; Fullerton, 2014; Hunicke, LeBlanc, & Zubek, 2004). However, with the exception of games based on role play, research dealing with hybrid and pervasive games, particularly investigating narrative construction and development, is relatively underdeveloped. Narrative is often overlooked in favor of other aspects—such as technological issues, mechanics, dynamics, and aesthetics—that tend to prevail in the game design process. In response, we focus on the benefits and implications of building LBMGs that rely heavily on narratives to communicate specific topics.

Our initial rumination regarded the issue of "thresholds," with the term understood as the sum of game elements and mechanics that make it possible to switch between the ordinary and the extraordinary, and sought to identify shrewd ways to turn the limits and constraints that characterize these games into further design opportunities with the potential to enrich play(er) experiences. As we will see, every threshold, as a boundary (Star & Griesemer, 1989), can play a key narrative role. Our goal is to discuss how such thresholds can be wisely and coherently designed, consciously integrated, and intertwined within hybrid game elements. Adopting such a perspective also requires us to carefully question the idea that such games should limit the role of mobile devices by including physical elements as gateways that strengthen the meaningfulness of the game experience. Such physical elements need to be coherently designed if they are to be aligned and consistent with the game's narrative world.

Thresholds as design possibilities

The concept of threshold is central to our investigation. We understand threshold beyond its traditional meaning of using mobile devices as a gateway (hence a first threshold) for accessing digital worlds. Instead, we consider physical spaces, objects, and people as boundaries between the two realms.

The role of the game environment, and that of the objects and people players may encounter, is often overlooked and neglected in LBMG design. Indeed, some well-known games seem to primarily focus on hybridizing the physical and fictional game worlds through the mobile device and superimposing contextual information, tasks, and game mechanics on the physical environment. Examples are the well-known *Pokémon Go* (2016) and *Ingress* (2012) by Niantic. They both use in-situ interactions, but only the first capitalizes on the cultural heritage of the places that are points of interest in the gameplay. Specific places are characterized by particular species of Pokémon, for instance. *Ingress*, by contrast, uses cities as mere locations: Its portals could be moved to other places and the game would remain the same. Unlike the two cases mentioned earlier, Niantic's new title *Harry Potter: Wizard Unite* (2019) introduces narrative in a significant way, with characters who present parts of the story and invite the player to continue looking for elements in the digital world.

As we consider it important to capitalize on the cultural, social, or personal capital of space and enrich it with further meanings that players can access, we asked our students to design LBMGs with the specific goal of seamlessly integrating physical game elements and people in the play experience (Spallazzo & Mariani, 2018). To do that, we asked them to mix LBMGs with praxis from urban games (de Souza e Silva & Hjorth, 2009; Montola, Stenros, & Waern, 2009) and mixed-reality gaming performances (Ackermann, 2014; Benford & Giannachi, 2011) that tend to commonly employ props, actors, live performances, and installations.

The boundary between the physical and the fictional worlds, which is typical of LBMGs, is therefore played by threshold elements, *boundary objects*, to use Star and Griesemer's terminology (1989). Namely, these elements are plastic enough to adapt to the two worlds without losing their common identity (Star & Griesemer, 1989, p. 393) or at least while maintaining consistency in both realities. Star and Griesemer propose a classification of boundary objects into four categories: (i) Repository, (ii) ideal types, (iii) coincident boundaries, and (iv) standardized forms. These categories can be translated into the field of LBMGs. Repositories (i) are objects that people from different worlds can "borrow from the pile for their own purposes without having directly to negotiate differences in purpose" (Star & Griesemer, 1989, p. 410). Urban space, for example, can be thought of as a repository, a library of objects—trees, benches, lampposts—designers can employ in both worlds. Other elements can play the role of ideal types (ii), elements which are sufficiently blurred and abstracted from all domains that they can be easily adapted in both worlds. One example is an abstracted city map, either physical or digital, vague enough to be superimposed onto different urban settings. Designers can also exploit coincident boundaries (iii), providing the same element with different meanings according to the world in which it is employed. To follow up on the examples related to urban space, we could imagine having a lamppost in the physical world that functions as a meeting point or a portal for digital characters. Finally, designers could also employ elements that convey the same information regardless of the context, standardized forms (iv) according to Star and Griesemer's definition, or *immutable mobiles* in Bruno Latour's (1986) terminology. For instance, a city bench could be a place to rest for both players in the physical world and avatars in the digital one.

The rationale behind such classification shows that designers can employ a number of elements as thresholds serving to circumscribe the two worlds. In so doing, such elements act as interfaces which are capable of influencing our daily lives, defining how we perceive our spatial surroundings and social interaction (Johnson, 1997). de Souza e Silva's (2006) concept of *social interface* is particularly relevant here in that she argues that digital devices "intermediates relationships between two or more users" (pp. 261–262). She also underlines the role of cultural context in defining interfaces, since the social significance of an interface is not wholly reliant on technology alone but is the result of the way such an interface is integrated into social practices.

Therefore, the discourse on boundaries and thresholds must take into account all those elements that may act as interfaces between the two worlds across the entire play experience. This is to say, designers must be aware that the mobile device is not the only boundary element; rather, the environment, physical objects, and even people can be boundary elements between physical and digital worlds and these thresholds need to be coherently used and seamlessly integrated into the narrative.

A narrative perspective

Not all games entail or rely on stories (Juul, 2001, 2005). However, games are also a compelling area for researching storytelling systems that involve multiple instances of experimentation with interactive narratives (Koenitz et al., 2015; Young & Riedl, 2003). Although games themselves are not narrative-based by definition, narrative appears to be particularly relevant for certain genres of games, such as persuasive and adventure games, role-playing games (RPGs), and alternative reality games (ARGs) that largely revolve around stories and game content (Ip, 2011a, 2011b). Independent of the story's depth or branching, such games recognize and legitimize the role of narrative (Moser & Fang, 2015). By providing a sense of dramatic progress, stories grant a greater sense of meaning and immersion, and they nurture emotional satisfaction (Adams, 2010, pp. 155–156). On the other hand, those games that rely more on mechanics than narrative display a fairly solid tendency to relegate narrative to a mere design possibility. Examples are games such as the abovementioned *Pokémon Go* (2016) and *Ingress* (2012) by Niantic, or *Can You See Me Now?* (2001) by Blast Theory and Mixed Reality Lab: technology-mediated games that use spatial movements, localization, and in-situ interaction to progress in the game without the need for a narrative. When they are present, narratives are often used to provide a setting rather than being a constituting element of which players might take full advantage: In such cases, narratives appear as an interchangeable element of the gameplay included to make it appealing and fascinating, but they remain unattached and even disposable.

Our goal largely relies on the potential of narrative as a way to immerse players in the fictional game world (Wolf, 2012). Many scholars and practitioners have described a good game as one that allows its players to *immerse* themselves (Csikszentmihalyi, 1991; Murray, 1997; Ryan, 2001) and get lost in the game and its narrative, resulting in a sort of escape from reality. However, in LBMGs and hybrid games, such a situation is challenged by the fact that the game is taking place in the physical space as well as in the digital world. Instead of escaping from the physical world, such games can—and in our opinion *should*—take advantage of thresholds, enhancing them with further meaning. As a result, rather than being potential weak points or elements of friction between what is part of the game and what is not, elements of division between physical and digital, such as the device, the space itself, its objects, and people can—and should—be invested with narrative, in-game meaning, thereby further nurturing immersion in the game as a holistic experience characterized by consistency and coherence (Wolf, 2012).

As a result, there are many aspects that make it difficult to design these games in a way that makes proper use of their potentiality, such as being geo-localized and able to rely on interaction with physical elements spread throughout the space in which the game takes place. In this context, the thresholds introduced earlier serve a key function. However, if they are not shrewdly designed, they can damage the overall experience, becoming possible exit points from the flow of the game. Examples include physical spaces that are not recognized as narratively consistent with what is taking place in the digital dimension, boundary objects that are not acknowledged as game elements, and people who should trigger specific interactions but are not identified as part of the game.

A well-built narrative can create a game experience that is satisfying, engaging, and significant. Indeed, narrativity can facilitate immersion and encourage players to engage in meaning-making. Ryan (2001), for instance, discusses the role immersion and interactivity play in helping the audience along the process of reconstructing both worlds and their features while at the same time activating a comparison between a fictional world and the physical one. Narrative is pivotal when dealing with communication. However, transcending the often straightforward, functional, solution-oriented approach typical of the design discipline, a wise use of narrative can both evoke and create meanings (triggering meaning-making). Stories can be embedded, conveying messages through their elements: the fictional world, roles/characters, game objects, the story itself, and its missions, but also the mechanics and places through which players are led to move can be built as parts of an ecosystem of metaphors (Spallazzo & Mariani, 2018). In terms of game design, such a use of narrative elements and narrative creates an opportunity for exploiting narrative potentialities and making the most of its ability to encourage players to reason about the topic being presented. In so doing, we can say that the game is producing knowledge through its elements, on the basis of the fact that players continuously interpret what they consume.

We embrace a design perspective to highlight how narrative might be skillfully—and wisely—used in designing LBMGs as complex rhetorical structures in which different components can convey meanings that are reciprocally consistent. Designing games that take place between the physical and the digital entails integrating concepts and meanings into elements that already have a complex function, that of constituting thresholds between two dimensions.

In light of this reasoning, after defining the research methodology underlying our study, we proceed to unpack how the various elements involved in LBMGs as complex ecosystems can play the role of meaningful thresholds with the capacity to enrich the game experience by making sharp and consistent use of narrative logics.

Context and methodology of the empirical research

The observations we present in this section are grounded in the results of an empirical research we conducted, analyzing the processes of both designing and playtesting 57 LBMGs created as final student projects for the BSc course "Augmented Reality and Mobile Experience" in the School of Design at Politecnico di Milano. From 2013 to 2017, a total of 240 students—about 60 each year—were involved in designing, prototyping, and testing LBMGs addressing contemporary societal problems.

The aim of our study was to research how these games can function as engaging communication systems with the capacity to involve players while also transmitting information. We observed and examined our sample of LBMGs through ethnographic analysis and interpretative research. The study employed a mixed methods approach, collecting multiple forms of data and applying a triangulation of methods (Creswell, 2008).

During the iterative design cycles, which lasted three consecutive months each academic year, we performed interpretative ethnography and participant observation (Musante & DeWalt, 2002; Stake, 1995). Rapid ethnographies, shadowing, questionnaires, and informal interviews with students were carried out in parallel to complement the results of the above-described methods and reduce eventual biases and weakness. These strategies were selected in light of two main premises, namely that games are artifacts which (i) require designers to consider a broad range of elements and interplays, and (ii) lead players to have hands-on experiences of *play*. By participating in the entire process of ideating, creating, and testing the 57 LBMGs analyzed in our study, we were able to understand designers' needs in terms of knowledge and tools, on the one hand, and how players received games and made sense of them, on the other.

The design dimension of distributed thresholds: device, spaces, objects, and people

The aim of our study is to broaden the concept of threshold to extend beyond the idea that mobile devices are the *only* interface between the ordinary and the ludic in LBMGs. Analyzing LBMGs as objects of study shows that designers have adopted diverse strategies in terms of using the mobile device for narrative purposes. Several games employ the mobile device as a guide through the game's points of interest; in other words, the mobile device can also function as a narrator, a companion following players through the story and urban space that delivers narrative pieces to the players, following the progression of the game and players' triggering of game mechanics by moving in space. The situatedness of the narrative entails a close relationship between locations and story: Consequently, mobile technology nurtures the fictional world layer by continuously mixing the physical and digital realms.

From a design perspective, this requires looking at games as a set in which multiple layers intertwine, such as the story, gameplay, spaces, objects, and trigger elements. Designing such a game, therefore, involves (i) unpacking the storyline and outlining specific fragments of story, (ii) identifying meaningful locations, (iii) distributing the narrative in significant places, (iv) defining how to convey each part of the story, and (v) determining their trigger, namely whether (and, if so, which) specific game elements or the geo-localization itself will function as points of access to the story, causing the player to progress in the gameplay (Figure 2.1).

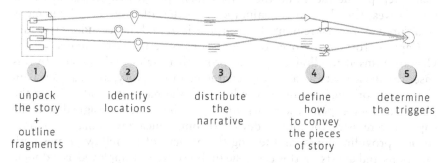

1	2	3	4	5
unpack the story + outline fragments	identify locations	distribute the narrative	define how to convey the pieces of story	determine the triggers

Figure 2.1 The design process, focusing on the connection between the elements. Copyright: Davide Spallazzo and Ilaria Mariani.

Figure 2.2 The Lost Papyrus (Benedetti et al., 2015). Copyright: Davide Spallazzo and Ilaria Mariani.

The device as a storyteller

In many cases, the smartphone is employed as an omniscient narrator that chronicles the events in an impartial way from outside the story, without taking on the role of a character inside the story. It provides the player with suggestions regarding the correct position of clues and proposes dilemmas to be solved in order to progress in the gameplay. An example is *The Lost Papyrus* (Benedetti et al., 2015), designed to raise awareness about the impact of Alzheimer's disease on the everyday activities of sick people and those who live with them. In this game, the mobile device is used as an all-seeing narrator directing the four players, while the players take on the roles of expert archaeologists and their bold assistants exploring an as-yet-undiscovered tomb to find a renowned papyrus. In their search to recover valuable ancient artifacts, players face increasingly difficult quests that symbolize the degeneration of the illness (Figure 2.2).

In other games, the mobile device takes on the role of storyteller, entering the story as a character. In *The Treasures of Captain Torment* (Boni, Frizzi, & Taccola, 2015), the mobile device embodies the spirit of a pirate captain named Torment who guides the players to his hidden treasures. The game deals with the mental condition of depressed people and aims to raise awareness about the challenges facing individuals struggling with depression, specifically the feelings of inadequacy, melancholy, and hopelessness that often plague them and their consequent progressive marginalization by relatives, friends, and acquaintances. As the title suggests, the game is structured as a treasure hunt. The purpose is to find the legendary treasure of Captain Torment by overcoming a series of tests masterminded by the Captain himself to allow players to prove their valor and bravery. In this case, the device acts as an active character in the story, and as such is in charge of both introducing and advancing the narrative and guiding the players as they explore their surroundings. The game is designed as if the captain were using the mobile device to communicate with players, telling stories, providing hints, and testing the bravery of his fellow pirates with questions and quests. In this case, the mobile device is employed as a double threshold: It is the storyteller that grounds the narrative in urban space and the portal that connects players with the spirit of the captain.

The mobile device can also be employed as a *mentor,* reminiscent of the archetypal narrative role detailed in Campbell's (1949) and Vogler's (1992) works, namely a wise character who helps, trains, or instructs the *hero,* the main character of the story. The smartphone becomes an influential voice, leading the player not only through the game but also toward a specific behavior. The game *The 10 Commandments* (Culla et al., 2014) seeks to immerse players in the daily life of a person struggling with anorexia, stressing both the mental and physical discomfort, to inform people and raise awareness about eating disorders as a contemporary and widespread phenomenon. Equipped with a smartphone and a game kit containing dilemma cards and instructions, players retrace a day in the life of a girl who has to attend a casting call. The mobile device provides the players with ten commandments they must follow in order to have a "perfect slim body," unconsciously inducing the players, within the safe space of the game, to follow harmful rules based on real online blogs asserting the so-called "Pro-Anorexia" (Pro-Ana) behavior and presenting anorexia as a positive life philosophy. The progression of the game narrative is designed to make players feel more and more doubtful about the validity of the behavior of the character with whom they have identified. In so doing, Ana's 10 commandments presented at the beginning of the game as rules to be followed end up being called into question one by one, and the mobile device is no longer perceived as a mentor who accompanies and guides players, but rather as a *shapeshifter* (a character that blurs the line between ally and enemy) as well as a *shadow* (villains in the story) (Vogler, 1992) who underhandedly fools the player. Leading to certain failure and even a possible game over, designers harnessed the potential of the mobile device as an authoritative voice to puzzle players with a final plot twist that calls into question the credibility of the narrative voice. Indeed, it is impossible for players to ultimately reach the casting call: At the end of the day, they simply do not have enough energy to open the door of the photo studio.

The examples discussed earlier highlight the role that the mobile device can play as a threshold, linking players to the story. Nevertheless, mobile technology in LBMGs is just one of multiple possible bridges: All game elements can be key in transferring meaning and sustaining the narrative of the game. Consequently, each element, be it physical or digital, and the way it is understood can impact on players' perceptions of the story and more broadly on the overall coherence and consistency of the way the game conveys its messages.

A complex interplay between spaces, objects, and people

Space is also a powerful threshold in LBMGs. Indeed, linking the gaming experience to specific places means granting those places a role within the story and transforming them into a bridge to the fictional world. This is especially true in *local games* (Montola, 2011), that is, games in which the gameplay is closely related to the setting in which the game takes place.[1]

On the flipside, narratives may be fully exploited in *local games* since every place, as well as the objects it contains, has the potential to act as a threshold between the two worlds. *The Treasures of Captain Torment* (Boni, Frizzi, & Taccola, 2015), for example, turns objects in the university campus into elements that support the game story. In the game, the paved road is transformed into a sea, the flowerbeds become rocks, the fire-fighting stairs are cliffs to be climbed, and the university garden is the treasure island. Regardless of whether their use is metaphorical/symbolic or literal, places always signify something.

Both the environment and the objects populating the game acquire a double meaning: one in the physical world, and the other in the story's fictional world. Consequently, we analyze the different functions that objects can play as game elements by unpacking the relationship between these objects and the context in which they are positioned. We outline three categories of game objects: *ordinary objects*, *common objects*, and *bespoke objects*.

Ordinary objects are physical elements that are perfectly integrated into the space and only acquire a new significance for the players, specifically. These objects might previously exist in the game space or be placed there on purpose, but they are not perceived as alien or extraneous to the context since they do not appear to be part of a game; however, they have a different meaning depending on whether the person viewing them is a player or non-player. An example of this category is found in *The Fellowship of the Umbrella* (Bianchini et al., 2014), a game that tackles the sensitive topic of physical disabilities by exploring its related issues, creating a fictional world that is a metaphoric transposition of certain traits of the obstacles people with disabilities face on a daily basis. Set in Middle-earth, the game tells the story of a group of four gifted individuals—an extraordinary magician, a wise dwarf, a powerful beech, and a sharp elf—and their adventures to reach a treasure. The magician who cannot speak because he is "in a water world" is actually mute, the beech tree has a motor disability, the elf is visually impaired, and the dwarf is deaf.

In this context, a regular garbage bag left on the top of or next to a trash bin in the physical world is viewed as a forgotten item by unsuspecting passers-by, while for players it represents a fundamental element of the game in that the player performing the role of the beech has to wear it. Within this specific game, the garbage bag is a physical prop the player has to wear. The game elements that we have categorized as *ordinary objects* generate a different interpretation depending on the user who is looking at them. While they do not exert any influence over non-players, they are of major significance to players. They act as boundary objects, and in particular as *coincident boundary objects*, recalling the studies of Star and Griesemer (1989), since they acquire different meanings according to the world in which they are employed.

The second category, c*ommon objects*, refers to those game elements that are actually common objects but are recognized as being out of context by both passers-by and players themselves. For example, in *Drop.it* (Bonfim Bandeira et al., 2016), common ampoules filled with water are hung on trees, waiting to be collected by players. Although no one would describe them as unusual if they were located in a kitchen, the fact that they are hanging from trees makes them stand out by virtue of being out of place. However, only the players grasp their meaning and contextual role. Another example is found in the aforementioned *The Fellowship of the Umbrella* (Bianchini et al., 2014). Among the items that players wear to perform the different game roles is a mask with snorkel. The object is intended for the Wizard, who cannot actually talk since he is wearing the snorkel and represents the condition of mute people. While a mask with snorkel would not be out of context on a beach, it is conspicuous and definitely out of place in this context, considering the fact that the game is location-specific and located in the North of Milan, where there are neither beaches nor sea. Although these objects are clearly not integrated into the space in which they are located, they do not openly declare themselves to be necessarily "gameful." The fact that they are "out of place" does not make them so powerful as to be immediately and without exception identified as game elements. However, within the fictional world of the game and its narrative, they make sense and hence are recognized as game objects.

The third category, *bespoke objects*, includes those elements that are perceived as specifically designed and manufactured for the game. In *The Origins of Forging* (Belloni et al., 2016), players take on the role of Greek Gods who are asked to re-discover their mythological roots—roots which are bound to contemporary works of craftsmanship. Aimed at conveying the practices and values of handicraft, the game invites its players to explore their surroundings by interacting with several artifacts and props placed in different places of the gamespace. Such interactions and activities are part of the missions that players need to complete to earn the status of in-game Gods. These props include cardboard cutouts of wild animals such as wolves and bears. These objects are clearly game elements and are identifiable as such by both players and non-players, with the only difference being that players know what they mean. The elements of this category transmit the same information regardless of the user observing them and, as such, they constitute *standardized forms* (Star & Griesemer, 1989), *immutable mobiles* (Latour, 1986) capable of connecting the two worlds.

To understand how these objects are perceived and interpreted, a fundamental step in designing LBMGs has to do with defining the interactions. In particular, we have identified three main types of interaction: *direct*, *mediated*, and *metaphorical*. *Direct interaction* involves the direct manipulation of physical objects such as game elements. Such objects can be a representation or a metaphor, but the interaction that they require takes place in the physical world without being translated into the digital. They might be elements that players are asked to collect and assemble, as in the aforementioned *The Origin of Forgings* (Belloni et al., 2016) where players must gather physical objects and gradually assemble them to form an element symbolizing the role played in the game, for example pieces of Poseidon's trident. They might also be props to use during the game, as in *The Treasures of Captain Torment* (Boni, Frizzi, & Taccola, 2015) where players are equipped with various objects, depending on their in-game role, as well as with a cardboard boat they have to step inside in order to navigate the sea. In these cases, the physical objects have a plain and evident function that corresponds to their narrative: The boat represents a boat and it is used as such (Figure 2.3).

Mediated interaction requires players to manipulate physical elements to achieve results in the digital world. The interaction is defined as *mediated* because physical objects are used to trigger activities on the mobile device. Examples are objects built, manipulated, or even destroyed to gather information and advance in the game. In *The Rapture* (Conti et al., 2015), the physical objects are a styrofoam car, colored balloons, and a piñata. They are the receptacles of hidden codes that players must type into the digital interface of the game to progress in the story. To unlock the necessary information, each

Figure 2.3 The Treasures of Captain Torment (Boni, Frizzi, & Taccola, 2015). Copyright: Davide Spallazzo and Ilaria Mariani.

object needs to be destroyed. However, a powerful action of this kind needs to be properly sustained by the narrative, lest players perceive it as unnecessary or even inappropriate. In this specific case, breaking objects was particularly in tune with the game narrative, a critical commentary on how people often think that certain ends and ideals justify the means. Players, indeed, think that they are acting like superheroes, while in the end, they discover that they have been acting like common vandals. In the example discussed earlier, the game elements are boundary objects that play the role of real thresholds, preventing the player from entering the digital part of the game, hence advancing in the story and gameplay, until they have been solved.

The last type, *metaphorical interaction*, involves objects that explicitly represent or symbolize something else. A well-known example is the way players use bananas and coffee as guns and poison in assassin games, the live-role play games commonly played in university campuses (Montola, Stenros, & Waern, 2009, pp. 34–35). In such cases, the similarity in shape or nature between certain objects leads players to make use of one object to represent another. By embedding meaning in objects through metaphors, the designer transforms them into a threshold that the player must first decipher and then use.

Players and non-players alike can also function as thresholds. In *local games*, for example, people can be purposely placed at specific locations to allow or trigger players' action. An example can be seen in *Rewind* (Gubbiani et al., 2014). Designed to raise awareness about aging issues, the game carries players back in time like in *The Curious Case of Benjamin Button* and asks them to collect memories in order to cause time to flow in the correct direction. The designers leveraged the uncertainty of the Global Positioning System (GPS) to encourage players to go into the various stores located in the surroundings and strike up conversations with the shopkeepers. In this case, the players' aim is to find a password to proceed in the game and to collect memories. Only one of the stores has an aware actor, who provides players with the right clue, while the others are real outsiders. Clearly, the aware actor is the threshold that discloses its role as part of the game, while the other, unaware shopkeepers can potentially play the same role in the eye of the player.

While it is true that actors' involvement in the game may result in several advantages, such as a more vivid play experience, increased immersion, and eventually a better way of solving the problems players may encounter (providing situated help), such involvement may also affect the replicability and longevity of the game, configuring it as performances and events. On the other hand, *Rewind* (Gubbiani et al., 2014) suggests that, as long as the narrative implies such a possibility, players might just perceive every person on the playground as a threshold. This may be the case of *global* LBMGs which, by their very nature, cannot cover the entire world with actors, but they can cause players to think that bystanders are part of the game. For instance, they can suggest that other players are nearby or exploit some elements of urban space that are very likely to be present. An example is *Chain Reaction* (2006), a non-digital locative game designed to make people get lost in the city in a modern *dérive* by asking players to change direction every time they bump into a real-world pedestrian walking with a specific item—such as a red bag—or find a certain kind of store, such as a bakery or a shoe store.

Both the narrative and the game mechanics stand out by virtue of their potential to transform people into thresholds and make players perceive elements which are not part of the game as if they actually were part of it. As a matter of fact, the story may become so pervasive and consistent as to lead players to attribute meaning and significance to elements present in the environment which, although not originally part of the game, end up being understood as such.

In a nutshell

In this chapter, we have discussed how meaningful narrative and metaphorical elements can be included in the design of LBMGs. We have analyzed these games as complex rhetorical structures, which convey coherent and consistent meanings. Designing a game that takes place between the physical and the digital entails integrating new meanings into elements that already have a complex function, that of thresholds between two worlds. The very presence of these elements requires players to capture, interpret, and grant meaning to an experience taking place across thresholds. In terms of design, this means trying to eliminate any possible narrative-cognitive friction in favor of a roundness of meanings and overall smoothness. Such complexity stems not only from the physical elements of the game. Since we are dealing with geo-localized games that are spatially situated, the space itself is meaningful and indeed the very space in which the game takes place is a source of further value. In light of this insight, LBMG designers would do well to create narratives that valorize places, rather than using places as mere gamespaces.

Note

1 In global games such as *Pokémon GO* (Niantic, 2016), a close relationship of this kind is almost impossible since designers cannot foresee where the game will be actually played and must rely on algorithms to associate pieces of gameplay, characters, and mechanics with places. As a consequence, the device assumes a leading role as the main threshold, and the environment is deprived of a specific meaning, detached from the story and employed as a mere setting for the play experience.

References

Ackermann, J. (2014). Digital games und hybrid reality theatre. *New Game Plus: Perspektiven Der Game Studies. Genres-Künste-Diskurse, 3,* 63.

Adams, E. (2010). *Fundamentals of Game Design.* San Francisco, CA: New Riders.

Belloni, E., Bucalossi, C., Mazzoleni, C., & Menini, M. (2016). *The Origins of Forging* [LBMG]. Milano: Politecnico di Milano.

Benedetti, A., Franco Conesa, C., De Marco, A., & Piatti, J. (2015). *The Lost Papyrus* [LBMG]. Milano: Politecnico di Milano.

Benford, S., & Giannachi, G. (2011). *Performing Mixed Reality*. Cambridge, MA/ London: The MIT Press.

Bianchini, S., Mor, L., Princigalli, V., & Sciannamé, M. (2014). *The Fellowship of the Umbrella* [LBMG]. Milano: Politecnico di Milano.

Bonfim Bandeira, F., Marcon, S., Namias, C., & Paris, M. (2016). *Drop.it* [LBMG]. Milano: Politecnico di Milano.

Boni, A., Frizzi, G., & Taccola, S. (2015). *The Treasures of Captain Torment* [LBMG]. Milano: Politecnico di Milano.

Botfighters [MMORPG]. (2001). Stockholm, Sweden: It's Alive.

Caillois, R. (1958). *Les jeux et les hommes: le masque et le virtige*. Paris: Gallimard.

Campbell, J. K. (1949). *The Hero with a Thousand Faces*. Princeton, NJ: Princeton University.

Can You See Me Now? [Hybrid game]. (2001). London, UK: Blast Theory and Mixed Reality Lab.

Conti, G., Saracino, G., Serbanescu, A., & Valente, N. (2015). *The Rapture* [LBMG]. Milano: Politecnico di Milano.

Creswell, J. W. (2008). *Research Design: Qualitative, Quantitative, and Mixed Methods Approaches*. Beverly Hills, CA: Sage.

Csikszentmihalyi, M. (1991). *Flow: The Psychology of Optimal Experience*. New York, NY: Harper Perennial.

Culla, L. A., Di Filippo, L., Frisia, C., & Golan, M. (2014). *The 10 Commandments* [LBMG]. Milano: Politecnico di Milano.

de Souza e Silva, A. (2006). Re-conceptualizing the mobile phone – from telephone to collective interfaces. *Society, 4*(2), 108–127.

de Souza e Silva, A., & Delacruz, G. C. (2006). Hybrid reality games reframed: Potential uses in educational contexts. *Games and Culture, 1*(3), 231–251.

de Souza e Silva, A., & Hjorth, L. (2009). Playful urban spaces: A historical approach to mobile games. *Simulation & Gaming, 40*(5), 602–625.

de Souza e Silva, A., & Sutko, D. M. (2011). Theorizing locative media through philosophies of the virtual. *Communication Theory, 21*(1), 23–42.

Ermi, L., & Mäyrä, F. (2005). Fundamental components of the gameplay experience: Analysing immersion. *Worlds in Play: International Perspectives on Digital Games Research, 37*, 88–115.

Flanagan, M. (2009). *Critical Play: Radical Game Design*. Cambridge, MA: The MIT Press.

Flintham, M., Benford, S., Anastasi, R., Hemmings, T., Crabtree, A., Greenhalgh, C., … Row-Farr, J. (2003). Where on-line meets on the streets: Experiences with mobile mixed reality games. *Proceedings of the SIGCHI Conference on Human Factors in Computing Systems*, 569–576, New York: ACM.

Fullerton, T. (2014). *Game Design Workshop: A Playcentric Approach to Creating Innovative Games*. New York, NY: CRC press.

Gubbiani, G., Rico-Sanchez, M., Ronchi, E., Rosti, A., & Tabasso, I. (2014). *Rewind* [LBMG]. Milano: Politecnico di Milano.

Harry Potter: Wizard Unite [LBMG]. (2019). San Francisco, CA: Niantic.

Hunicke, R., LeBlanc, M., & Zubek, R. (2004). MDA: A formal approach to game design and game research. *Proceedings of the AAAI Workshop on Challenges in Game AI, 4*, 1772.

Ingress [LBMG]. (2012). San Francisco, CA: Niantic.

Ip, B. (2011a). Narrative structures in computer and video games: Part 1: Context, definitions, and initial findings. *Games and Culture, 6*(2), 103–134.

Ip, B. (2011b). Narrative structures in computer and video games: Part 2: Emotions, structures, and archetypes. *Games and Culture, 6*(3), 203–244.

Jacob, J., da Silva, H., Coelho, A., & Rodrigues, R. (2012). Towards location-based augmented reality games. *Procedia Computer Science, 15*(Supplement C), 318–319.

Johnson, S. (1997). *Interface Culture: How New Technology Transforms the Way We Create and Communicate* (1st ed.). San Francisco, CA: Harper San Francisco.

Juul, J. (2001). Games telling stories? – A brief note on games and narratives. *Game Studies, 1*(1), 45.

Juul, J. (2005). *Half-Real: Video Games between Real Rules and Fictional Worlds.* Cambridge, MA: The MIT Press.

Kaufman, G., & Flanagan, M. (2015). A psychologically "embedded" approach to designing games for prosocial causes. *Cyberpsychology: Journal of Psychosocial Research on Cyberspace, 9*(3), 1–18.

Koenitz, H., Ferri, G., Haahr, M., Sezen, D., & Sezen, T. İ. (2015). *Interactive Digital Narrative: History, Theory and Practice.* New York, NY: Routledge.

Latour, B. (1986). Visualization and cognition: Drawing things together. In H. Kuklick (Ed.), *Knowledge and Society Studies in the Sociology of Culture Past and Present.* Greenwich: Jai Press.

Mariani, I. (2016). Meaningful negative experiences within games for social change. *Designing and Analysing Games as Persuasive Communication Systems.* PhD Thesis, Milano: Politecnico di Milano.

Montola, M. (2011). A ludological view on the pervasive mixed-reality game research paradigm. *Personal and Ubiquitous Computing, 15*(1), 3–12.

Montola, M., Stenros, J., & Waern, A. (2009). *Pervasive Games: Theory and Design.* Burlington, MA: Morgan Kaufmann Publishers.

Moser, C., & Fang, X. (2015). Narrative structure and player experience in role-playing games. *International Journal of Human-Computer Interaction, 31*(2), 146–156.

Murray, J. H. (1997). *Hamlet on the Holodeck: The Future of Narrative in Cyberspace.* Cambridge, MA: The MIT Press.

Musante, K., & DeWalt, B. R. (2002). *Participant Observation: A Guide for Fieldworkers.* Lanham, MD: AltaMira Press.

Pokémon Go [LBMG]. (2016). San Francisco, CA: Niantic.

Ryan, M. L. (2001). *Narrative as Virtual Reality: Immersion and Interactivity in Literature and Electronic Media.* Baltimore, MD: Johns Hopkins University Press.

Smith, S. (2006). *Chain Reaction* [Urban game]. New York, NY and Westwood, LA: Samara Smith.

Spallazzo, D., & Mariani, I. (2017). LBMGs and boundary objects. Negotiation of meaning between real and unreal. *6th STS Italia Conference, Sociotechnical Environments,* 645–659. Trento: STS Italia Publishing.

Spallazzo, D., & Mariani, I. (2018). *Location-based Mobile Games: Design Perspectives.* Cham: Springer.

Squire, K. D., Jan, M., Matthews, J., Wagler, M., Devane, B., & Holden, C. (2007). Wherever you Go, there you are: Place-based augmented reality games for learning.

In B. E. Shelton & D. A. Wiley (Eds.), *The Design and Use of Simulation Computer Games in Education* (pp. 273–304). Boston, MA: Sense Publisher.

Stake, R. E. (1995). *The Art of Case Study Research*. Thousand Oaks, CA: Sage.

Star, S. L., & Griesemer, J. R. (1989). Institutional ecology, 'translations' and boundary objects: Amateurs and professionals in Berkeley's museum of vertebrate Zoology, 1907–39. *Social Studies of Science, 19*(3), 387–420.

Vogler, C. (1992). *The Writer's Journey: Mythic Structures for Screenwriters and Storytellers*. Studio City, CA: Michael Wiese Productions.

Wolf, M. J. P. (2012). *Building Imaginary Worlds: The Theory and History of Subcreation*. New York, NY: Routledge.

Young, R. M., & Riedl, M. (2003). Towards an architecture for intelligent control of narrative in interactive virtual worlds. *Proceedings of the 8th International Conference on Intelligent User Interfaces*, 310–312. New York: ACM.

3 Training perceptions through play

A case for building interactive autoethnographic experiences through Twine

Kristina Bell

In 2009, Chris Klimas developed Twine, an open-source tool for building hyperlinked, interactive narratives. With this tool, users with little coding experience could build text-based stories, and those with advanced skills could employ HTML, CSS, and Javascript to add multimedia and modify the design. Since its creation, many of Twine's content creators have not sought commodification. Instead, they have created "pay-what-you-can" games out of an intrinsic motivation to connect with others and express themselves. For this reason, Twine has historically been used to queer traditional texts, that is, Twine has been used to create "radical, experimental, and non-normative development, stories, and mechanics" (Harvey, 2014, p. 99). In this chapter, I argue that these qualities serve autoethnography's approach of telling marginalized stories from a highly personal standpoint.

Autoethnography is a hybrid method that combines autobiographical creative writing and rigorous research. It requires an organizational pattern and style that blends story and study of the self to help us reevaluate the identities constructed by and for us, to provide a means "to write about the poetics of living" (Goodall, 2007, p. 188), and to emotionally connect and heal audiences and authors. Autoethnography provides an outlet to express the pain of stigmatized identities (Bochner & Ellis, 2006), and connects those who suffer with the stories of others like them by providing an opportunity for audiences to reflect and learn from others' experiences. Autoethnographers consider their stories "gifts to the world" (Poulos, 2008a p. 64), since they give voice to multiple lived experiences, often underrepresented within the social sciences (Bochner, 2001). For this reason, autoethnographic writing often brings attention to the oppression of marginalized groups and pushes back against institutionalized racism and sexism found in many publications and citation practices (Chakravartty, Kuo, Grubbs, & McIlwain, 2018). Further, autoethnographies are often more accessible and immersive because they employ a writing style that includes both storytelling techniques and emotionally descriptive language to produce an experience that is performative and evocative.

Twine's interactivity and customization serve autoethnography's goals of immersive storytelling, as authors can include game-like mechanics, sound effects, images, and branching narratives. Through Twine, the author is able to appeal to two seemingly competing player motivations: to learn and to play. Play has been defined by scholars such as Caillois (1961) as being separate from work, seriousness, and ordinary life. However, play is an experience that is networked, connected with other experiences—no matter how trite; "play is essentially part of (all) life," the ordinary, the mundane, and the banal (de Souza e Silva & Sutko, 2008). All acts of play are hybrids of the game's virtual world and the player's physical world (a.k.a "meatspace") as the player's own bodily responses (such as needing to go to the bathroom), technological hardware (controllers, keyboard), and cultural constructions and social engagements directly influence their performance in the game (Taylor, Kampe, & Bell, 2015).

In this chapter, I explore how autoethnography, as a hybrid method, can be paired with Twine to form playable, immersive hybrid experiences. I explore four different forms of hybridity in relation to play: (1) the hybridity of the researcher as a game designer and subject, (2) the hybridity of play and academic research, (3) the hybridity of highly personal writing as something to be played, and (4) the hybridity of play with the ordinary or the mundane. Through both a textual analysis of genre-defining Twine works such as Anna Anthropy's *Queers in Love at the End of the World (QED)* (2013) and Zoe Quinn's *Depression Quest* (2013), and an examination of my own interactive autoethnography, I detail themes and approaches that are shared by autoethnographers and Twine authors. I examine the hybrid roles I performed during my own Twine project's creation, which included researcher, subject, and game designer. Further, I explore how these hybrid roles pushed me to organize my research differently and to include more elements, like pathos and playful experimentation, compared to what I would typically include in my research and writing.

What follows is a textual analysis of similar themes that some Twine games and autoethnographies share, ending with a discussion of how I incorporated these themes in my interactive autoethnography. This is not intended to be a generalizable or comprehensive study. I selected Twine stories that I have previously researched and written about in my autoethnographic work, which I later discuss as a case study. The Twine stories were found via Google searches, recommendations from colleagues and students, and books about indie game design (Anthropy, 2012; kopas, 2015). Twine games are hypertexts (Hayles, 2002); they include hyperlinks that players click to advance and change the story (Aarseth, 1997; Ryan, 2011). They have roots in *Choose Your Own Adventure Books* and early text adventure games like *Zork* (Infocom, 1977) and *Adventure* (Crowther, 1977) (Montfort, 2011). Early literature (Aarseth, 1997; Montfort, 2011) has referred to these types of texts as "interactive fiction." Here, I refer to these works as "interactive narratives."

Several of Twine's texts are autobiographical in part or in their entirety. The interactive narratives I gathered shared many of the following themes: They were personal, diverse stories (which included, at times, an attention to the ordinary); they engaged the player through design and encouraged learning through choice. The themes here are not representative of *all* Twine games or autoethnographies, and only speak to the possibilities the medium offers to autoethnography.

Personal, diverse stories

Many Twine games and autoethnographies focus on personal stories with deep self-disclosure. Anna Anthropy, a queer, transgendered, do-it-yourself (DIY) game maker, is credited for creating a "Twine Revolution" among independent, marginalized game designers (Harvey, 2014) and ushering in a "personal games movement" (Alexander, 2013; Bernardi, 2013; Harvey, 2014; kopas, 2015), as many of the Twine stories from this time focused on the authors' private lives. These include Pratt's *Anhedonia* (2014a) piece about mental illness; Freeman's *Mangia* (2014) about chronic illness; and Sampat's *Nineteen* (2014) about suicide. kopas (2015) has also examined difficult topics such as childhood abuse and consensual sadomasochism, as a means to process her emotions and work through "personal and political struggles" (p. 6).

Like Twine, autoethnography provides an outlet for researchers to disclose intimate stories of trauma to expose life's "shadow places" (Richardson, 1992, p. 131) and spark discussion (Fox, 1996). Fox (1996) utilized autoethnography as a tool to educate and talk about childhood sexual abuse, Olson (2004) discussed her survival of domestic abuse, Tillmann-Healy (1996) worked through her life-long struggle with an eating disorder, and Poulos (2002) examined the trauma of the September 11th terrorist attacks. The disclosing of traumatic experience helps to contextualize intimate stories within broader social and cultural structures.

For kopas (2015), writing served a hybrid role as it worked toward community-building. She shared her work with like-minded others and became part of the "queer games scene" community that wrote and shared interactive stories about their "messy lives" (p. 7). Twine helped queer the "hegemonic culture of game design" (Harvey, 2014), as it provided an accessible outlet for marginalized groups to make games. At the time of Twine's 2009 release, few games told the stories of characters who were non-white and non-male (Williams, Martins, Consalvo, & Ivory, 2009), and game companies were reluctant to include homosexual relationships out of fear that gamers were homophobic (Shaw, 2009). The lack of representation contributed to a "symbolic annihilation" of groups (Shaw, 2009); the selective exclusion communicated that the voices, lives, and culture of these underrepresented groups were insignificant to American culture.

This was partially the result of a lack of gender diversity within the mainstream game industry. A 2015 survey by the International Game Developers

Association (IGDA) found that 75% of all game developers identify as male, and 76% are white. Twine provided an outlet for marginalized players who sought interactive experiences beyond the normative mainstream experience provided by AAA titles (large studio and budget). Anthropy (2012), an independent game designer and author, wrote of her desire to create games outside of the "single culture" of the games industry and how Twine could be used (among other tools) to make games about something other than "men shooting men in the face" (p. 3).

Like the Twine authors, ethnographers have used autoethnography as a tool to tell stories through diverse, underrepresented standpoints that celebrate the personal and subjective perspectives and encourage those who are silenced to voice their secrets to heal. Autoethnography provides a means to explore identity in-depth, making emotional, personal, and provocative texts about cultural phenomena available to readers inside and outside academia, in hopes that the readers become connected, healed, and challenged through narrative (Bochner & Ellis, 2006; Ellis & Bochner, 2000; Poulos, 2008a). For some, though, it is challenging to practice that degree of self-disclosure, as this makes the author vulnerable (Olson, 2004) and, in turn, can shape the author's creative practices. If an author is using Twine and feels nervous when expressing deep self-disclosure, these intimate passages can be "buried" through choices and unlocked only after certain actions. A Twine game can be designed, so audiences have to "prove" themselves before unlocking sensitive content. It can also give the audience agency over whether or not (and at what point) they experience self-disclosure. From this perspective, the experience of Twine games exists as a series of negotiated interactions between the author and the audience.

Nevertheless, many Twine stories are published online to reach audiences outside of academia and, as such, there are risks for the authors. This was evident in Gamergate (2014), a massive harassment campaign against independent female game designers, critics, and academics who dared to create non-traditional games or who critiqued stereotypical representation (Wagner, 2014). Gamergaters sent rape, bomb, and death threats; obtained and shared highly personal information (addresses, photos); photoshopped sexual and violent imagery portraying the victims; and sent harassing messages to the victims, their employers, and their families that included misogynistic, racist, xenophobic, and anti-semitic language. While examples, like Gamergate, point to the risks of Twine, there are benefits to using such an unconventional tool when writing deeply personal accounts. For instance, Twine's interface, which allows users to write across interlinked passages, felt less intimidating to merrit kopas (2015) than trying to organize separate thoughts in one long linear document in a word processor. The novelty of this new tool worked to prevent writer's block and free her from the struggles of perfectionism. She writes:

> I'd been writing in an analytic mode for so long that I couldn't look at a blank page without my mind struggling to put things in order

before I got a single word down. When I opened up Twine, I felt free to just start writing fragments, each in their own passage (kopas, 2015, p. 7).

kopas' statement suggests that we often become so enmeshed in our systems, organizations, and structures of writing that we don't step back and question their effectiveness. Sometimes it takes breaking down them all and experimenting with a new method to gain clarity on what is useful and what is ineffective.

Yet another potential benefit is that videogames, including interactive narratives built on Twine, can embody human values (Flanagan & Nissenbaum, 2014) and may hybridize personal, emotional, and traumatic experiences with play in ways that promote empathy and understanding. For example, these hybrid texts include but are not limited to such experiences as loss of a parent (*The Walking Dead*, Telltale, 2012), loss of a child (*That Dragon, Cancer*, Numinous Games, 2016), mental illness (*Hellblade: Senua's Sacrifice*, Ninja Theory, 2017), childhood abuse (*Papa & Yo*, Minority Media Inc., 2012), coming out (*Coming out Simulator*, Nicky Case, 2014), and the trauma of War (*This War of Mine*, 11 Bit Studios, 2014). Through encountering these hybrid texts, players may be asked to make difficult choices and witness the repercussions of those choices, such as the manner in which a person might come out as gay to their homophobic father (*Coming Out Simulator*), or how they might respond in the last few minutes of their life, knowing that the world is coming to an end (*QED*). This pushes players to have a relationship with the text that is much more intimate as they perform a role that is "more than a mere audience member" (Galloway, 2006). Because most Twine games are written from a first-person perspective, players are encouraged to role-play through their avatar and become immersed in a different reality (Dormans, 2006). This increased immersion within a hybrid text provides opportunities to allow players to experience different perspectives, lives, and worlds in more intimate ways (Galloway, 2006).

It must be noted that not all autoethnographies and Twine games focus on the tragic and emotional moments in life. Many focus on the everyday and the ordinary, the playful and the mundane (Goodall, 2007). There are autoethnographic pieces about an "accidental" dialogic moment between father and son (Poulos, 2008a), gendered engagement with a remote control (Uotinen, 2010), performance of one's identity through karaoke (Drew, 2001), and experience of play within a poker game with Ferrari culture (Goodall, 2004). There are also several interactive stories that focus on topics and phenomena "considered 'too boring' to be portrayed in mainstream games" (kopas, 2015). *Scarfmemory* (Brough, 2013), for example, focuses on the grief of losing a favorite scarf; *Detritus* (Hamilton, 2013) looks at the act of packing up and moving; and *Bee* (Short, 2012) shows a child practicing for an upcoming spelling bee. There is value in writing about smaller, more ordinary moments. These moments can make us feel connected to strangers as they highlight the characters' humanity and make them feel more like real people who struggle and overcome minor, daily obstacles just like us. The ability to connect to others' experiences similar to our own may help us feel less alone and isolated. These ordinary moments may work to build empathy by teaching us about the other, as they can provide insight into our inherent similarities and differences. They may unpack cultural misunderstandings by teaching and normalizing cultural and religious rituals. They can also highlight and detail the gendered division of domestic labor and the incessant implicit bias that builds and weighs on oppressed individuals. Finally, they can share and process the dialogical and serendipitous moments that transform and shape a person (Poulos, 2008b).

Engaging the reader/player through design

Twine games and autoethnographic studies both play with style, organization, and immersive storytelling techniques. Autoethnographers work toward immersion by using "thick descriptions" in their writing, by describing the context around the observed phenomena using evocative and visual language. This poetic approach to discussing research can be found in pieces by Goodall (2007), Tillmann-Healy (1996), Olson (2004), and Poulos (2008a, 2008b, 2012): "In any event, one cannot forever escape the intrusion of the shadow into everyday life (Zweig & Abrams, 1991). The secrets come up—in the wind, in flashes, in whispers, in torrents, in waves" (Poulos, 2008a, p. 62). Autoethnographers embrace the persuasiveness and evocative nature of style and believe that it makes their work more accessible, through the powerful pull of stories (Poulos, 2008a).

Similar to autoethnographies, Twine games often include evocative and descriptive language in their stories. They have the capability to push design and style further because the medium allows them to experiment with nonlinear storytelling, sound, and visual effects. As kopas (2015) writes, "Authors are doing things with Twine that aren't possible with traditional text. And at the same time, they're using interactive media to tell stories that mainstream videogames couldn't dream of telling" (p. 11). This is partially made possible by Twine's hypertextual structure (Ryan, 2011) of separate chunks of information connected by hyperlinks. This form frees the author from more conventional storytelling techniques and allows them to play with maze-like structures (Ryan, 2011), providing more player agency.

Lutz, an author of Twine horror games, uses sound effects in *The Uncle Who Works at Nintendo* (2014) and *My Father's Long, Long Legs* (2013) to set mood through ambience. He also incorporates visual effects, such as a usable flashlight feature (Figure 3.1) to increase immersion. Likewise, Crows Crows Crows' (2016) satirical *The Temple of No* includes atmospheric sounds and synchronous sound effects, such as a "splat" when a

Figure 3.1 My Father's Long Long Legs. Copyright: Michael Lutz.

drawing of a book appears. Sound and music can influence a player's interpretation and enjoyment of a game, such as whether/to what extent players experience immersion during play (Wharton & Collins, 2011). Players may become more (or less) anxious depending on the musical score; it can alter their heart rate and make them play more cautiously or uninhibited (Wharton & Collins, 2011). Music can be used within an autoethnographic piece to signal changes between voices or time/locations (e.g. as the narrator shifts from a research to an autobiographical voice or makes a jump forward in time and space).

Pratt's (2014a) piece on mental illness, *Anhedonia*, includes typography and animated graphics to symbolize her mental turmoil and depression. Pratt uses game mechanics to express her rumination and mimic the frustration and anxiety she experiences during panic attacks (Pratt, 2014b). For example, Pratt explains in her analysis of the game that as the players experience *Anhedonia*, they have to repeatedly click to progress through the story. When the phrase "this is not a rational response" appears, the player can choose to click on "rational" or "response." If they click on rational, that one word is replaced thrice, first by "healthy," then "reasonable," then "sane," before they can progress (Pratt, 2014b). Pratt also forces the audience to pause with timed responses, as the clickable options will appear later than the rest of the text, adding dramatic emphasis and creating a sense of loss and confusion in the player.

St. Germain's (2017) Lovecraftian horror story *The Terror of Thetford* reveals the inner-workings of a first-person narrator who, over the course of the playthrough, loses their humanity and morphs into a monster. The game, told through a first-person perspective, includes rich descriptions of

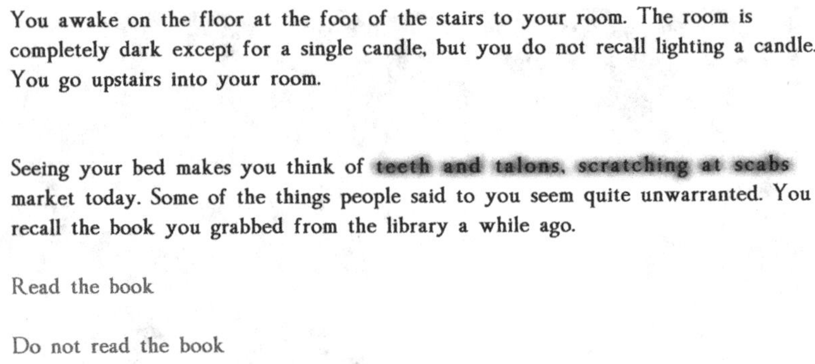

You awake on the floor at the foot of the stairs to your room. The room is completely dark except for a single candle, but you do not recall lighting a candle. You go upstairs into your room.

Seeing your bed makes you think of teeth and talons, scratching at scabs market today. Some of the things people said to you seem quite unwarranted. You recall the book you grabbed from the library a while ago.

Read the book

Do not read the book

Figure 3.2 The Terror of Thetford. Copyright: Dan St. Germain.

the world, similar to what was found in early text-based adventure games like *Zork* (1977) and *Adventure* (1976). Unlike those early games, however, it does not permit exploration and directional movement. Instead, players make choices of how to engage with characters and items around them. As the game progresses, the choices and subsequent actions morph—each day becoming darker and more crazed. A player may start off with selecting polite dialogue options, like "Good day, Mr. Harte, I'll need your best cut of beef today," or they may participate in civil activities, such as to play a "rousing" game of chess with a local townsperson. The next day, some of the choices become indecipherable, blurred, and written backward in a medieval typeface. The options at this point are still largely unchanged, but the townspeople's reactions differ dramatically: A request for beef turns into the butcher begging you to put down the knife in your hands. The day after that, blurred, shaking text is juxtaposed in the repeated descriptions of your daily life (Figure 3.2) and the interaction with the townsfolk turns into something much more sinister.

The Twine games described earlier are two hybridizations: one of text with movement and sound, and the other of play with seriousness. Twine's playful design elements could provide autoethnographic authors with opportunities to add additional layers of emotional and symbolic meaning in their work and push their piece to be more or less immersive. For example, an author could build a world through sound effects, such as the clock chiming and digging sound effects within Lutz's (2013, 2014) works. They can be used to represent a character's unique perspective, like the warped text found in Terror of Thetford. They could also be used to pull you out of a story, like the obvious sound effects found in Crows Crows Crows' (2016) satirical game. These elements have the potential to trigger shifts of affiliation with the avatar and other in-game elements (Taylor et al., 2015), allowing players to experience a story through a multitude of perspectives, that of their character, their self, or a hybrid of their character and self simultaneously.

Learning through choice

Twine's interactive capabilities push the players to engage with the hybrid narrative differently than if they were reading a static text. Landow (1992) writes, in his early work on hypertext, that hypertextual work "blurs the boundaries between reader and writer, allowing the reader to play a hybrid role as creator and spectator as the reader creates their own path through the interlinked content" (p. 5). Authors can include external links to other online content to draw attention to the piece's intertextuality, a networking of texts with cultural signs and symbols (Landow, 1992), such as what is often found in online journalism stories. An author can make a cultural or historical reference and connect it with a demonstration or article about its origination. They can draw attention to the network surrounding their writing, to build a "dialogic, polyphonic, and multivocal" text (Landow, 1992) that includes an attention to difference consciousnesses and perspectives. Authors can be used to provide multiple points of view or present an interconnected stream of consciousness (Bolter & Joyce, 1987). They can also include internal links to draw attention to the connections within their own ideas and characters. Johnson (1997) describes how Dickens created a world of literature in which all of its characters are interconnected regardless of class; if Dickens had the ability to add hyperlinks, he could highlight their interconnectedness and carve out spaces for more backstory.

One feature that shows great potential is the ability to add a choice-based mechanic, similar to a *Choose Your Own Adventure Book*. For example, a story could start with:

> *You turn the corner and find a monster.*
> *[[fight]]*
> *[[run]]*
> *[[introduce yourself]]*

Each of these very different bracketed choices will appear as hyperlinked options for the player, automatically generating different cards that the designer can type into and continue the story. These choices give audience agency but can be designed in a way that the player has less agency and the character has more. Instead of the previous example, one can write:

> *You turn the corner and find a monster.*
> *[[punch them in the nose]]*
> *[[unsheathe your sword]]*
> *[[raise your axe]]*

In this scenario, the player still has agency; yet, the choices are limited to reflect more of the character's personality and beliefs. For instance, Anthropy's Twine game *QED* (2013) relies heavily on this choice-based mechanic.

After beginning the game, players have 10 seconds before the game's world ends. They can choose to kiss their partner, hold her, take her hand, or tell her "I love you." Each of these choices is limited to the character's desire to express her love; players only have agency over the way she expresses it. Each of the choices will unlock subsequent choices until eventually, the player runs out of time and everything is wiped away. There is a sense of urgency as players race to do and communicate as much as possible before the end of the game. No matter what the player chooses, the world still ends—but the way the player/character experiences that end differs.

Independent game designer and critic Brice (2014, June 28) writes in her discussion of *QED* that most of these text-based games are not really about the choices you have but rather, how the games "aim to train your perception, get you to understand the architecture of your thoughts, the reason why you chose the things you do" (para 7). It's not the outcome of the choices that matter; it's what happens to the player during the process of making those choices. The game encourages players to analyze the rationale behind their decisions, shedding insight into their hidden beliefs and values, and their past experiences and privileges that inform those ideologies. This could help autoethnographers work toward their goals of helping the audience work out problems (Goodall, 2007), understand and shape their identities (Berry, 2006; Goodall, 2007), and experience and empathize with underrepresented standpoints (Goodall, 2007).

Zoe Quinn uses a choice-based system in *Depression Quest* (2014) to demonstrate the experiences of living with depression. In one scene, the playable character's mother asks, "So what's going on with you lately?" The narrator gives the player an option to discuss their illness but warns that it will drain them. Depending on the player's previous decisions, some options may not be available to them. For example, in one of my playthroughs, the player is given the option to say everything is fine or change the subject. The two more productive choices "Let her know that you've been feeling down lately, and that you appreciate her concern" and "Try to be honest with her anyway" are red and crossed out. If the player had made more prosocial choices, like connecting with their partner and attending a party, they would have been given access to those more productive options. This mechanic works on two levels. First, it teaches players that people with depression, because of their symptoms, may struggle to act in prosocial ways that work toward minimizing their symptoms. In other words, it shows that it's not easy to get help and treatment. Second, it illustrates that the more often they reject resources and support systems, the harder it is for them to make productive choices. This mechanic works toward helping players without depression better understand and empathize with those that do and, further, it helps players with depression understand their illness and feel less alone.

The "illusion of choice" mechanic could be useful in autoethnographic work, as it can reveal to the audience the consequences of their choices and constructions of reality. It has the potential for helping players experience understanding and empathy through active experience. Some autoethnographers view their work as a "reciprocal conversation" designed to "re-create the interpretive anchors that so powerfully shape how we constitute ourselves and experiences" (Berry, 2006, p. 10). The inclusion of interactive elements heightens the reciprocal nature of performative narrative work, creating a narrative that is co-constructed, influenced by both the designer and the player. Game designers can structure choices to push audiences to become more aware of their hybrid experience of multiple roles, including a character/agent in the world, a competent and skilled player, a real-world person with physical needs and individual perspectives, and a storyteller. This hybridity, as demonstrated in Anthropy's (2013) and Quinn's (2013) work, has the potential to produce understanding through experience. I explored this kind of hybridity in an interactive autoethnographic piece I built on Twine, in which I included personal and ordinary stories to engage the player through design and choice.

"A New World": a case study

"A New World": An autoethnographic telling of motherhood and Telltale's The Walking Dead (Bell, 2018) explores how my experience as a new mother influenced my playthrough of *The Walking Dead* series (*TWD*) (Telltale, 2012–2019). *TWD* is a narrative adventure game about a little girl who comes to age during the zombie apocalypse in the southern United States. I worked to build a piece that was a hybrid of a narrative game and rigorous research to serve different audiences: Some could choose to skip branches that focused on personal reflection and storytelling; others, uninterested in research, could choose to only stay on the surface of academic divergences; and yet others could enjoy a balance of both. I served a dual role of artist and researcher, as I had to practice and improve my creative writing and experimentation. I often got dizzyingly lost in my interconnected passages (Figure 3.3).

In the end, I learned to think more like a game designer who is player-centered. I worked to include player agency and developed an organizational system that works for an interactive game. My final piece dances between my two voices, as some passages are devoted to autobiographical tellings, and others focus on research and analysis. This is reminiscent of the organizational approach found in Olson's (2004) autoethnography; her reflections were italicized, separating it from the main body. Twine allows me to push this separation further by fractioning off entire pieces, accessible only by clicking a hyperlink. This separation worked toward minimizing my vulnerability, as I was able to "hide" the self-disclosure about my troubled relationship with my disabled and alcoholic father deep in the game via hyperlinks. I buried the increasingly personal moments of self-disclosure over five different passages, and I used symbolic colors to offer a visual warning to my audience about the content with which they were about to interact.

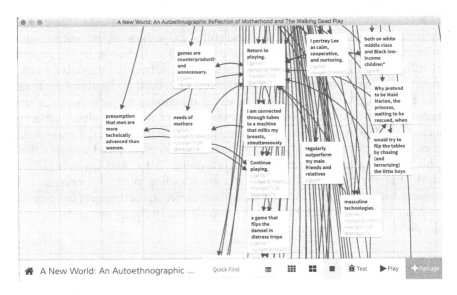

Figure 3.3 A New World on Twine. Copyright: Kristina Bell; Twine copyright: Chris Klimas.

I also used other aesthetic and aural cues to work toward making my story more immersive. I included audio of my newborn son suckling and snoring, audio of me pumping breast milk while playing the game, and I included video of gameplay and personal images (such as my son's ultrasound). I added interactive effects to enhance immersion and further push the "illusion of choice." At one point in the game, toward the end, I describe the final moments in *TWD: Season One*. Lee is dying, and his adoptive daughter has to make a choice: Does she walk away and allow him to become a zombie, or does she shoot and kill someone she loves like a father? I provide the two dialogue options, formatted like blue hyperlinks: "Leave me," and "You have to shoot me." If the reader hovers over or tries to click on "Leave me," the option disappears, fades away from the screen, leaving them only the option: to shoot Lee. In this moment, their ability to choose a path is merely an illusion, a reference to the "illusion of choice" (Brice, 2014) these types of games often rely on.

My reasoning, within this mechanic, is to remind audiences that all games, including mine, are a co-construction. Player input is essential, and some games, like *TWD*, provide great opportunities to shape characters, change relationships, and experience starkly different narrative endings. Yet, these options are limited, carefully constructed by the narrative designer to engage and shape within the confines of the character. Since I was essentially an avatar (considering that the player is experiencing the narrative through me), I could only provide an option that was true to what I, as the character, would choose. I would not have let Lee walk away.

The "illusion" of choice brought attention to how a player's experience of playing through a character is a hybridization. Even though they may act as a participant in a narrative, they are always considered a hybrid, considering that their actions and interpretations are shaped by their personal experience and perception. For instance, if I had only provided the player with one choice—"You have to shoot me"—they would have clicked without much reflection and cognitive dissonance. However, because I offered the player another option, it encouraged them to reflect upon why they would have made a different choice than me and what it was, about my background and history, dissected in the text that fed into their gameplay experience.

My intent as the designer was not to create an ergodic experience (Aarseth, 1997) that enables players to win points and achieve a "perfect play" or to build a story that permits audiences to "sit back as spectators" (Bochner & Ellis, 2006, p. 120). Rather, I worked to enhance the dialogical" nature of autoethnographic work (Goodall, 2000) and to encourage readers to serve a hybrid role of spectator and active participant in the conversation/narrative. Similar to narrative games discussed in this chapter such as *QED* (Anthropy, 2013) and autoethnographic works by authors such as Poulos (2008a, 2008b, 2012), Tillman-Healy (1996), Fox (1996), and Olson (2004), I worked to recreate and shape the players' (and my own) "interpretative anchors" (Berry, 2006, p. 10). I utilized evocative narrative writing, intersectional and critical feminist theory, and interactive elements (e.g. choice-based mechanics) to encourage self-awareness through reflection and critical thought. In doing so, I worked to disrupt certain interpretative positions to push toward transformation within the reader.

Finally, I included the everyday, mundane moments in my life. I spent several passages discussing pumping breast milk, as it was interconnected to my play experience and relevant to my discussions in the piece of technologies as gendered. I wrote about small moments in my life that shaped my perspective and became turning points in my life. This included the experience of microaggression after beating another child at a game, a playful moment on the playground, moments of "accidental dialogue" (Poulos, 2008b) with my family, and encouragements and engagements from my father as I played on the computer—all because they informed my relationship to games, my father, and my cultural understandings of gender.

My approach to research and writing changed as I worked to build this hybrid text. I began to see connections between details, and I built in an excessive amount of hyperlinks that I later thinned out during editing. Twine's layout of interconnected cards gave me permission to fragment my writing into separate chapters or vignettes. I would create a link and a new blank card would open, a blank slate to play with a new approach or idea. This feature, coupled with the design features that I could change from page to page, liberated me to switch writing styles at my leisure. This is an advantage and a disadvantage, as I needed considerable editing to unite the passages and make the changes justifiable. Although, at times I found myself lost in a maze of words and code, I created a piece that was more sprawling and twisted than I had intended.

I performed multiple hybrid roles during the creation of my game. First, as an autoethnographer, I was a researcher/subject as I collected data, reflected on my subjectivity, and selected my theoretical framework. Second, I was a player/researcher, as I played the game, sometimes enjoyably, other times regretfully (such as when I had to prioritize play as work), all while noting my observations and reflecting on my findings. Third, I was an academic/game designer, as I worked on research writing and style while brainstorming interactive engagement and player-centered design. Finally, I served as play-tester/editor as I checked sources, looked for broken links, and critiqued its interactivity.

My hybrid roles forced me to consider the project differently than if I was only the researcher. As a subject, I was concerned about my degree of self-disclosure and how it would be perceived; as a game designer, I was concerned with its accessibility and entertainment. At times, I found myself in contradiction, particularly when I was tasked with editing down the project. There would be a vignette that was engaging and immersive, yet also requiring a great deal of disclosure that made me (as a participant) feel uncomfortable; there would be another that discussed important prior research, yet it was long and dry. I worked to achieve a balance of rigor and engagement, while also maintaining a level of disclosure that I felt comfortable with.

Conclusion

Twine is useful in creating hybrid play experiences which work to destabilize boundaries between identities and disrupt homogenous thought processes by providing players with (limited) choices through which they can play out the repercussions. This chapter discussed four forms of hybridity in relation to play: (1) the hybridity of the researcher as a game designer and subject, (2) the hybridity of play and academic research, (3) the hybridity of highly personal writing as something to be played, and (4) the hybridity of play with the ordinary and mundane. Using my interactive autoethnographic experiment about motherhood and *TWD*, as a case study, I examined each of these hybridizations.

When building my game, I merged the themes found from previous Twine works into my design. I worked to engage the audience through my design by building an immersive experience of sound and description. I pushed players to learn from my experiences and knowledge through an illusion of choice; I relinquished my need to control my audience's perception and experience and, instead, allowed them to explore my life by providing them with hyperlinks to interconnected passages. I included choice-based mechanics to make them aware of how my in-game choices clashed with theirs and how their perceptions influenced their experience of the game. Finally, I wove in a history of my personal gaming practices that included the everyday and the mundane to paint a well-rounded understanding of my engagements with videogames.

My goal was to create a piece that encouraged critical thinking, specifically regarding gendered perceptions of technology and parenting, yet also engaging and accessible. Therefore, I worked to build a hybrid play experience that had serious elements of research and critical reflections as well as sound effects and game mechanics. I performed a hybrid role as I worked to tell a story, *my story*, which was personal and underrepresented in academia, of a new mother, struggling with breastfeeding, pumping, and post-partum anxiety. Through its creation, I ended with a piece that examined multiple field-sites, online and off (Marcus, 1998), and was a multi-layered construction of the various phenomena relevant to my playthrough of the game. This points to the potential of Twine to serve other ethnographers who wish to tame the unbridled complexity of the phenomena they are studying. In all, I ended this project believing that the hybridization of ethnographic research with play offers creative capabilities, audience engagement, and an immersive nature that could add nuance to research in the humanities and social sciences.

References

Aarseth, E. J. (1997). *Cybertext: Perspectives on Ergodic Literature*. Baltimore, MD: The John Hopkins University Press.

Alexander, L. (2013, June 17). Playing outside. *The New Inquiry*. Retrieved from https://thenewinquiry.com/playing-outside/.

Anthropy, A. (2012). *Rise of Videogame Zinesters: How Freaks, Normals, Amateurs, Artists, Dreamers, Drop-Outs, Queers, Housewives, and People Like You are Taking Back an Art Form*. New York, NY: Seven Stories Press.

Anthropy, A. (2013). *Queers at the End of the World*. [Video Game].

Bell, K. (2018). *A New World: An Autoethnographic Reflection of Motherhood and The Walking Dead Play*. [Video Game].

Bernardi, J. (2013, Feb 19). Choose your own adventure-maker: Twine and the art of personal games. *Motherboard*. Retrieved from https://www.vice.com/en_us/article/xyyp9a/twine-and-the-art-of-personal-games.

Berry, K. (2006). Implicated audience member seeks understanding: Reexamining the "gift" of autoethnography. *International Journal of Qualitative Methods*, 5(3), 94–108.

11 Bit Studios. (2014). *This War of Mine*. [Video Game].

Bochner, A. (2001). Narrative's virtues. *Qualitative Inquiry*, 7(2), 131–157.

Bochner, A., & Ellis, C. (2006). Communication as autoethnography. In G. J. Shepherd, J. St. John, & T. Striphas (Eds.), *Communication as ... Perspectives on Theory* (pp. 110–122). Thousand Oaks, CA: Sage.

Bolter, J., & Joyce, M. (1987). Hypertext and creative Writing. Proceedings from *Hypertext '87 Papers* (pp. 41–50). Chapel Hill, NC: University of North Carolina. Retrieved from https://dl.acm.org/citation.cfm?id=317431.

Brice, M. (2014, June 28). Countdown: Thinking of time in text games. *Mattie Brice Alternate Ending. Justice.* Retrieved from http://www.mattiebrice.com/countdown-thinking-of-time-in-text-games/.

Brough, M. (2013). *Scarfmemory.* [Video Game].

Caillois, R. (1961). *Man, Play and Games.* Urbana and Chicago: University of Illinois Press.

Case, N. (2014). *Coming Out Simulator.* [Video Game].

Chakravartty, P., Kuo, R., Grubbs, V., & McIlwain, C. (2018). #Communications-SoWhite. *Journal of Communication*, 68(2), 254–266.

Crows Crows Crows. (2016). *The Temple of No.* [Video Game].

Crowther, W. (1977). *Adventure.* [Video Game].

de Souza e Silva, A., & Sutko, D. (2008). Playing life and living play: How hybrid reality games reframe space, play, and the ordinary. *Critical Studies in Media Communication*, 25 (5), 447–465.

Dormans, J. (2006). On the role of the die: A brief ludologic study of pen-and-paper roleplaying games and their rules. *Game Studies*, 6(1). Retrieved from http://gamestudies.org/0601/articles/dormans

Drew, R. (2001). *Karaoke Nights: An Ethnographic Rhapsody.* Lanham, MD: AltaMira.

Ellis, C., & Bochner, A. (2000). Autoethnography, personal narrative, reflexivity. In N. Denzin & Y. Lincoln (Eds.), *Handbook of Qualitative Research.* Thousand Oaks, CA: Sage.

Flanagan, M., & Nissenbaum, H. (2014). *Values at Play in Digital Games.* Cambridge, MA: MIT Press.

Fox, K. (1996). Silent voices: A subversive reading of child sexual abuse. In C. Ellis & A. Bochner (Eds.), *Composing Ethnography.* Walnut Creek, CA: AltaMira.

Freeman, N. (2014). *Mangia.* [Video Game].

Galloway, A. R. (2006) *Gaming: Essays on Algorithmic Culture.* Minneapolis, MN: University of Minnesota Press.

Goodall, H. L. (2000). *Writing the New Ethnography.* Lanham, MA: AltaMira.

Goodall, H. L. (2004). Deep play in a poker rally: A Sunday among the ferraristi of Long Island. *Qualitative Inquiry*, 10, 1–36.

Goodall, H. L. (2007). Commentary: Narrative ethnography as applied communication research. *Journal of Applied Communication Research*, 32(3), 185–194.

Hamilton, M. (2013). *Detritus.* [Video Game].

Harvey, A., (2014). Twine's revolution: Democratization, depoliticization, and the queering of game design. *Game Journal*, 3, 95–107.

Hayles, K. (2002). *Writing Machines.* Cambridge, MA: MIT Press.

Infocom. (1977). *Zork.* [Video Game].

Johnson, S. (1997). *Interface Culture: How New Technology Transforms the Way we Create and Communicate.* San Francisco, CA: Harper.

kopas, m. (2015). Introduction. In m. kopas (Ed.), *Videogames for Humans: Twine Authors in Conversation.* New York: Instar Books.

Landow, G. (1992). *Hypertext: The Convergence of Contemporary Critical Theory and Technology.* Baltimore, MD: The Johns Hopkins University Press.

Lutz, M. (2013). *My Father's Long, Long, Legs.* [Video Game].

Lutz, M. (2014). *The Uncle Who Works at Nintendo.* [Video Game].

Marcus, G. (1998). Ethnography in/of the world system: The emergence of multi-sited ethnography. In G. Marcus (Ed.), *Ethnography Through Thick and Thin* (pp. 79–104). Princeton, NJ: Princeton University Press.

Minority Media Inc. (2012). *Papa & Yo.* [Video Game].

Montfort, N. (2011). Toward a theory of interactive fiction. In K. Jackson-Mead & J. Robinson Wheeler (Eds.), *IF Theory Reader.* Boston, MA: Transcript on Press.

Ninja Theory. (2017). *Hellblade: Senua's Sacrifice.* [Video Game].

Numinous Games. (2016). *That Dragon, Cancer.* [Video Game].

Olson, L. (2004). The role of voice in the (Re) construction of a battered woman's identity: An autoethnography of one woman's experiences of abuse. *Women's Studies in Communication,* 27(1), 1–33.

Poulos, C. (2002). The death of ordinariness: Living, learning, and relating in the age of anxiety. *Qualitative Inquiry,* 8, 288–301.

Poulos, C. N. (2008a). Narrative conscience and the autoethnographic adventure. *Qualitative Inquiry,* 14(1), 46–66.

Poulos, C. N. (2008b). Accidental dialogue. *Communication Theory,* 18, 117–138.

Poulos, C. N. (2012). Stumbling into relating: Writing a relationship with my father. *Qualitative Inquiry,* 18(2), 197–202.

Pratt, M. (2014a). *Anhedonia.* [Video Game].

Pratt, M. (2014b, August 13). Anhedonia and hypertext. *The Rumpus.* Retrieved from https://therumpus.net/2014/08/anhedonia-and-hypertext/.

Quinn, Z. (2013). *Depression Quest.* [Video Game].

Richardson, L. (1992). The consequences of poetic representation: Writing the other, rewriting the self. In C. Ellis & M. Flahery (Eds.), *Investigative Subjectivity: Research on Lived Experience.* Newbury Park, CA: Sage Publications.

Ryan, M. L. (2011). The interactive onion: Layers of user participation in digital narrative texts. In R. Page & B. Thomas (Eds.), *New Narratives: Stories and Storytelling in the Digital Age* (pp. 35–62). Lincoln: University of Nebraska Press.

Sampat, E. (2014). *Nineteen.* [Video Game].

Shaw, A. (2009). Putting the gay in games: Cultural production and GLBT content in video games. *Games and Culture,* 4(3), 228–253.

Short, E. (2012). *Bee.* [Video Game].

St. Germain, D. (2017). *The Terror of Thetford.* [Video Game].

Taylor, N., Kampe, C., & Bell, K. (2015). Me and Lee: Identification and the play of attraction in The Walking Dead. *Game Studies,* 15. Retrieved from http://gamestudies.org/1501/articles/taylor.

Telltale Games. 2012. *The Walking Dead: Series.* [Video Game]. San Rafael, CA: Telltale Games.

Tillmann-Healy, L. (1996). A secret life in a culture of thinness. In C. Ellis & A. Bochner (Eds.), *Composing Ethnography.* Walnut Creek, CA: AltaMira.

Uotinen, J. (2010). Digital television and the machine that goes "PING!": Autoethnography as a method for cultural studies of technology. *Journal for Cultural Research,* 14(2), 161–175.

Wagner, K. (2014, October 14). The future of the culture wars is here, and it's gamergate. *Deadspin.* Retrieved from https://deadspin.com/the-future-of-the-culture-wars-is-here-and-its-gamerga-1646145844.

Wharton, A., & Collins, K. (2011). Subjective measures of the influence of music customization on the video game play experience: A Pilot study. *Game Studies*, 11(2). Retrieved from http://gamestudies.org/1102/articles/wharton_collins.

Williams, D., Martins, N., Consalvo, M. & Ivory, J. (2009). The virtual census: Representations of gender, race and age in video games. *New Media Society*, 11(5), 851–834.

Zweig, C., & Abrams, J. (1991). *Meeting the Shadow: The Hidden Power of the Dark Side of Human Nature*. Los Angeles, CA: TarcherPerigee.

4 En(Twine)d

A feminist software analysis

Sarah Evans

Code and software studies emerged as interdisciplinary research fields to interrogate the "black box" that computer software and other digital technologies represent to non-experts. These humanities-based approaches take many forms but most tend to investigate code as a specific kind of text (Manovich, 2001; Hayles, 2004; Marino, 2006; Fuller, 2008; Berry, 2011). Overall, this undertaking of code and software studies adopts an overdetermining "power of the programmer" (Chun, 2008, p. 227), meaning code is often analyzed separately from the contexts of its use. As such, these approaches extrapolate data and knowledge from individual lines of code without addressing how the code is experienced by the end-user. Most digital technology users will only see and use a software's interface, the product of code, but never the code itself. When code is treated as text that can be read in isolation, it evokes an imagined user, one that often reflects a hegemonic populous. This is an issue because without qualitative data, it is difficult to assume how any "typical" user may interact with software or, further, who that typical user may be. Abstracting code from its situated uses ignores the user experiences of non-dominant populations, such as women or people of color, thereby making conclusions garnered via these methods incomplete. This chapter offers an alternative, nuanced, and context-specific method of software analysis that attempts to capture a more holistic experience of how end-users experience and interact with code via a novel, hybridized analysis of the beginner game design/interactive fiction software program Twine.

Specifically, I propose a feminist method to cultivate *in situ* analyses of what a program like Twine makes (im)possible for beginner users in a formal learning environment. Feminism is employed here for multiple reasons. First, it allows me to account for and respect the varied experiences that diverse populations encounter when using this tool. Second, it offers a lens through which to analyze the software and its uses, one that foregrounds values of inclusivity and accessibility over other values, such as mastery or prestige. Normative game design cultures typify men and boys as the default producers and consumers of video games, particularly games that reinforce themes of militarism, domination, and power. To break up these norms and diversify both the pool of producers and games available to consumers, new methods of inquiry and analysis are necessary.

This feminist software analysis comprises two parts. First, I undertake a critical, textual, and analytic investigation of Twine to determine its suitability for participants. Second, I pair that analysis with qualitative insights around how Twine was used by participants in a university classroom setting. To that end, I designed and facilitated an in-classroom study of beginner Twine users to interrogate some of the underlying biases coded into the program. Overall, I investigate how feminist efforts *might* be articulated through interactions between game design tools, contexts, people, and larger ideological structures. I consider the ways that software, such as Twine, when used in service of feminist efforts do (or do not) support inclusive practices, such as diversifying access to game design and exploring non-capitalistic motivations for designing games.

To investigate the hybrid[1] roles of nonhuman elements such as software, environment, and social norms, I cultivated and used a novel, interdisciplinary feminist research method that combines ethnography with a close reading of the nonlinear narrative-building software, Twine. These methods, when combined, constitute what might be called *feminist software analysis*. As such, the purpose of this chapter is two-fold: (1) to analyze the feminist capacities of the program Twine, and (2) to establish *feminist software analysis* as a distinct mode of inquiry capable of generating an empirically driven understanding of the capacity for low-barrier game design tools to be used toward destabilizing entrenched hierarchies in game design.

In the following sections, I first provide background information on Twine and describe extant methodological precursors and influences behind the proposed feminist software analysis. Next, I assess Twine in terms of its features, and also through qualitative evidence of its use in a classroom context. This multi-pronged approach is meant to access the feminist potential of these tools *in situ*, as one way to resist reproducing the exclusivity of normative game design cultures.

Connecting with Twine

Twine was designed in 2009 by Chris Klimas, a web developer, game designer, and writer. This free, browser-based tool uses simplified HTML to allow users to create interactive, branching stories reminiscent of *Choose Your Own Adventure* novels or hypertext fiction (Aarseth, 1997). One of the most well-known Twine games is Zoe Quinn's *Depression Quest*, a text-based adventure which asks players to make everyday decisions from the perspective of a person suffering from depression. To make a Twine game, users connect a series of hyperlinked boxes of text (called passages) by typing a set of double brackets around a word or phrase in one box, corresponding to the title/tag of another box. Twine's visual interface is straightforward: Connections between text boxes are shown via lined arrows drawn between them. Twine does not require computer processing power, it is compatible with both Windows and Mac, and the file sizes it creates are very small, easy to export and share via e-mail.

It is possible to make a complex and professional-looking game using basic Twine functions. Despite its initial simplicity, the range of expression that Twine facilitates is immense. Twine's learning curve is low, and users are able to create high-quality games with the platform, therefore challenging expected norms of game design where games are produced using expensive, complex platforms and large teams. Harvey (2014) asserts that Twine's affordances as a tool paired with its supportive online community and wealth of free, user-generated development resources have allowed Twine games to "challenge mainstream standards by subverting the celebration of difficulty, in both production and play, as [Twine games] are often quick to both make and play" (p. 99). This quality runs counter to the masculine trope of "dumbing down" as negative since easing access and use of technologies could make mastery, a trait associated with masculinity, less impressive. Instead, Twine games and the online Twine community reinvented the genre by celebrating accessibility and perceived simplicity.

Twine boasts a range of customization options to create a broad array of different games, from entirely text-based to multimedia experiences, puzzles, and more. By copying and pasting different pieces of the modified HTML that undergirds Twine from any of the free online resources, a user can change fonts' color, typeface, size, and add special effects like shudder or shadow. Copying and pasting also work to add media to games via the embed codes from YouTube videos, GIFs, or online-hosted images. Advanced mechanics such as variables,[2] text prompts, and even rudimentary animation can also be included. Twine is open to almost anyone with a computer and internet connection. Because of its open-endedness as a text-based program, it is entirely upon the user to create the game content. Its text-based interface and workflow make Twine a useful tool for the kind of interventionist work with non-experts that I undertook to study due to its accessibility for non-programmers.

Twine was not originally created *for* game making; it was rather for designing nonlinear stories. As a result, it lacks some of the baggage that game design tools hold. Using Twine for game design was a shift led by online queer communities, particularly game designer, Anna Anthropy. Through her online presence and book, *Rise of the Video Game Zinesters* (2012), Twine's potential as a game development tool grew to attract wide attention since it gives users experience with procedural logics that undergird more advanced programming languages. The importance of Twine as a cultural artifact that catalyzed a movement of experimental game designers making personal games is well covered in popular culture outlets (Ellison, 2013; Hudson, 2014) and particularly in Alison Harvey's (2014) article on Twine's democratization of game design and in the book *Video Games for Humans* (Kopas, 2016). What is worth interrogating about Twine, however, is not necessarily the product, but the processes and ways of being that it affords.

Can software be feminist?

I am not analyzing "feminist software." Such an identification or evalua-
tion is impossible and erroneous because the "feminism" of a technology
cannot be isolated and/or extrapolated. Past efforts to determine the feminist capacities of software have proven inadequate, in part because artifacts
in and of themselves cannot be understood without their contexts. To be
clear, technologies and tools are *always* embedded with politics, often stal-
wartly reflecting those of the dominant ideology. For example, the home
pregnancy test may provide empowerment to a woman who deeply desires
knowledge about her body, but may also work as a tool of oppression in the
hands of an abusive partner enforcing regular pregnancy testing as an act of
control (Layne, Vostral, & Boyer, 2010). Therefore, understanding specific
contexts of use is paramount. Layne, Vostral, and Boyer (2010) conclude
that attempting to define feminist technologies is fruitless since some technologies that may be viewed as liberators by one person might be viewed
as oppressive to others. Therein lies the problem with assessing technology
without context. As continuously evidenced by feminist strands of theory
from posthumanism to intersectionality to ethnographic methodology, part
of the work of feminism[3] lies precisely in understanding oppression as a relational, contingent dynamic (Collins, 2000; Barad, 2003). Likewise, feminism itself is relational, not a property of things.

As such, it is not enough to only evaluate the affordances of a software when
considering how game design tools intersect with feminist goals. Twine embodies specific principles and affordances that have feminist potential (such as accessibility via cost, simplicity, etc.), but they also have the potential to reproduce
patriarchal, sexist, and racist products and practices (as will be shown later in
my analysis). We need this "situated knowledge" (Haraway, 1988) of the tool
at work *in situ* to more fully understand this technology as an assemblage.

Assemblage theory provides the theoretical underpinning for examining tools like software as not simply *artifacts*, but rather as some of many
agentic objects coexisting within a network (Latour, 2005). Technology as
assemblage cuts through the practice and artifact dichotomy to cultivate a
stronger means of assessing if something is feminist. For Slack and Wise,
assemblage is a network of relations produced through a conglomeration
of context-specific actors. Drawing from Deleuze and Guattari (1980), they
describe the ways technology can be understood as assemblage in relation
to another concept, articulation:

> Technology as articulation draws attention to the practices, representa-
> tions, experiences, and affects that constitute technology. Technology
> as assemblage adds to this understanding by drawing attention to the
> ways that these practices, representations, experiences, and affects ar-
> ticulate to take a particular dynamic form with broader cultural conse-
> quences (Slack & Wise, 2005, p. 156).

Therefore, to understand the ways in which game design tools work for, with, and/or against participants—and particularly in this case, for, with, and/or against certain feminist goals—I take into account the multiple and varied factors that comprise a specific context within which they are deployed (in this case, a university classroom in the U.S. South) and consequently influence the associated products, practices, and processes that are produced with it (in this case, creating Twine games for a graded assignment). Although other methods might work to attach more granularity to the tools and practices involved in game design undertaken by novices, my task is an effort to *build*. By this, I mean that I am trying to bring together a set of practices, knowledges, and structures that might offer not only intellectual insights but, more importantly, opportunities for diversifying access to the myriad of benefits (such as increased digital literacy, creative expression, and job opportunities) that game design skills can provide.

Methodological foundations and constraints

When code began being interrogated by humanities scholars, many chose to look at it as a text, thereby limiting the types of analyses and outcomes garnered through these investigations (Manovich, 2001; Hayles, 2004; Marino, 2006; Fuller, 2008; Berry, 2011; Marino, 2014). However, looking at code in isolation from its context leads to fetishizing code (Chun, 2011), which means that one understands code as the singular most important factor in any interaction with software, thus ignoring user experiences and other potential uses unintended by the code. Under this assumption, code can be viewed as a form of control (Kittler, 2008), where it has power over the outcome of any user interaction. This understanding disregards other factors, such as subversive uses of code, like hacking, modding, or repurposing outputs.

A few methodological approaches take into account the context in which code is inserted and, therefore, set the groundwork for this chapter's methodology of *feminist software studies*. One such method is critical code studies (CCS), which emerged as a way to contextualize code within its attendant apparatuses. Marino (2014) writes:

> Rather than examining source code to the exclusion of these other aspects of technology (i.e., the platforms, network, or interoperating software), CCS emphasizes the code layer in response to a lack of critical methodologies and vocabulary for exploring code through this cultural lens.

In other words, in CCS, the software processes constructed by code are considered in relation to adjacent technologies and settings, including aspects such as the markup language and the intended end-users (Dilger &

Rice, 2010). Marino (2014) sums it up, saying "the effects of software are read against its processes (para. 26)."

Another approach that also looks at code but more closely also considers the physicality of software is platform studies. Hayles (2004) asks us to consider the materiality of code to address issues with decontextualized, isolated analyses that exclude user data from the equation. Materiality, for Hayles, refers to both the "real-world" effects of code—that is, outputs like an image or interface—and the physical hardware that makes code possible—such as microchips, processors, and switches. Montfort and Bogost (2009) describe why platform studies are a necessary addition to analyzing software:

> When digital media creators choose a platform, they simplify develop-ment and delivery in many ways…Work that is built for a platform is supported and constrained by what the chosen platform can do. Some-times the influence is obvious: a monochrome platform can't display color, for instance, and a videogame console without a keyboard can't accept typed input (p. 3).

Succinctly, platforms play a powerful role in limiting or expanding poten-tials for what both users and designers can accomplish with/through it.

Platform studies have drawn attention to many heretofore ignored mate-rial interfaces. In the simplest example, Pold (2008) discusses buttons and how they force users to make binary choices, since a button has only two states: pushed or not pushed. There is no nuance that buttons are beholden to; they switch on or off. Moreover, console design directly influences socio-political constructs. For example, the new controller and style of gameplay introduced by *Guitar Hero* (Jenson & de Castell, 2011) and the Nintendo Wii broadened the profile of gamers through their novel, more representa-tional and therefore easy-to-learn controllers (Jones & Thiruvathukal, 2012). Such shifts are not merely the product of code but also platforms, human actors, and sociopolitical contexts. Platform studies offer a way of understanding code in context. In sum, responses to the criticisms of code studies take several forms including distant reading (aggregating and analyzing larger bodies of similar software) (Fuller, 2008) and critique (problematizing the contexts and practices of coding) (Sample, 2016) such as through platform studies (Montfort & Bogost, 2009) or CCS.

Hacking into the matrix: study and method details

In the fall of 2015, I conducted an IRB-approved qualitative study on how university classroom students used beginner-centric game design tools in an upper-level Game Studies class offered by my institution's Department of Communication. The course was theory and practice driven where stu-dents learned histories, perspectives, and issues related to gaming and got hands-on experience designing games. We met once per week in the late afternoon. During the first class, I described the study and gave students the opportunity to participate, stating that their participation was voluntary and had no bearing on their grade or their relationship with me. No incentive was offered for participation. Upon receiving signed informed consent forms, I distributed questionnaires soliciting their demographic information, previous experience (if any) playing games, using game design software, or other forms of digital media production. 21 students (out of 23 total) chose to participate in the study; four identified as women, the rest men.

Students were asked to design a Twine game with a partner for their midterm exam that used between five and ten advanced techniques (defined here as design techniques that move beyond the basic passage linking). The game was supposed to use minimally 35 passages in length, and thematically disrupt some gaming norm. For example, one group designed a game that never ended (most games are supposed to end eventually), while another asked players to experience the game world as a shopkeeper, which is a non-playable character (a character whose actions the player cannot control). Assignments analyzed for data in this study included student-designed Twine games, weekly process journals, final reflection papers, and in-class observations. My process was to look through these documents and identify recurrent themes, standout stories, or sentiments that may have affected design or experiential outcomes. The analysis at hand remains on the representational level because the users I worked with started at a novice competency level, and, therefore, understood the game design tool Twine at a surface level. Pseudonyms are used to protect the privacy of participants when individuals are quoted or referenced. In the next section, I perform the feminist software analysis.

Applying *feminist software analysis*

Throughout the course of the study, it was clear that some of the very features that made Twine a desirable and useful tool for novices were also features that could result in frustration or disappointments. Among the many such tensions that participants reported, the four main frustrations were the text-based interface, the obtuse advanced features, the "versioning problem" (explained below), and difficulty with collaboration.

Several participants mentioned the lack of a visual interface and limited support for in-game graphics as a feature that is both desirable and undesirable. Because Twine is text-based, it reduces complexity by eliminating the need to access and manipulate graphics. However, this same feature limits the range of game genres possible and can be experienced as a restriction or increased burden to the novice designer's creativity. Zeke, a first-time game designer, describes this ambivalence:

> It is nice to have my first experience with designing a game come in a simple form. Specifically, Twine doesn't require image generation or

detailed mechanics. This will definitely make the design process more streamlined and will allow me to create a game that is focused heavily on story. On the other hand, I am a little nervous about the limitations of doing a text-based game. Due to the lack of imagery and detailed mechanics in a game like this, it will require a great plot, superb writing, and a working knowledge of Twine. As someone who is not the best writer and inexperienced with Twine, this will be a bit of a challenge for me.

Such responses were common among participants upon using the tool for the first time. The accessibility of the interface was lauded. Peter, a first-time designer, said his first impression of Twine was that, "the interface is simple, easy to use, and straightforward. The editing feature is extremely simple and will make game creation rather quick." After using the tool, he maintained this sentiment but added that the more advanced features were tough to implement. He said:

It was rather difficult to insert a formatted style sheet.[4] I was eager to do this in order to change things up and express myself, yet we ran into several problems in doing so. It may have simply been my lack of knowledge about coded systems and computer talk. The only creative element I could figure out how to work, besides inserting graphics, was changing the font. After finding out what style sheets were and how they could enhance a game, I was disappointed with this result.

This response reflects how it may be the case that the basics of Twine are simple to pick up by these participants, but the more advanced techniques are obtuse, and the interface hinders the ease of use since it is text-based and comprised of many single-view windows. Emphasizing this point, Jenna, a self-described "non-gamer" and first-time designer, said:

I wish twine had a way to keep multiple windows within the program open at once. For example, when I was adding a background photo to various passages in my twine, I kept having to open and close the stylesheet and passage to either copy and paste a code, check and see what the tag for the image was in the passage, etc.

Like Jenna, several participants disliked the design interface saying that it looked messy and at times unwieldy when they started making larger, more complex stories.

Another feature that resulted in frustration is what I call the "versioning problem," namely that Twine has five distinct story format options which vary in many ways and can end up confusing first-time designers. Each of the five options allows different versions of the tool that require different commands, have different norms for input/use, make certain things easier/harder, and change the default graphic interface. Formats include from most to least recent: Harlowe 2.1.0, Harlowe 1.2.4, Snowman 1.3.0, SugarCube 2.21.0, and SugarCube 1.0.35. Moreover, the scripting language (based in HTML) associated with each story format is not only unique to Twine, but also differs per version. The earlier versions, called SugarCube, rely more heavily on prior HTML scripting knowledge and, therefore, are less accessible to beginners, albeit still accessible. Twine boasts a solid community of dedicated users who post tutorials, ask and answer questions on the official forums, and share resources. This versioning problem, although meant to help grow the tool to make it more and more accessible, flexible, and user-friendly, means that stable resources are not possible, making learning the tool more time consuming than it could otherwise be. In this study, the versioning problem tripped up first-time designers, and especially those with more advanced knowledge of computer coding in some other capacity. Greg, a first-time game designer with some prior Java experience, said:

> Having three different versions that work in fundamentally different ways is really unhelpful when trying to find resources online. I can't tell you how many times I would try and look something up only to find that it wasn't for Harlowe.

The most frequent complaint among participants was about the difficulty to complete collaborative work using this tool. Margaret, a first-time game designer, reflected: "It was extremely difficult to collaborate with other people on Twine. I wish it offered some sort of option that allowed multiple people to work and edit on one story at the same time." Granted, the fact that the assignment was group-based rather than individually executed did prime participants for this kind of comment. Nevertheless, this frustration with the poor collaboration potential of Twine was brought up by many participants and elucidates an important aspect of game design practices that will be discussed later.

Despite their individual issues with the tool, all students completed and turned in Twine games that exhibited degrees of creativity and expertise with the tool. Some students performed the minimum requirements, while other exceeded expectations and used Twine in novel ways. For example, one first-time game designer made an image of a book into a clickable link, allowing the book to appear and disappear along a vertical path, essentially creating an animation of the book falling. Users were tasked with catching it by clicking it at the right time. This level of creativity and resourcefulness exhibited by a first-time game designer is a testament to the approachability and power of Twine as an introductory game design tool for some people, in some contexts—a comment I will return to and expand upon in the discussion.

Feminist futures

The tools available in the status quo afford some level of reflexive subversion, but we can look forward to technologies that embed feminism more deeply in their processes. Tools can be made such that they more closely reflect the work for which they are being used. Some work is already being done toward this effort, as Schlesinger (2014) argues:

> By combining the disciplines of feminism and computing, there is an opportunity to construct technology that perpetuates a non-normative philosophy. This means that technology can be built that intentionally does not reify patriarchal, neoliberal structures or monolithic, normative Western cultural values (p. 2).

As established at the start of this chapter, feminist technologies cannot exist (in isolation), since any artifact can be used nefariously. However, feminism and gaming are ready for accessible tools and practices that allow women to enjoy game design experiences that do not reproduce the harms of capitalist patriarchy. Through employing *feminist software analysis* in my limited context, I was able to identify some of the limitations of the tool that could be improved upon to enhance its inclusivity.

Examining Twine as a *networked agent* rather than an isolated *artifact* allowed me to analyze not the code itself, but rather the functioning of code and how it adds to or detracts from my effort to make game design more accessible, since it was situated within the context of the users' experience with the functional aspects of the programs. The process of designing a game results from a network of actants that vary from context to context. Almost every context will include some variation of a person or group of people who aim to design a game and a tool (or a few tools) to aid the endeavor. Identifying the full assemblage of actants in a particular context, as well as considering what the ideological intention of the game design process is, gives us a viable entry for judging a tool's efficacy as an agentic part of that network.

In this case, Twine succeeded in allowing students with no STEM background and no prior game design experience to make their first game. This worked in service of feminism since it broadened access to the medium. However, I found that students who were not intrinsically motivated by a personal interest in video games did the required minimum to pass the assignment and this resulted in their games being derivative. Imitation is not inherently negative but, in this context, students unintentionally reproduced some of the problematic norms typical in mainstream game production. For example, many students defaulted to designing a white male playable character, an industry norm that hinders equitable representation in video games. This may indicate that despite the inclusive curriculum I offered in the course, some norms are so deeply rooted that they are difficult to break away.

The biases, affordances, and constraints inherent to game design programs like Twine are also actants in game design (especially for novices), as they influence how and what gets made and further provide insight into the political ramifications associated with such processes and products. As an example, Twine does not support concurrent, collaborative work. This means that students often worked individually and passed versions of the game file back and forth until they were finished, rather than being able to work together remotely. In the classroom where I assigned the Twine game as a project for pairs, this became an issue. My hope was that they could find time to work together in person, but multiple students stated that it was a difficulty due to busy schedules. This quality slightly limits Twine's potential as a collaborative tool for classroom use, although this could be remedied by redesigning the curriculum to allow in-class time for collaboration. This change would emphasize the value of mutual collaboration as a desirable quality in game design contexts, rather than reinforce the norm of individuals working on parts of the project in isolation. A more holistic making practice that includes mutual collaboration allows people to practice and learn about the whole process of how a game comes together. This stands in contrast to the Fordist model that dominates typical game design studios where one person/department writes the narrative, another draws characters, another codes, etc., thereby subtly reinforcing potentially toxic qualities like hierarchy, competition, and isolation.

Moreover, we can purposefully situate tools like Twine within particular networks in order to increase their usefulness as means to feminist ends. It is true that some game design platforms may have the potential to overdetermine outcomes "in the wild," but when combined with appropriate structures such as expertly led discussion and reflection can still be put toward feminist efforts. In this instance, I assessed how Twine could be used for the feminist work of diversifying the pool of people who can reasonably access digital game design by introducing it to individuals with no coding or game design experience. Thus, this tool, by and large, *is* doing feminist work by lowering the bar to entry, though expanding access via "lowering the bar" will not qualify as a feminist goal into itself in every context.

Feminist engagement with technology, in the context of *this* study, meant allowing participants to create games with minimal explication from expert, institutionalized/hierarchized relations of knowledge. However, in other game design contexts—for instance, in communities in which this kind of initiative has more firmly taken hold—what counts as feminist will certainly not (or not simply) be something that is *easy to use*. In other words, "simple to use" and/or "easy to learn" are not always appropriate measures of whether something is feminist, since the critic must first contextualize the tool and its role in a particular group whose expertise and intentions will vary.

While discussing technology that eases the technological burden of storytelling, Noah Wardrip-Fruin (2012) stated that "the crafting of special purpose authoring environments—from game engines to interactive animation software...can make some tasks much easier and others impossible" (p. 233). It is programs that achieve this, the streamlining of various computer programming processes, that make game design easier for beginners but also constrains these early designers in potentially harmful ways. Building context around the sites and procedures of using these tools can mitigate some of their entrenched issues. By bringing attention to the problems inherent to a software program, such as its time needs or discriminatory content, these shortcomings can be used as discussion points while still allowing users to benefit from the advantages the tools offer.

Therefore, it *is* possible to use programs like Twine subversively to produce games that challenge the status quo, bolster outside-the-norm design practices as well as broaden who can access game design. While the technology does contain biases and constraints that have the potential to do harm, my study explored the limits and opportunities associated with employing specific software objects for use toward disrupting entrenched hierarchies in game design. Therefore, one way forward for feminist efforts is to acknowledge that technological complexity does not produce better or more compelling games. A tool that invites more diverse bodies into a practice is more likely to foster innovation since new voices and perspectives can be shared.

Following this, *feminist software analysis* can reveal the impacts of biases embedded in software as they play out in particular contexts. The analysis needs to be called *feminist* software analysis, not something else, because it pays homage to the history and vigor of the work that has persisted through so much. I intend the method to be an adaptable, flexible tool for others to use in order to accumulate knowledge about the use of software tools for carrying out feminist projects. This is one methodological option among many, and provides grounds for unique insights into how technology and users act through and on each other in networked, messy ways.

Conclusion

This chapter offered a distinct method to interpret the roles game design tools play in bringing feminist change to gaming practices. I offered a feminist software analysis that begins with the assumption that technology is an assemblage, while intentionally leaving the door open for additional modes and practices for other feminist software analyses. To this end, I identified the role(s) this technology played across the contexts of my study and how they facilitated, and in some instances restrained, the potential for participants to express themselves through computational and interactive media. Looking at the relations a tool engenders that support feminist efforts such as accessibility, collaboration, and expression rather than just the tools as self-contained artifacts opens new pathways for both researchers and digital media practitioners like game designers or artists. Put simply, artifacts can be subverted through use, but by looking at artifacts *in use*, one can more holistically assess their value. This points to the importance of understanding tools in use with particular audiences. It is my hope that the mode of analysis deployed in this chapter may be used in the future with other technological assemblages to better understand their affordances and constraints across a variety of contexts and users.

Notes

1 Here, hybrid applies to the objects of study, video games designed through the partnership between human and software; the methods, a joining of divergent methodological traditions; and my overall approach, an amalgam of activism and scholarship. Through this lens, we move closer to understanding and thereby alleviating the various discriminations and oppressions that both human and nonhuman apparatuses may pose for those hoping design games.

2 Variables, in particular, allow Twine to be used for more gamic experiences as they are traditionally understood. Variables can be understood as "information containers" to store data that may be referenced and called up throughout an entire program.

3 More accurately, I use "feminisms," plural, here since multiple forms exist and my use of the term is not universal. There are multiple, identity-based layers of oppression that contribute to the very phenomenon I describe earlier. Identity features like race, class, etc., contribute to this complicated relational dynamic of feminist theories and real women's lives.

4 A formatted style sheet changes the visual style of the entire Twine.

References

Aarseth, E. J. (1997). *Cybertext: Perspectives on ergodic literature.* Baltimore: John Hopkins University Press.

Anthropy, A. (2012). *Rise of the videogame zinesters: How freaks, normal, amateurs, artists, dreamers, drop-outs, queers, housewives, and people like you are taking back an art.* New York: Seven Stories Press.

Barad, K. (2003). Posthumanist performativity: Toward an understanding of how matter comes to matter. *Signs: Journal of Women in Culture and Society,* 28(3), 801–831.

Berry, D. M. (2011). The computational turn: Thinking about the digital humanities. *Culture Machine,* 12, 1–12.

Chun, W. (2008). Programmability. In Fuller, M. (Ed.), *Software studies: A lexicon* (pp. 224–228). Cambridge: MIT Press.

Chun, W. (2011). *Programmed visions: Software and memory.* Cambridge: MIT Press.

Collins, P. H. (2000). Gender, black feminism, and black political economy. *The Annals of the American Academy of Political and Social Science,* 568(1), 41–53.

Deleuze, G.& Guattari, F. (1980). *A thousand plateaus.* Minneapolis: University of Minnesota Press.

Dilger, B., & Rice, J. (2010). *From A to <A>: Keywords in HTML and writing.* Minneapolis: University of Minnesota Press.

Ellison, C. (2013). https://www.theguardian.com/technology/gamesblog/2013/apr/10/anna-anthropy-twine-revolution.

Fuller, M. (Ed.). (2008). *Software studies: A lexicon*. Cambridge: MIT Press.

Haraway, D. (1988). Situated knowledges: The science question in feminism and the privilege of partial perspective. *Feminist Studies, 14*(3), 575–599.

Harvey, A. (2014). Twine's revolution: Democratization, depoliticization and the queering of game design. *GAME Journal: The Italian Journal of Game Studies, 1*(3), 95–107.

Hayles, N. K. (2004). Print is flat, code is deep: The importance of media-specific analysis. *Poetics Today, 25*(1), 67–90.

Hudson, L. (2014). https://www.nytimes.com/2014/11/23/magazine/twine-the-video-game-technology-for-all.html

Jenson, J., & de Castell, S. (2011). Girls@Play. *Feminist Media Studies, 11*(2), 167–179. doi:10.1080/14680777.2010.521625.

Jones, S. E., & Thiruvathukal, G. K. (2012). *Codename revolution: The Nintendo Wii platform*. Cambridge: MIT Press.

Kittler, F. (2008). Code. In Fuller, M. (Ed.) *Software studies: A lexicon* (pp. 40–47). Cambridge: MIT Press.

Kopas, M. (2016). *Video Games for Humans*. New York: Instar Books.

Latour, B. (2005). *Reassembling the social: An introduction to actor-network-theory*. Oxford: Oxford University Press.

Layne, L. L., Vostral, S. L., & Boyer, K. (2010). *Feminist technology*. Chicago: University of Illinois Press.

Manovich, L. (2001). *The language of new media*. Cambridge: MIT Press.

Marino, M. C. (2006). *Critical code studies*. Electronic Book Review. http://www.electronicbookreview.com/thread/electropoetics/codology

Marino, M. C. (2014). Field report for critical code studies, 2014. *Computational Culture—A Journal of Software Studies, 4*.

Montfort, N., & Bogost, I. (2009). *Racing the beam: The Atari video computer system*. Cambridge: MIT Press.

Pold, S. (2008). Preferences/settings/options/control panels. In Fuller, M. (Ed.) *Software studies: A lexicon*. Cambridge: MIT Press.

Sample, M. (2016). Code. In Guins, R., & Lowood, H. (Eds.) *Debugging game history: A critical lexicon* (pp. 53–62). Cambridge: MIT Press.

Schlesinger, A. (2014). *Human values in code: Integrating feminism and computer science*. SIGCHI.

Slack, J. D., & Wise, J. M. (2005). *Culture+ technology: A primer*. Switzerland: Peter Lang.Wardrip-Fruin, N. (2012). *Expressive processing: Digital fictions, computer games, and software studies*. Cambridge: MIT Press.

Part II
Hybrid subjects

5 The hybrid agency of hybrid play

Frans Mäyrä

When we engage in play, we become playing subjects—play changes us. When our style of play changes, it also has consequences on how we change while playing. One of the more notable changes in the hybridization of play in recent decades involves blurring and intermixing the boundary between play involving physical objects and play that is primarily engaged with virtual objects, born out of digital computing and media technologies. This chapter discusses play in this hybrid, boundary condition and focuses particularly on the consequences it has for the playing subject by asking: What are the hybrid characteristics of agency in hybrid play?

The situation of all human agency engaged in play is rather complex. Like philosopher Hans-Georg Gadamer (2004) famously argued, "all playing is being-played" (p. 106). When we become playing beings, we are being redefined and framed by the rules and structures of the game in question—player becomes subjected to the game, and game "plays the player." In mixed reality and hybrid games such as *Pokémon GO* (a location-based game) or *Skylanders* (a physical-digital hybrid game), the situation of human subjectivity is even more complex. This relates to the multiple frames and multiple layered dimensions of reality that overlap in a hybrid play situation. The everyday, social roles of persons engaged in hybrid play can potentially conflict with the in-game roles that they hold as participants in the play reality: Think, for example, a college student who is, at the same time, in an everyday social role as a student in a classroom while also being an "assassin" in a pervasive live-action game. Some of these overlaps take place through modern technologies such as Global Positioning System (GPS), the radio navigation system owned by the US government, which define certain novel conditions for location-based hybrid play. Given these conditions, the underlying aim of this chapter is to discuss the constitution of agency of hybrid play by alerting us to the power dynamics involved in human-technological systems. Hybrid play with location-based mobile games is the paramount contemporary example of such developments, but there are also other important forms of play that will be addressed by this discussion, such as play with digitally augmented physical toys or physically augmented digital games.

I discuss agency in hybrid play first through the fundamental hybridity underlying all play situations. Particularly, I consider the role of imagination and the potential of play to mean several things at the same time, when approached from different frames of reference or points of view. After a brief philosophical introduction, I address several historical examples that help to highlight the construction and operation of hybrid play agency in practice. These include the introduction of digital technologies into classical, non-digital forms of play and games, the further hybridization of play in various toy-game hybrids, and location-based mobile play. The themes of empowerment and confinement run through this discussion: The effects of hybrid play on player's agency appear in this investigation to be somewhat mixed and ambiguous in the end.

The roots of hybrid play

The philosophers and theorists of play have long debated how to properly address the fundamental character of play. The pervasive and even somewhat "banal" character of play possibly has made it harder to comprehend the full complexity of play—after all, play is commonly associated with something that children do (and adults do less), and there is plenty of evidence of many animal species also engaging in play behaviors—particularly young mammals play, but there is evidence of play even among non-mammals, such as spiders (Riechert, 1978). The agency of animals who engage in play might appear a relatively simple starting point, but it also might shed light to the agency of hybrid human play. Arguably, as symbol-using, cultural beings, humans are the only species to definitely act and play simultaneously in multiple, hybrid realities. Jean Piaget (1951), for example, strongly argued that early play scholars like Karl Groos (1898) were guilty of "anthropomorphic abuse" by attributing make-believe play to animals. In this line of thinking, only humans would truly be able to maintain two realities imposed on top of each other and derive enjoyment of the subsequent playful hybrid experience. The make-believe activities of higher animals such as dogs play-fighting nevertheless remain as a borderline case here (Piaget, 1951).

Philosophically, the roots of hybrid play are ancient, as arguably all play is fundamentally hybrid play. The basic reality of play has a hybrid dimension, which can be approached, for example, from work done in understanding animal play. The scholars of animal play studies recognize the fundamental difference between play and other behaviors that animals engage in, and they note that all play is something that appears to be spontaneous, rewarding in itself, and marked by some features that set it apart from "normal" (or "serious") behaviors—for example, the play versions of animals' behavioral repertoire are often somehow incomplete, or exaggerated versions of non-playful behaviors; an example might be a dog and deer playing "hunting" without being serious and complete in their "hunting" or "escaping" antics (Bateson &

Martin, 2013). The biological foundations of animals—and humans—appear to include play as an additional dimension into their experience of reality: We all have the capacity to settle into a frame or mindset which includes non-productive and non-serious behaviors that are done just for fun. In this line of thinking, play is a behavior that is intrinsically motivated, rewarding, and appears to have its goal in itself. In terms of its ontology, the basic character of play can be found in it being a compound activity that both differentiates and combines two realities into a single hybrid one: the experience of inhabiting a particular mixture of first the physical and serious reality of purpose-driven activities, and, second, the non-serious and playful reality that tends to dominate while engaged in play activities. It should be noted that ontologically, both of these "realities" are primarily mindsets—modes of behaving and thinking that modify our relationship to both material and immaterial dimensions of existence.

When we step beyond the most elementary forms of play which some animal species evidence, and go into games and play of humans, the play situation complicates further: Human play is not only biologically motivated or determined, but it also has many play-related cultural traditions, norms, and values that are passed from generation to generation, and which are also constantly creatively modified. For example, there are classic forms of outdoor play such as hide-and-seek and tag, which appear rather universal, but also change constantly and are accompanied by the invention of new outdoor games. The economic conditions, organization of work and leisure, and conceptions of what is proper behavior for children and adults also affect the forms that play takes in cultures (Sutton-Smith, 1989; Virtanen, 1972). It is important to study what characterizes and defines the cultural agency of human play—and particularly the contemporary forms of playful agency that are emerging in the era of hybrid media and information systems.

Cultural agency of play

In this hybrid context, even coming up with a clear and precise definition of "culture" might be a bit tricky. Generally speaking, there are at least two major traditions of thought that deal with culture: One is based on association of "arts and culture," and the other is rooted in anthropological traditions of thought. A classic definition in the latter tradition is provided by the pioneering anthropologist Edward Burnett Tylor, who, in his work *Primitive Culture* (1871), defines culture as "that complex whole which includes knowledge, belief, art, morals, law, custom, and any other capabilities and habits acquired by man as a member of society" (p. 1). This is a very wide understanding of "culture" and underlines the many ways in which the different aspects of culture are deeply integrated into our lives and agency as "cultural beings." It is difficult to think about a human without culture, even while the accounts of "feral children" that are raised by animals and have lived isolated from any human contact seem to provide an interesting test case for developmental psychology and philosophy alike. The limited evidence that these individuals can provide seems to suggest that "humans without culture" appear to grow up as fundamentally disabled compared to our norms of human agency; for example, their inability to learn language and adopt "civilized" behaviors and practices makes them seem both mentally impaired and socially misfit when brought back to human contact and community (Candland, 1995; Newton, 2003). Considering this, all studies of human agency are also studies into cultural agency—a fundamentally hybrid phenomenon, including both biological and genetic, as well as socially transmitted and constructed components. There are also no distinctive criteria that would allow differentiating "culture" from "society," for example. From an anthropological perspective, one can, however, study "cultures" in plural: Adopting this approach, it should, therefore, be possible to study the intersections of societal and cultural changes within the late modernity when it interfaces with pervasive technologies and novel play forms that they allow.

The other tradition of thinking about culture does allow certain qualitative distinctions to be made within cultures themselves. In everyday speech, it is this understanding of culture as "the arts and other manifestations of human intellectual achievement" that is the most commonly used (see, e.g., *Oxford English Dictionaries*). Among all human practices and behaviors, the cultivation of arts and culture is something distinctive and usually highly valued. The cultural history is recorded and taught to the next generation. There can also be differences in cultural agency in this line of thinking: Someone can be more "cultured" than someone else. This has been discussed by sociologist Pierre Bourdieu in his theory of cultural distinctions. According to Bourdieu (1984), people can cumulate and possess different kinds of "cultural capital" that features in their lives in important ways, as it is the foundation for how knowledgeable or sophisticated they appear in various social contexts. For example, the "game cultural agency" in contemporary societies comes with similar kinds of qualifiers. There is distinctive "game cultural capital" that one can achieve by evolving as a football fan, as a golfer—or as an expert in online role-playing games or a particular video game series with a cult following (Consalvo, 2007). Like with other cultural practices, enculturation into game cultures involves development of certain knowledge and skills: in this case something that is often called "ludic literacy." Cultural critics and scholars of games emphasize that being able to just play and having a "naïve understanding" of games has its limits. At a deeper level, game cultural agency also comes with expectations of historical and critical knowledge and "analytical know-how," which enables a subject to provide grounds for her critique of games (Mäyrä, 2008; Zagal, 2010). As games are an evolving cultural form, the criteria for this kind of educated game cultural agency are also constantly changing.

Perhaps the most fundamental dimension of understanding and skills in terms of games and play relates to being able to understand that these are forms of "play culture" from the start. Johan Huizinga, a classic of cultural game scholarship, included in his work *Homo Ludens* (1938/1955) as a key argument the claim that there is a fundamental "play element" in all cultures. Furthermore, Huizinga saw the effects of the play element as wide-ranging and pervasive; in this perspective, play is something that should be taken into account when discussing diverse cultural phenomena such as art, law, war, and philosophy. Huizinga emphasized how play, while a free activity, is "standing quite consciously outside 'ordinary' life" and that it "proceeds within its own proper boundaries of time and space" (p. 13)—which produces a symbolic and functional demarcation of games and play that has become known in later scholarship as the "magic circle" of play and games. While the magic circle of Huizinga has been repeatedly criticized and, arguably, also often understood too literally (Stenros, 2014), his discussion of "illusion" and "make-believe" of play has received less attention. However, it is crucial to see how the cultural agency of play relies on certain underlying understanding of fantasy: Play takes place within a layer or dimension of reality that is built on imagination. The object and actions that are taken into play gain their particular meaning precisely due to this "what if" dynamics. A pinecone can be a dragon; a wooden stick can be a magic sword. In the state and mindset of play, multiple realities are simultaneously created and maintained in order to give birth for a new hybrid reality of play. This understanding of cultural hybridity as a consequence of our innate capacity for fantasy and imagination forms the starting point for the following discussion of hybrid games and play.

Power, subversion, and fantasy in play

The cultural analysis of play has from the early stages paid attention to the interesting relationship play has with power in a society. On the one hand, play can appear as something that the powerless do; it is "mere play," after all, rather than real power over the basic life realities—it is unlikely that play can overturn social hierarchies, redistribute wealth, or effect changes in the fundamental ways in which the society operates, for example. On the other hand, it is in playful versions of such "revolutionary" potentials where pleasure and fascination of play reside, to a certain degree. Like Huizinga, Russian literary scholar Mikhail Bakhtin (1984) studied the cultural roles of humor, play, and playfulness in history, and his discussion of the "carnivalesque" is particularly important for understanding the roots of contemporary hybrid street games, among many other things. Bakhtin refers to the ancient history of folk humor, fantasy, and the grotesque, and suggests that the medieval carnivals are a form of speech and action that is relevant for understanding an important subversive cultural tradition that continues even today. Drawing from the traditions of parody and travesty, the carnival is here seen as a cultural site for experimenting and playing with alternative visions of social reality: The regular order of things was overturned, as the dominant tone was changed to one of comic parody and exaggeration. For a while, the fools were kings, and the kings (and all things sacred) were drawn into foolery. Bakhtin speaks about how a carnival "built a second world and a second life outside officialdom" (p. 6) and says that consideration of this "two-world condition" is crucial for understanding the medieval cultural consciousness and the ensuing culture of the Renaissance. Today, the multi-layered character of "ludic realities" overlapping and mixing with the everyday, more utilitarian social realities holds potential for interacting with structurally somewhat similar, carnivalesque phenomena. The agency of hybrid play is the one that is capable of keeping contact with such, multiple and even conflicting spheres of reality.

Many contemporary game genres and play forms display influence from literary traditions or the fine arts. One particularly important cultural influence for hybrid play relates to the tradition of fantasy, or the fantastic, in the arts. This is a wider topic than "fantasy games"; yet, it is true that the milieu and game characters in many adventure and role-playing games in particular are drawn from fantastic fiction with dragons, elves, and magic. The deeper, underlying connection with the fantastic concerns the ways in which the agency of game play includes the repertoire of detecting and communicating something as play. Named as "metacommunication" by Gregory Bateson (2000), the play actions carry with them signs that signal: "These actions which we now engage do not denote what those actions *for which they stand* would denote" (p. 180). The play actions as carried out by a hybrid, playful agent are always also parts of a fantasy reality, where an attack, or struggle, for example, becomes an enjoyable and exciting experience, rather than threatening one.

Ample use of imagination, and particularly mixing it with the everyday social reality, comes with its own potential conflicts and ambiguities. Even the linguistic and etymological roots of "fantasy" suggest that it is a loaded concept; on the one hand, "fantasy" (as derived from Greek *phan'*, "to appear or seem") is used to discuss something that is imagined or dreamed—a highly desirable reality. On the other hand, "fantasy" is also used like the "phantasma," to discuss "delusions" and "figments of the imagination"—something irrelevant or even dangerous. The fantastic tradition in the arts is popular yet conflicting in its reception and cultural status. The fantastic elements of ancient myths, for example, have been the target of critique and (loving) satire at least since Lucian of Samosata and his second century A.D. satirical fantasy work *A True Story* (Ἀληθῆ διηγήματα). Literary scholar Rosemary Jackson (1981) writes about fantasy as "the literature of subversion" and notes that while it is the cultural role of fantasy to provide opportunities for exploring "taboo" topics and evoking the (often subconscious) conflicts that underlie our socially and culturally constructed "selves," fantasy often frequently serves (as in the case of Gothic fiction) to reconfirm institutional order of things. The fantasy can work as a temporary escape from this shared normative reality by supplying "vicarious fulfilment of desire" and "neutralizing an urge towards transgression" in the end (Jackson, 1981, p. 41).

The dynamics of contemporary hybrid games come embedded within similar, culturally ambiguous power dynamics. It is indeed typical for play and games to provide incentive for the creation of "alternative orders" and operational logistics. This is a dimension that has been raised into headlines by the proponents of "gamification" in particular. For example, Jane McGonigal (2011) has argued that our current social reality is "broken" (dysfunctional and unsatisfactory) and, if lessons of good game design would be applied in the context of real-life problems rather than just ludic fantasy, there could be immense potential for societal and individual transformation through game play. There are indeed ongoing efforts to design services and experiences that would be as engaging as good games, while also providing multiple benefits in addition to enjoyment derived from the fantasy dimensions of games. The most popular hybrid games of today nevertheless continue to prioritize the engaging and enjoyable character of imaginative play realities over the real-life goals or consequences.

Physical and digital in hybrid play

The engaging and enjoyable character of hybrid play is interesting in itself. As noted earlier in this chapter, all play is hybrid by character, and the cultural character of ludic agency is fundamentally rooted in our ability to combine and negotiate between multiple dimensions of constructed reality, some playful, some less so. But it is with the rise of digital, computer, and video games where the concept of hybrid games and play started to gain broader relevance. The veritable Renaissance of game design and new ways of playing that followed the early experiments and the first generations of video games meant that there were suddenly both new kinds of implementations of traditional games and completely new kinds of experiences available that were made possible by the advances in computing and digital audiovisual technologies. In 1952, it was possible for the first time to play tic-tac-toe, a simple paper-and-pencil game on a computer terminal (OXO), then in 1958 to play simplified tennis (*Tennis for Two*) on an oscilloscope screen, and in 1962 a computer game designed to simulate fighting spaceships (*Spacewar!*) was released to a select audience of early mainframe computer users. In all these cases, the experience of traditional games was fundamentally altered by the technical requirements of computing hardware: There was no physical paper used by the tic-tac-toe players, nor physical rackets in the electronic tennis version (Kent, 2001). In the case of *Spacewar!*, there were no direct predecessors among traditional games (as autonomously moving playing pieces were not part of classical games), and it should also be noted that the closest earlier game forms such as miniature wargames differ fundamentally in their tactile nature.

It is in the nature of physical toys to naturally support and encourage hybrid play: the mapping of imaginative characteristics or fantasy reality with associated playful functionalities on physical objects (Heljakka, 2019). For a long time, computer and video games developed into an opposite direction. The digital game player needed to internalize the button-presses, typed keyboard commands, or other arbitrary operations that the computerized user interface required. During the early decades of computer and video games, there were few attempts at bridging the digital and physical realities in a more intuitive manner, for example by developing games that used plastic "light guns" for shooting at targets in the monitor display. Such combinations of physical and digital play started to expand in two ways, starting in the 1980s and entering mainstream in the early 2000s. First, the handheld video gaming devices, such as Nintendo's Game & Watch series (from 1980 onward, followed eventually by the first Game Boy device in 1989) started to feature digital game play that was also increasingly connected with mobile experiences. In 1997, the first known mobile phone game—*Snake* by Nokia—appeared preinstalled in mobile handsets (Mäyrä, 2015). Second, the introduction of multiple different sensor types (such as accelerometer, gyroscope, heart rate, and touchscreen sensors) allowed techniques for implementing game play that tied the physical reality more intimately with the digital dimensions. In the area of video game consoles, Nintendo was again in the forefront. In 2006, the Nintendo Wii console was released, including a new type of game control, the Wii Remote. This control device was designed to track the natural motions of players' hands with the help of an accelerometer and optical sensor. With this technology, it was possible, for example, to play tennis in a virtual tennis court by physically simulating the hand movements and the trajectory needed to make a successful serve in a real-life tennis game. The virtual, in-game agency that is represented by the player's avatar on-screen is in this case (more or less accurately) reflecting the embodied agency of the playing subject. In reality, many players soon noticed that it was relatively easy to "fool" the system, if so desired, and play the games with very minimal physical movements, while sitting on a sofa. The in-game realities thus still remained fundamentally disconnected from the embodied and physical realities of the players, even while the hybridization involved increasingly close, parallel developments in physical and digital, simulated or virtual domains.

The potential for combining physical and digital in novel, hybrid experiences has continued to evolve, particularly as it has become easier to embed tiny sensors in all kinds of physical objects, implement touch-sensitivity into multiple objects and surfaces, link embedded microphones and voice commands to programmed functionalities, use light-sensors and cameras to make objects react to proximity, and implement types of pattern recognition. When such technological developments are combined with low-power wireless connectivity, the option for implementing a sort of "Internet of Playful Things" starts to open up. The conventional industry-driven vision of "Internet of Things" (IoT) is focused on implementing home automation, remote monitoring, or health solutions with wearable technology (Ometov et al., 2017). But the same basic technologies are open for exploitation into games, toys, and playful designs of other sorts.

Studies of hybrid play: toys and games

At Tampere University, our research group in the Game Research Lab has studied hybrid play forms and game experiences from the early 2000s, and this work has been informed by the technological changes outlined earlier. We have noted the increasing hybridization of such, previously relatively distinct play and game types as gambling and gaming, mobile phone play and video game play, social media usage, and online gaming (Mäyrä et al., 2017). A series of studies on such emerging fields led into a two-year research project to study the hybridization of physical and digital playthings ("Hybridex," 2012–2014). Under such closer analysis, the blurring and hybridization of play appeared as a wide-ranging and quickly evolving phenomenon. We could detect how the game industry and toy manufacturing were intermixing with franchises such as Activision's *Skylanders* (2011–) product line, which was followed by other toy-augmented videogame products, the Disney *Infinity* (2013–) series and Nintendo's *Amiibo* toys (2014–). The popular construction toy company, LEGO, also introduced its own hybrid toy-game product line, *Lego Dimensions*, in 2015. These products provide the players with diverse experiences, including collecting and controlling experiences that are derived from tangible toys, set within the context of digital, video game play. The crossing of boundary lines between physical toy and digital game is typically implemented with the use of sensors: e.g., in a *Skylanders* game, there is an RFID chip embedded into a toy-game figure, which is then used to access the in-game digital version of same character when placed on the provided "Portal of Power"—which is technically just an RFID reader that communicates between the physical toy and the digital game world. When the hybrid experiences in this wide, emerging category are analyzed, certain design patterns can be detected, e.g., implementation of hybrid play by synchronizing or asynchronizing the physical and digital dimension of play; or by making the physical or digital play dimension either dependent or independent of the other play dimension; or by implementing "open play" or "closed play" in a complementary manner in the physical and digital game-toy dimensions (Tyni et al., 2016).

From the perspective of hybrid play agency, the augmentation of digital game designs with tangible toys and other physical additions may appear like an empowering direction of development. After all, while some digital games are open for creative inputs from players—e.g., the open world, "sandbox" style games, and games that support "modding" or sharing user-created content—in many cases the game design imposes a certain actionable script on the player.

The toy designs can be empowering or limiting in terms of player agency. The LEGO construction toys are one interesting example of this. The central idea of plastic bricks is focused on open-ended construction play and the creation of playful, self-created designs as play. This idea was changed in the late 1990s, when LEGO Company reacted to the increasing mediatization and technologization of children's (and indeed almost everyone's) experiential reality by starting to introduce tie-in products such as *Star Wars* themed LEGO sets (Hjarvard, 2004). The new sets also came with more "preformed" parts, rather than just the basic brick shapes. Like Maaike Lauwaert (2009) writes, this had the consequence of inviting media-inspired play with LEGOs, but also of decreasing the play options: Once constructed according to the provided instructions, the new LEGO pieces were no longer as open for completely new, open designs as the older LEGO pieces with the basic designs were. Marsha Kinder (1993) has discussed the wider implications of this changing toy and media landscape for the play agency. She argues that the popular transmedia franchises are designed to position the children in ambiguous state of "consumerist interactivity"; they are both empowered and limited by the dual form of spectatorship, where they are both invited to passively watch the television series or movies and then to act out the preformed scripts with the tie-in toys, video games, and action figures.

The blending of play: location-based gaming

Location-based games are another example where the emerging hybrid play agency is becoming realized in ambiguous and internally conflicted manners. The classic forms of location-play such as organizing outdoors treasure hunts go back a long time in history. For instance, the "letterboxing" hobby was popular as early as the 1850s. In the Dartmoor moors in England, people would initially amuse other hikers by placing boxes with a letter or postcard hidden inside. Since then, the number of practitioners in this kind of (adult) outdoor play has grown, and it is typical to make an imprint of the stamp found in a letterbox in one's personal notebook, as a proof of having found the box. The interest in letterboxing might stem from the diverse forms of playful activities that it brings together: outdoor exercise, orienteering, puzzle solving, and forms of arts and crafts. The hobby of geocaching is another modern variant where the digital technologies bring along a particular added hybrid dimension into the experience and practices of play. Geocaching is based on playful appropriation of GPS. GPS was originally developed for military uses by the U.S. Department of Defense in 1973; however, civilian uses were allowed in 1980s, albeit with degraded GPS signals—for "national security reasons." This practice was discontinued in May 2000, after which it became possible to play games that rely on precise positioning with the help of GPS (GPS.org, 2018). It is nevertheless an illustrative example of the ways in which power relations operate: The underlying systemic power is often unequally distributed between different actors in hybrid play.

A technology-centric perspective into hybrid play is to a certain degree valuable in highlighting the historical change and development in the field; yet, as such, it remains insufficient in the end. An alternative is provided by Ville Kankainen et al. (2017) in their definition of hybrid games that relies on conceptual blending theory. Rather than being defined by the "hybridizing capabilities" of some novel technology, hybrid games emerge as a novel ludic category only when they bring together and combine two previously unconnected conceptual domains in a new way; these might be previously non-connected domains of art and entertainment, as in combination of playing music with playing instruments and playing arcade video games, as in case of *Guitar Hero* and *Rock Band* style of rhythm video games that feature instrument-shaped gaming peripherals. The source domains can, however, be even further apart from each other in how our everyday concepts and experiences are organized. The ensuing "conceptual blending" thus opens up a new cognitive (and cultural) category, which expands the operative range of play agency. From this perspective, when analyzing hybrid play in digital games, it is not particularly useful to focus only on the use of physical controllers or special peripherals. Every game is in any case embedded within a material reality, so if the game experience does not gain a particularly added conceptual dimension from the mixing of previously disconnected conceptual and experiential domains, the game play experience itself is not particularly "hybrid." The examples that Kankainen et al. (2017) discuss include *XCOM: The Board Game* (2012)—a game that carries the tagline "You are humanity's last hope" and which sets players fighting against imminent alien invasion. In this game, players use both a selection of physical objects (play tokens, cards, a gaming board) and a smartphone app, which is used to control in-game time, resources, and some game events. *XCOM* demonstrates how the functionalities, experiences, and conceptual mindsets involved in playing video games and board games can be blended to produce a novel type of hybrid board game play. Similarly, the *Skylanders* series of games relies on the hybrid blending of toy play and video game play, where both toys and games are involved in and intermingled into a new kind of hybrid: The player alternates from manipulating the physical character miniatures to manipulating their animated and interactive digital counterparts—and the ensuing playful blend includes both of these dimensions (Figure 5.1). From the perspective of hybrid play agency, it is important to note that such conceptual blends also involve blending of functionalities: In a physical *Skylander* toy, there are also "hidden," digital functionalities that become playable in the context of compatible video game; such key functions that are not immediately visible from just looking at the toy figure are activating virtual version of toy character and saving the digital game state inside the physical toy. Hybrid player agency is empowered and expected to engage in play behaviors that relate to multiple dimensions of hybrid games, or their play realities, simultaneously.

Figure 5.1 Skylanders: a physical toy figure activates the corresponding digital game character. Copyright: Frans Mäyrä.

Coming back to the example of location-based play and games, the agency of traditional treasure hunt style of game is enabled and confined within the playful appropriation of physical spaces. As such, the traditional outdoor player is subject to the laws and norms that govern the use of public and private spaces in a local area. The fantasy of hiding and locating treasures in surprising locations can motivate the players, but there are laws or norms that stop hiding such play treasures inside a grave or into a church, for example, or for setting up a treasure hunt inside a supermarket without permission. The negotiations about the use of space for physical play are embedded in power relations that are economic, political, and also ideological by nature. For example, the inquisitive adventures of the so-called "urban explorers" (urbex) appropriate urban wastelands such as ruined buildings into playgrounds. Doing that, the urbex practitioners (or players) may frequently step into contested areas in the use of abandoned or overlooked spaces that might be off limits or out-of-bounds for the general public. However, like Carrie Mott and Susan M. Roberts (2014) have noted, this re-appropriating and potentially radical practice of "urbex" is embedded within ideological power structures; the agency of urban exploration is often rather masculinist (rich with the rhetoric of "penetration"), and the social privileges and entitlements characterizing the body of urban explorer have so far been largely ignored (p. 10).

When a dimension of digital play is added to location-based activities, additional dimensions also emerge for design and playful exploration. As we argued in an earlier study (Mäyrä & Lankoski, 2009), the experiential and cultural potential of mixed reality in location-based gaming is inherently liberating and enriching for the playful subjects, and even for the community. There are innumerable novel perspectives and opportunities for meaning-making that open up when "non-tangible" information is made accessible and shared in real-world, physical locations, and played within social settings. Based on our early 2003–2004 experiments with location-based mobile multiplayer gaming, culminating in *The Songs of North* (a shamanistic-themed mobile location-based multiplayer game implemented as part of the MOGAME project), we argued that these new forms of hybrid play have the potential to bring games and play back to public spaces, from the confines of private homes where digital gaming has been isolated, at least to a certain degree. Furthermore, the hybrid play holds potential for providing playful incentive and better sense of control for using and creating connections between the domains of digital information systems and everyday environments (Mäyrä & Lankoski, 2009, pp. 141–145). A recent study (Koskinen et al., 2019) about the memorable and meaningful experiences that players have had while playing *Pokémon GO* (2016) suggests that these potentials have started to become realized: In addition to interacting with engaging fantasy gaming content, it was the interactions with other people and social experiences in shared spaces that provided the largest numbers of memorable experiences. The hybrid play provided additional incentive and empowerment for talking with strangers in the streets or for coming up with new ways to interact with familiar environments.

Yet, the hybrid play agency in games such as *Pokémon GO* is framed by tensions and power relations that include most of the ones that were already discussed in the context of physical location-based play (like treasure hunting or urban exploration), but with additional limitations of its own. Playing hybrid games in sparsely populated urban or suburban areas does not come with equal opportunities for males and females, or for minors and adults. There are also important asymmetries in power when the technical and creative aspects of hybrid play agency are discussed. The costs of location services and online access can be prohibitive for some, depending on the mobile phone plans they are able to access. The unlimited mobile data plans are not yet the standard, nor affordable option in many places. The urban emphasis in this style of hybrid play is also a limitation for many. Living in a sparsely populated country with little cultural landmarks or tourist attractions that are far apart has consequences for what is being registered into the in-game location database of Niantic (company which created *Pokémon GO* and its predecessor, *Ingress*). Typical game play of *Pokémon GO*, for example, revolves around "Pokéstops" and "Gyms" that are key in-game locations for collecting game resources or for engaging in player-vs-player sessions. And those key game spots are anchored in real-life urban landmarks and attractions. The solitary players, particularly in the countryside, have for a long time been missing out. Something that could help them to have meaningful play experiences would be to give them the power to propose their local points of interest, vantage points, nature trails, or hiking landmarks as in-game landmarks (*Pokéstops or Gyms*) from within the game. As of this writing (in Summer 2019), there is not yet an in-game system for submitting Pokéstop locations—except for level 40 players in a few specific countries—nor (most importantly) for a solid review process to guarantee fair distribution of such key locations. Future versions of location-based games will indeed need to open up more opportunities for user-created content for truly global reach and equal opportunities in hybrid play to become reality. The fundamental imbalance in hybrid play relates particularly to the limitations that these games impose on creative play agency. While a physical treasure hunt is relatively easy to set up in almost any area (taking into account factors such as the behavioral norms, safety concerns, and the ability to find other co-located players), the programmed digital dimensions in hybrid play still remain rather inflexible. Modifications and "house rules" that are typical for many forms of adaptive, traditional games are a problem for massively multiplayer digital games that are designed with the eye toward large player populations and related concerns of "cheating." The hesitation of Niantic to open up *Pokémon GO* for their millions of players to submit places to be nominated as Pokéstop or Gym sites might be explained by the unfair advantages such openness might provide for some: Some players might possibly get their school, home, or work places registered as such key sites of the game, leading to tilted in-game resource distribution. An opposite, altruistic example is the player-created practice of city-based *Pokémon Go* players "adopting" rural players by trading them rare Pokémon as gifts (Stefansky, 2019).

It must be remembered that while hybrid play is a complex phenomenon, it can be in various ways empowering. Yet, it also has built-in potentials for power imbalance and abuse. Regardless of the type of technology employed, there will also always be cultural, behavioral, and community-related conflicts and challenges that any hybrid game needs to overcome. For example, finding like-minded people who share compatible ideas of what are interesting, fair, and fun ways to play together remains as a human challenge that new technologies can solve only to limited degree.

Conclusion: power and ambiguity of hybrid play

In the end, on the basis of aforementioned discussion, we can conclude that there are at least two sorts of consequences from the blending of digital and physical dimensions in contemporary hybrid play. First, these games and play forms act as a valuable reminder about the fundamental hybridity concealed in all play: The digital and virtual elements of modern toy-game hybrids or location-based mobile games make more visible how all play is rooted in negotiating and intermingling of multiple realities—some material, some immaterial. The hybrid play agency from this perspective is the one that is creative and empowered: The hybrid play enables access and blending of fantasy with reality with even potentially transgressive consequences. Second, the contemporary hybrid game and play forms are also tied with technology in a manner that confines the hybrid play agency. The asymmetric power relations that are not exclusive to but aggravated in technologically augmented play forms limit the players' ability to create their own game content, or to design own "house rules" for play, and they steer players into pre-scripted and commercially motivated narratives and behaviors. In this sense, the empowerment of contemporary hybrid play agency is the one that is also subjected to multiple framings: technological, economic, and ideological. Hans-Georg Gadamer's (2004) claim that all playing is also "being played" (p. 106) is consequently particularly true in the case of hybrid games and play: The players of hybrid games are simultaneously embedded within multiple frames of reference that have both empowering and confining consequences for their agency. All this contributes in different ways to their fascinating characteristics and to their significance as subjects of study.

References

Bakhtin, M. M. (1984). *Rabelais and His World*. Bloomington: Indiana University Press.

Bateson, G. (2000). *Steps to an Ecology of Mind: Collected Essays in Anthropology, Psychiatry, Evolution, and Epistemology*. Chicago: University of Chicago Press.

Bateson, P. & Martin, P. (2013). *Play, Playfulness, Creativity and Innovation*. Cambridge: Cambridge University Press.

Bourdieu, P. (1984). *Distinction: A Social Critique of the Judgement of Taste*. Cambridge, MA: Harvard University Press.

Candland, D. K. (1995). *Feral Children and Clever Animals: Reflections on Human Nature*. Oxford: Oxford University Press.

Consalvo, M. (2007). *Cheating: Gaining Advantage in Videogames*. Cambridge, MA: The MIT Press.

Gadamer, H.-G. (2004). *Truth and Method*. London & New York: Continuum International.

GPS.org (2018). Selective Availability. *GPS.Gov* (web site). https://www.gps.gov/systems/gps/modernization/sa/.

Groos, K. (1898). *The Play of Animals*. London: Chapman and Hall.

Heljakka, K. (2019). Toys and Universal Guidelines for Design: A Designerly Perspective on Playability of Character Toys. In: *Proceedings of Universal Design 2019*. Presented March 5, 2019, Universal Design 2019, Bangkok.

Hjarvard, S. (2004). From Bricks to Bytes: The Mediatization of a Global Toy Industry. In *European Culture and the Media*, edited by I. Bondebjerg & P. Golding, 43–63. Bristol: Intellect Books.

Jackson, R. (1981). *Fantasy, the Literature of Subversion*. London: Methuen.

Kankainen, V., Arjoranta, J. & Nummenmaa, T. (2017). Games as Blends: Understanding Hybrid Games. *Journal of Virtual Reality and Broadcasting*, 14 (4). https://www.jvrb.org/past-issues/14.2017/4694.

Kent, S. L. (2001). *The Ultimate History of Video Games: The Story Behind the Craze That Touched Our Lives and Changed the World*. New York: Three Rivers Press.

Kinder, M. (1993). *Playing with Power in Movies, Television, and Video Games: From Muppet Babies to Teenage Mutant Ninja Turtles*. Berkeley: University of California Press.

Koskinen, E., Leorke, D., Alha, K. & Paavilainen, J. (2019). Player Experiences in Location-Based Games: Memorable Moments with Pokémon GO. In *Augmented Reality Games I: Understanding the Pokémon GO Phenomenon*, edited by V. Geroimenko, 95–116. Cham: Springer International Publishing.

Lauwaert, M. (2009). *The Place of Play: Toys and Digital Cultures*. Amsterdam: Amsterdam University Press.

Mäyrä, F. (2008). *An Introduction to Game Studies: Games in Culture*. London & New York: Sage Publications.

Mäyrä, F. (2015). Mobile Games. In *International Encyclopedia of Digital Communication & Society*, edited by Robin Mansell et al. Hoboken, NJ: Wiley-Blackwell.

Mäyrä, F. & Lankoski, P. (2009). Play in a Hybrid Reality: Alternative Approaches into Game Design. In *Digital Cityscapes: Merging Digital and Urban Playspaces*, edited by A. de Souza & D. Sutko, 129–147. New York: Peter Lang.

Mäyrä, F., Stenros, J., Paavilainen, J. & Kultima, A. (2017). From Social Play to Social Games and Back: The Emergence and Development of Social Network Games. In *New Perspectives on the Social Aspects of Digital Gaming: Multiplayer 2*, edited by R. Kowert & T. Quandt, 11–31. New York: Routledge.

McGonigal, J. (2011). *Reality Is Broken: Why Games Make Us Better and How They Can Change the World*. New York: Penguin Press.

Mott, C. & Roberts, S. M. (2014). Not Everyone Has (the) Balls: Urban Exploration and the Persistence of Masculinist Geography. *Antipode*, 46 (1): 229–245.

Newton, M. (2003). *Savage Girls and Wild Boys: A History of Feral Children*. London: Faber & Faber.

Ometov, A., Bezzateev, S. V., Kannisto, J., Harju, J., Andreev, S. & Koucheryavy, Y. (2017). Facilitating the Delegation of Use for Private Devices in the Era of the Internet of Wearable Things. *IEEE Internet of Things Journal*, 4 (4): 843–854.

Piaget, J. (1951). *Play, Dreams and Imitation in Childhood*. London: Heinemann.

Riechert, S. E. (1978). Games Spiders Play: Behavioral Variability in Territorial Disputes. *Behavioral Ecology and Sociobiology*, 3 (2): 135–162.

Stefansky, E. (2019). Who's Still Playing Pokémon GO Three Years Later? *Thrillist*, 22 June 2019. https://www.thrillist.com/entertainment/nation/pokemon-go-who-still-plays-three-years-later.

Stenros, J. (2014). In Defence of a Magic Circle: The Social, Mental and Cultural Boundaries of Play. *Transactions of the Digital Games Research Association*, 1 (2), 147–185.

Sutton-Smith, B. (1989). Children's Folk Games as Customs. *Western Folklore*, 48 (1), 33–42.

Tylor, E. B. (1871). *Primitive Culture: Researches into the Development of Mythology, Philosophy, Religion, Art and Custom*. London: John Murray.

Tyni, H., Kultima, A., Nummenmaa, T., Alha, K., Kankainen, V. & Mäyrä, F. (2016). *Hybrid Playful Experiences: Playing between Material and Digital – Hybridex Project, Final Report*. Tampere: University of Tampere. http://tampub.uta.fi/handle/10024/98900.

Virtanen, L. (1972). *Antti pantti pakana: kouluikäisten nykyperinne*. Porvoo & Helsinki: WSOY.

Zagal, J. P. (2010). *Ludoliteracy: Defining, Understanding, and Supporting Games Education*. 1 edition. Pittsburgh, PA: ETC Press.

6 Casual bodies are hybrid bodies

Shira Chess

We live in a casual world.

We live in a world that privileges the ease and accessibility of what is often referred to as "casual play." This is my start point, because I think it's often easy to get lost in the weeds when talking about video games. The category of "casual games" is an industry term that is often used derisively or dismissively—it's a catch-all meant to indicate a style of play but is often deployed like a genre. The term increasingly infers a discursive list of game genres: match-3, invest/express, hidden object, and puzzle games that all fall under the purview of what is often considered "casual." The video game industry and dominant gaming culture often express a great deal of ambivalence toward these games and their players—both hoping to monetize off an emerging audience but simultaneously deploying memes like "filthy casuals" that remind players of a gamic pecking order.

The hybridity of casual games is at the core of what games have the potential to become. The world we live in, the world we play in, is a "casual" one that privileges casual temporal encounters with our mobile devices, the primary vector for these games. Our casual gaming bodies are composed of seemingly contradictory hybrids: work/play, expansion/constriction, and freedom/captivity. Because of these hybrid modes, casual bodies can reclaim gaming as a medium for all.

The immenseness, budgets, and coverage of massive games, such as *Metal Gear Solid,* make them easier, in many ways, to analyze[1] than the quiet resilience of match-3 games like *Two Dots,* wherein the players are tasked with the simple job of matching multicolored dots in specific patterns in order to clear a board. This, in turn, makes it easy to overlook some games in favor of other games. The anti-industry decrying topics such as video game violence or addiction encompass the medium so broadly that it is sometimes difficult to make room to talk about the quiet elegance of everyday casual games, that in many ways get more play than a big budget game like *Call of Duty.* However, games like *Candy Crush Saga, Clash of Clans,* and *Kim Kardashian: Hollywood* (all of which are considered casual games by industry nomenclature) make a lot in revenue and occupy a great deal of emotional and intellectual space with their players. They serve an important purpose, both at the consumer and industry levels. In short, they diversify the consumer base by broadening *who* plays games, and they force the industry to consider new styles of play in order to attract this broader audience.

I define these terms—hardcore and casual—a little more rigorously in the subsequent sections of this essay. But for now, let us take for granted that these terms define and align with the zeitgeist of video games as a media industry. When we talk about "video games," the image produced is typically one of the "hardcore gamer"—a human, most likely masculinized and necessarily playing in long, hard spans of time on difficult console systems within complex algorithmic universes.

Yet, by ignoring casual games, we are doing a disservice to the future of what video games can be—because in exploring the importance of casual games, we can truly understand the innate potential of digital gaming as a mass and artistic medium. "Casual," as I outline in this chapter, is the state with which we can access our bodies in infinitely more clever ways. Casual bodies are hybrid bodies; they are bodies that can access play in a multitude of situations and can shift between states of work and play more seamlessly than the body of a typical "hardcore" gamer. Thus, by tapping into the bodily complexity of casual games, we can better understand the potential for how the video game industry can disrupt, improve, and expand our lives. By pushing back against the industry rhetoric that privileges the staunch structure of console gaming over the hybrid aesthetic of the casual, we can witness a shift wherein more bodies can transform into hybrid gaming bodies.

In order to demonstrate this, I begin by unpacking the term "casual" as it is deployed by the industry and give examples of casual games to elaborate on the complexities of the category. I specifically talk about the mobile aspect of many casual games as a way to consider the hybrid potential as a vector of change within the video game industry and as a way to rethink and influence our bodily negotiations with games. I then break down the similarities between casual bodies and hybridity, talking through three different hybrid states of casual: work/play, spatial expansion/construction, and freedom/captivity. These hybrid distinctions are meant not as a final resting place for how we can think about the hybrid potential of casual, but as a starting point for understanding how casual gaming has continued to create change within the video game industry at large.

Casual, hardcore, and industry ambivalence

Until this point, I've been using the word "casual" a bit, shall we say, *casually*. The terms "casual" and "hardcore" are industry monikers; they are imperfect in every way, yet impossible to escape. The term "casual game" is an industry label that is often used derisively or dismissively to describe games that can be played in shorter or longer periods of time, are cheap or free, and are easy to learn but perhaps difficult to master (Casual Games Association, 2007). In his breakdown on how the idea of "casual games" is deployed in the video game industry, Jesper Juul (2010) has argued that players and game creators typically assign certain kinds of emotional affect with the play of casual games in terms of narrative style. In short, per Juul, the casual game player is typically associated with "positive and pleasant fictions" (p. 8). Likewise, John Vanderhoef (2013) has argued that casual games are typically feminized leaving the casual market to often be overlooked as a niche space.

Casual games are typically put in a binary opposition to "hardcore" games. To this point, hardcore games are usually considered big budget (sometimes referred to as AAA) games, meant for console systems or PCs. They require a great deal of money, time, and skill, both on the side of creation as well as in terms of commitment toward play (Chess & Paul, 2019). They are games for those who feel a resolute commitment to the video game industry and the products that they produce. When the media talks about video games as a category, "hardcore" games are typically what they are referring to. Just as he defined the stereotypes and affective expectations of the casual player, Juul similarly analyzes perceptions of the hardcore player. In Juul's (2010) breakdown, we typically associate a hardcore gamer with several characteristics: "a preference for science fiction, zombies, and fantasy fictions, has played a large number of video games, will invest large amounts of time and resources toward playing video games, and enjoys difficult games" (p. 8).

The tricky part of understanding the label of both of these terms (hardcore and casual) is that they are imprecise. Casual is a label that is typically deployed in reference to other games—non-hardcore games.[2] So if the term "hardcore" is meant to reference some sort of intense masculine desire for *extreme* gaming, casual is meant to refer to dilettantes, those just playing lightly, and typically feminized via the same gendered binaries. It implies those who might not really matter in the larger scheme of the video game industry. An additional part of the messiness, here, is that the term "casual" is often used as a catch-all meant to indicate a style of play but is often deployed like a genre. The term increasingly infers a discursive list of game styles such as match-3 (games where players are asked to color match various shapes and colors to solve puzzles), invest/express (where a player invests time and money and is given the ability to express their style with design choices), hidden object (where a player finds objects in cluttered spaces), social networking games (where players can connect with friends and strangers playing with them asynchronously), walking simulators (where a player points and clicks to explore a space), and other kinds of smaller puzzle games. All of these games fall under the purview of what is often considered "casual," yet are dramatically different in play style. To this end, the moniker of casual becomes a kind of shorthand for games that are not taken seriously within the realm of digital play.

An additional problem with the deployment of "casual" via the video game industry is that there is some lack of precision between the play being described versus the player being alluded to. Theoretically, casual describes a style of play, but in reality, many people don't play casual games in casual ways. For example, anyone who has ever regularly played *Kim Kardashian: Hollywood* (*KK:H*) knows that casual games can be intense, infuriating, and time consuming. In *KK:H*, the player is not only tasked with completing "gigs," but must return to their screens repeatedly to do so, at varying intervals of time, tethering the player to the screen throughout the day.[3] *KK:H*, and other supposedly casual games like it are only occasionally played in ways and with behaviors that would be typically described as "casual" by a non-player. More often, they are played in bursts of time that require full and rapt attention. For instance, I might play *Polar Pop Mania*, a physics game where I shoot bubbles in match-3 style to release small baby seals from their own bubbles, in casual ways, but that does not necessarily describe the range of responses and emotions to all play in this category. This is all to say: Lived, bodily experiences are complicated, and the term "casual" is a poor descriptor for a vast number of games, play styles, and emotional responses to an experience of digital play. However, the early use of the term in the industry has stuck, making the label difficult to evade. Elsewhere, I have recommended we replace the term "casual" with "non-core" (to sit more adjacent to the term "hardcore") as a legitimate category (Chess & Paul, 2019); however, for now, "casual" is what is most commonly deployed in both industry and player contexts. For the remainder of this article, I use the word "casual" as an industry-based descriptor (a catch-all for games that are not hardcore and include all of the previously outlined categories), but not as a descriptor of *how* the games are played.

The examples, discussed earlier, are all played on mobile interfaces. However, not all casual games are mobile; I've been conflating a bit, thus far, but with good purpose. Mobile is an important vector in casual games; it demonstrates to us the versatility of casual. Casual games existed long before mobile interfaces: For example, hidden object games (where the player is tasked with finding specific things in a messy room) were first made for personal computers, and the earliest versions of the popular game *Diner Dash* (where the player is in the role of a waitress serving customers) first began as a casual computer game. However, while casual games can be played on many platforms, it is our mobile devices that have really pushed casual to the forefront of the conversation and have created an emerging potential within the video game industry.

To all of these points, the video game industry and dominant hegemonic gaming culture have often expressed a great deal of ambivalence toward casual games and their players—both hoping to monetize off an emerging audience while at the same time mocking the style or inclinations of those who prefer casual games over hardcore (Chess, 2017; Chess & Paul, 2019). For example, one 2010 article in *Fortune Magazine* suggested that the casual market would destroy gamers' desire to pay for any kind of games and only offered "small pleasures" (Mangalindan, 2010). Others have suggested that the casual market comprises women alternating between playing casuals and watching *Oprah* (Kato, 2007). In these hardcore spaces, industry advocates are constantly being reminded of a kind of gamic pecking order that occurs, and casual games are necessarily at the bottom of that scale. This has been quite clear in the larger industry dialogue referring to games played on consoles like Playstation and Xbox as "real games" while being often derisive and dismissive of social networking games (such as Zynga games like *FarmVille*), walking simulators (such as *Gone Home*), or free-to-play mechanics (games that are "free" to download, but in order to level up, players need to purchase bonuses) (Consalvo & Paul, 2019).[4]

This anti-casual sentiment plays out most clearly in internet forums (such as Reddit and 4chan) where the meme "filthy casuals" has become popularized. The meme actively derides the tastes of casual gamers, creating the not-so-subtext that casual gamers and their dilettante ways are destroying the video game industry (Amanda, 2008). The typical argument for this either suggests that the industry itself is pouring money into casuals, and thus no longer investing in hardcore, or that microtransactions of free-to-play games will destroy audience desire for big-budget games. This creates a tension, wherein those gamers, who have long been invested in this industry, suggest that they have been abandoned and deploy the "filthy casuals" meme, in kind. The very existence of this meme category shows the reluctance of the video game industry (as well as the culture around it) to consider the possibility that casual games and gamers might bring a positive change by creating diversity in game genres and aesthetics as well as by pushing the industry to think about the market beyond the desires of a core set of players. While these games and the different categories of players that come with them might not "ruin" the video game industry (as alluded to by the memes), they are indeed disrupting the status quo of the industry by fostering different games and play styles that are more flexible in terms of accessibility and the time spent playing. This disruption—without question— owes to the transformative power of casual games, and more specifically, mobile casual games.

The casual body and hybrid gaming

Video game industry statistics are often dated and hard to nail down, but it's worth thinking about *who* is playing casually. About half of all people who play video games are female (Chalk, 2014; Yee, 2017). Many of these players are older; a 2014 ESA survey found that the average age of game players is 35 years (Chalk, 2014). At the same time, many newer players in these demographics are specifically playing games that are typically labeled as casual games. And more important than the specific quantitative demographics, the emergence of mobile casuals, casual games exclusively played on mobile devices such as phones and tablets, is pivotal in building a safe space for novice players to try out the medium. Because of their accessibility and lack of complexity, mobile casual games help to introduce new players to gaming in low-stakes, inexpensive ways.

We are at a crucial moment for the video game industry, and the casual market is at the core of this change. Hardcore games require players to spend a considerable amount of money and have specialized skills; casual games, in turn, do not require the same level of dexterity and knowledge. They, instead, court novices and old hands, alike. While casual games may have started with mobile games like *Angry Birds*, we are witnessing the popularization of more hybrid games that are between what is typically characterized as casual games and those that are referred to as indie games.

"Indie" once referred to a specific way of producing a game. Indie games were made by small teams of individuals, whereas games labeled as "casual" were typically made by larger corporations. Now, however, "indie" is more clearly linked to a specific style, genre, or *zeitgeist* that follows with non-industry art and mechanics (Lipkin, 2013). "Indies" are often quirkier and visually distinct from other games in the industry: both hardcore and casual. For example, consider the difference between *Dinner Dash*, a typical casual game, and *Florence*, an indie game. *Diner Dash* is a time management casual game where the player waits on tables. *Florence*, in turn, is a story-game about first love and relationships. *Florence* is more novelistic and artful in its style and is meant as a one-time experience, whereas *Diner Dash* is a game meant to be played ongoing until the player tires of it and moves on to another game. Indie games typically sit outside of the "hardcore" or "casual" boundaries, but they are also a kind of "inside baseball"—in other words, those in the video game industry or culture are normally those who know about good indie games. This means that while indie games might be more accessible to broad audiences, these audiences don't always learn about the interesting, artful, and literary games that are available. However, the borderlines between indie and casual continue to shift, and the distinctions become less meaningful. An artful "indie" puzzle game such as a *Monument Valley* has many qualities of popular "casual" games.

Indie games are a kind of hybrid of their own; they seem to relish in the accessibility of casuals with the thematic largeness of console. As I continue through this essay, I will not distinguish mobile casual with mobile indie, because, to some degree, they seek the same end—a pushback against the primary AAA industry and a desire to capture a broader audience. Regardless of whether the games in question are labeled as indie or casual, they are transformative: They can invite in new players, they make audiences rethink what video games are, they foster innovative forms of gaming, and they allow players to play while mobile. Our mobile devices allow us to multitask and transform "dead time" into play time—or work and play simultaneously. The time that we used to spend doing other things (such as browsing magazines in a doctor's office or staring into space while waiting to pick up our kids) can now be spent playing a casual mobile game. As it has been noted by de Souza e Silva and Frith (2010), mobile devices can be used "in-between" and fulfill times in which we were previously commuting, waiting, or using other media, such as reading a book while on public transportation. Besides being able to play digital games in a wider variety of places and times, we no longer need to own a $300 console video game system and spend $60 per game in order to play. The play on our mobile devices does not involve the purchase of additional hardware. We can play anywhere, anytime, with things we already own.

For better or worse, this effect is truly transformative—both at the micro-level experiences of players (who can materialize play into any moment of their lives) and at the macro-level of the industry (where game creators are able to access more players in an ever-growing list of technologies). In short, the world we live in, the world we play in is a "casual"—one that privileges casual temporal encounters with our mobile devices. Many of us live busy lives, and most people don't have time to play hardcore games for several hours in a row. The majority of people can far more easily sneak play into interstitial moments, and that's what the mobile/casual market is really quite good at. As a result, an increasing number of people can fit more play into their everyday lives.

At the same time, our bodies are central to this discursive shift. In this, I mean that our mobile devices are extensions of our bodies (McLuhan, 1994), and the play that is done on these devices is a complex interplay of time and space. For example, Ito et al. (2006) demonstrate how mobile phones became integrated into Japanese culture, transforming both bodies and interpersonal relationships. In order to play on our mobile devices, we need to collapse our bodies, reform them, and mold them into the small space of our screens. We see this affect in the bodily circumstances of how we interact with our mobile devices. With a console system, our bodies are sprawling, fixed to a television but typically enacting the largeness of the screen we are inserting ourselves into. Yet, in mobile casual games, our bodies respond to the smallness of the space. When playing a mobile game, our bodies sit hunched, staring into the miniature screen and reducing our girth to fit into that screen. Of course, this is not necessarily the case with location-based games, where our screens expand outward into the world. But this distinction further elaborates on the hybridity offered by mobile platforms. Their mobility makes them capable of many things, simultaneously.

Play time and leisure, too, become reconstructed in mobile play. While console and hardcore systems imply a kind of endless play that may span hours (which, of course, is necessary to excel at those systems), our mobile devices decrease the time of play but add it into the smallness of everyday moments. Players don't all have time to sprawl into a three-hour time block of play, but our mobile devices infer that it is quite acceptable to decrease that time into small, stolen moments. We can see this most coherently in time management games such as *Diner Dash* where the player completes timed tasks in abbreviated moments, when play and work often collide in the game's diegesis.

Yet, in both temporal and bodily transformations, there is something expansive, something of deep potential to shift how we think about the everyday of our playful activities. In order to understand the cultural changes wrought by these playful opportunities, it is useful to think of our casual play in terms of their potential toward hybridity, as I demonstrate in the following sections. Casual gaming bodies are composed of seemingly contradictory hybrids, such as work/play, spatial expansion/constriction, and freedom/captivity. These casual bodies are transformed by the interplay necessitated by hybridity and allow for both an increased and decreased flexibility in how we play, when we play, and what we play. This is even more the case *because* so much of casual play occurs on mobile devices. Adriana de Souza e Silva (2006) writes that our mobile devices are more akin to microcomputers than phones, and "because mobile devices create a more dynamic relationship with the Internet embedding it in outdoor, everyday activities, we can no longer address the disconnection between physical and digital spaces" (p. 262). To this end, she clarifies that mobile devices are an emergent hybrid space, "merging the physical and digital" (2006, p. 265).

In thinking of hybridity, here, I am also lightly playing off Donna Haraway's (1991) famous invocation of hybridity as a vehicle for better conceptualizing the ambiguous nature of 20th-century humanity through the metaphor of the cyborg. She characterizes the cyborg through three "crucial boundary breakdowns" that have caused us to rethink the role of technology in our lives: human/animal, organism/machine, and physical/non-physical (Haraway, 1991, pp. 151–153). Building off of Haraway and de Souza e Silva, I reflect on three modes of hybridity that demonstrate the shift of our bodily experiences with mobile casual gaming: work/play, spatial expansion/constriction, and freedom/captivity.

Hybridity: work/play

The first category of hybrid modes of the mobile casual game is work/play. Of course, this intermingling of work/play is not new to discussions within video game studies. For example, in *Play Between Worlds*, T. L. Taylor (2006) argues that there is a notable intersection between work and play in terms of how power gamers in Massively Multiplayer Online Games (MMOGs) think about their labor. "Power gamers," according to Taylor (2006), are "gamers who play in ways that seem to outside observers as 'work'" (p. 10)—in other words, game-practices are often labor intensive, slow, and arduous and may not appear "fun" even while they occur in a game. While Taylor's definition functions as a way to think about gamers who invest long periods of time "grinding"[5] in game worlds, her observations of the fuzziness between work and play are useful for considering the labor-centric activities deployed by leisure activities. Similarly, Julian Kucklich (2005) deploys the term "playbour" to describe the nuanced activities of game modders[6] and their often complicated relationship between work and play. In other words, video game play practices sometimes look more like work than like play, particularly as players engage in intense and rigorous play schedules. Similarly, in *Life on the Screen,* Sherry Turkle (1997) describes the practices of MUD (multi-user domains/dungeons), who play on several screens simultaneously to co-work, communicate, and compose their fictional identities. This play, too, can be seen through a kind of hybridity of work/play wherein doing several things at once, whilst engaged in play, forces a kind of interstitial play similar to how one engages with casual games, today.

The player experiences described by Taylor (2006), Turkle (1997), and Kucklich (2005) are certainly evident within the work/play hybrid experienced within casual games. Yet, there is also a differentiation, specifically because the play we do on mobile devices so neatly slips into our everyday lives. Because we carry around our gaming systems, always, the transition between work and play becomes seamless and entangled in a never-ending number of ways, forcing us to work and then play in constant succession. With casual mobile devices, we have the freedom to play more—we are no longer bound to our homes, computers, or consoles to enjoy play. At the same time, that play becomes infinitely complicated; just as our play is more available, so is our work (and on the very same devices!). While MMOGs and console games may have had a grinding effect that makes play feel like work, the immediacy and proximity of work on our mobile devices do this to an even greater extent.

Certain games specifically play into this form of bodily hybridity, invoked by casual. Time Management Games and Invest/Express Games are both formats that force the player to reconcile with the work-like appeal of casual games. Whether the player is waiting on tables as Flo in *Diner Dash* (a Time Management Game) or farming in *FarmVille* (an Invest/Express game) the player finds themselves in game-work activities and, subsequently, likely pulled out for real work activities via other mobile apps. Location-based games, such as *Pokémon Go* and *Harry Potter: Wizards Unite*, facilitate that labor even further, encouraging players to walk, travel great distances, and join up with others to achieve in-game goals. Adriana de Souza e Silva and Daniel M. Sutko (2008) persuasively observe the hybrid potential of how these spaces intersect play with ordinarily life, making them inseparable. A hybridity of work and play is part of what has become inseparable here. And perhaps the designers of these games are on to something—by hybridizing play and work in literal ways, both might feel more manageable to people outside of the "hardcore" realm. In casual mobile gaming, play doesn't always need to look entirely like play.

Hybridity: spatial expansion/constriction

Given that we can play our mobile games anytime, anyhow, and anywhere our portable devices might bring us, mobile casuals additionally play with the contradictory hybrid of spatial expansion/constriction. The mobile devices we play on seem to give us freedom of space. At the same time, they also force our playing bodies to become smaller and more compact. In this, our spaces have reduced in size—compared to the expanse of consoles. No longer can we sprawl our play across a living room with half-a-dozen peripherals. In turn, rather than mobile play making us feel larger than life, it often makes us feel miniscule.

When we play in the casual/mobile market, we have more literal space, yet that space is more interiorly constricted. With our mobile devices, we can expand our play spaces out into the world. Yet, that world ends up being more inwardly focused, less expansive, and more contemplative—we are constricting ourselves inwardly. This effects how we physically think about mobile and casual play. Our tiny selves are untethered to a specific locale, as they would be with a console system. Location-based games, of course, make this more complex. We are tethered to finding hot-spots and algorithmically generated imaginary critters, but we may move freely throughout the world in order to find these locales. Often, however, that play becomes inward-facing play, meaning that our playful prisons travel with us, binding us to our screens.

The contradictory nature of this hybrid between spatial expansion and constriction means that newer audiences are likely to think about play in increasingly different ways. The smallness embedded in mobile devices still resonates with the physical demeanor of something hidden and private, rather than something powerfully extroverted. This point, of course, can be taken both ways: If we are playing a game in public, more people see us in the act of playing. Mobile phones can be seen as both embedded in public and private spaces; they move seamlessly through both. Yet, the specifics of what is on a player's screen are only available if that player chooses to share it with others, allowing people into their own intimate spaces. Playing a casual game like *Stardew Valley* (a farm game with a deeper and more robust narrative than *FarmVille*) on a console system such as Xbox or Playstation is a vastly different experience than playing it on a mobile phone. The latter feels private and hidden, whereas the former feels public, assuming, of course, that there are others in your immediate space. A game like *Stardew Valley*, available on many kinds of devices and gaming systems, helps to break down the false dichotomies of these hybrids. The sense of expansion and constriction we feel is not device dependent, but dependent on who we play around, who we invite in to observe our play, and how we choose to understand that play in our own lives. And, of course, *Stardew Valley* is also available on the Nintendo Switch—a device allowing both mobile and stationary plays. A platform like Nintendo Switch complicates the interplay of expansion/constriction allowing players to literally "switch" between modes of this hybrid depending on their mood. The Switch is the start of an industrial acknowledgment of the power of hybridity within the confines of the gaming market and a recognition that different players seek out different experiences from their play.

Hybridity: freedom/captivity

The first and second hybrids (work/play and spatial expansion/constriction) embody contradictions that lead to a third form of hybridity—a mashup of freedom and captivity. This hybrid goes beyond the spatial expansion/contraction I referenced to in the previous section. Freedom/captivity as a hybrid of casual gaming functions on a metaphorical level. The player of mobile casuals appears to have the freedom to play an increasing number of games, with smartphones and tablets changing the nature of the industry. But that freedom is still riddled with the captivity of how these games are treated within the context of that very industry. Furthermore, players are captive to the limitations of what is available on mobile devices, again, determined by industry assumptions about what casual players are willing to pay in order to play.

This smallness and constriction of the previous hybrid, of course, reflects back toward the negative rhetoric surrounding casual games. The players of a game, per critics in the gaming industry and culture,[7] are "filthy casuals" and thus need to hide the play, thereby constricting themselves. This constriction makes them captivated by a limited market. Per this rhetoric, casual play is not a *real* gamer identity and does not receive the media attention, nor praise that a player of a hardcore game might receive. The inferred smallness of the casual player, hiding their games in supermarket shopping lines and on the subway, sits in contrast to the wide berth of a console player sprawling across her living room. Thus, the constriction of the game is echoed in the market expression of that player.

Freedom is, of course, at the core of many casual games which are often "free-to-play" (read: an initial cost but the one that typically involves subsequent micro purchases). Many in the industry have pushed back against this mode of "freedom," suggesting that free-to-play games are unethical payment structures—they are often compared to gambling industries praying on a small number of "whales" to support products (Consalvo & Paul, 2019). In turn, many casual games may be "free to play," but play always comes at a cost. Specifically, free games are rarely free and often require additional in-app purchases in order to play *well*. This contradiction of free-to-play games is, of course, a healthy debate for the industry to have. This purchasing structure often can trick players into spending more money than they might have planned. Consequently, however, the free-to-play structure is the one that can be an easy and accessible entry point for those who are not necessarily regularly engaged in video game play. This cost is embedded in the epithet of "filthy casual." The casual gamer often remains trapped within their reputation within the video game industry—a reputation that casual mobile gamers are just dilettantes and that they support investment in a supposedly less demanding style of gaming that depletes the revenue put toward hardcore games. Until the video game industry breaks apart this final mode of hybridity and disentangles freedom/captivity from the reputation of a false binary that is presupposed in the casual/hardcore labels, novice players will continue to be treated as illegitimate players.

Conclusion: the hybridity of casual will save us all

Embracing hybridity helps us reconcile the contradictions that are embedded in mobile casual games. Hybridity has the capacity to bring both alike and dis-alike things together, consequently transforming them into new structures—ones we may not have previously seen. The mythological chimera may be monstrous but is also magical. We need this hybridity. We need it because, in reality, we need play that is flexible, that has a complex set of parameters, that make us feel like we are both safe and unsafe; productive and unproductive. Play is already full of hybridity and contradictions, and by embracing those contradictions inherent in the mobile casual market, we can reform and reimagine the contents of the video game industry. If we are going to expand both the industries, mainstreaming it to broader audiences, it is the hybrids of contradictions that will create that pathway.

To this point, hybridity, as I have already alluded to, has created a new set of games that increasingly take the ease and accessibility of mobile casuals and hybridize them with the epic storytelling styles already known to indie and hardcore video games. This, in part, is what the indie games market has brought to casual games; it has allowed them to have a reputation that exceeds "time wasting" and become a fulcrum for how we can move forward in thinking about what the video game market can look like. The Nintendo Switch is the first gaming system to truly acknowledge the power that hybrid gaming can have on the gamer. It is these games and systems that we should look closely at, because they are the games that have the most transformative power to convert non-gamers into game players and broaden what a video game looks like.

Thus, by pushing back against industry rhetoric that privileges the staunch structure of console gaming over the hybrid aesthetic of the casual, we can witness a shift wherein more bodies can transform into gaming bodies. The hybrid gamer is the gamer of the future, not stuck with these ridiculous labels of casual, hardcore, or indie. Hybrid games and gamers are on track to transform what we play, how we play, and when we play. These gamers get to revel in the contradictions, and be engaged in work and play, expanding and contracting, whilst free and captive, all at once.

Notes

1 AAA console games are easier to analyze in the sense that their longer, more robust narratives allow for more space for literary analysis. The breadth of many in-depth console games creates more opportunities and topics for interpretation and discussion.
2 A possible exception here is the label "indie games" which I will discuss in more detail later in this chapter.
3 This process is intense enough that many players have casually reported to me that they have set alarms on their phone to remember when to play to complete a task on time.
4 Certainly, hardcore games have experienced their share of being derided by media and popular press. We hear much of their violence, and non-gaming presses

often write of more salacious claims such as the allegedly addictive nature of games and their anti-social aspects. These debates in popular press typically address both hardcore and casual games. At the same time, what is unique about critiques of casual games is that they often come from inside the industry.
5 "Grinding" refers to the laborious process of slowly leveling up through time consuming play.
6 Game modders are those who change the content of a game, creating custom objects, levels, or characters.
7 Because of the nature of the internet, it is often difficult to know the specific identities of those using the "filthy casuals" meme. Presumably, it is a combination of those in video game culture (hardcore game players) and those who work in the industry. Obviously, at times, these things overlap.

References

Amanda, B. (2008). *Filthy Casual*. Retrieved February 24, 2019, from Know Your Meme website: https://knowyourmeme.com/memes/filthy-casual

Casual Games Association. (2007). *Casual Games Market Report 2007*. Retrieved from http://issuu.com/casualconnect/docs/casualgamesmarketreport-2007/6?e=2336319/1145366

Chalk, A. (2014, April 25). *ESA Survey Finds Nearly Half of All US Gamers are Female*. Retrieved from The Escapist website: http://www.escapistmagazine.com/news/view/134028-ESA-Survey-Finds-Nearly-Half-of-All-U-S-Gamers-Are-Female

Chess, S. (2017). *Ready Player Two: Women Gamers and Designed Identity*. Minneapolis: University of Minnesota Press.

Chess, S., & Paul, C. A. (2019). The End of Casual; Long Live Casual. *Games and Culture*, 14(2), 107–118.

Consalvo, M., & Paul, C. A. (2019). *Real Games: What's Legitimate and What's Note in Contemporary Video Games*. Cambridge, MA: MIT Press.

de Souza e Silva, A. (2006). From Cyber to Hybrid: Mobile Technologies as Interfaces of Hybrid Spaces. *Space and Culture*, 3, 261–278.

de Souza e Silva, A., & Frith, J. (2010). Locative Mobile Social Networks: Mapping Communication and Location in Urban Spaces. *Mobilities*, 5(4), 485–505.

de Souza e Silva, A. & Sutko, D. M. (2008). Playing Life and Living Play: How Hybrid Reality Games Reframe Space, Play, and the Ordinary. *Critical Studies in Media Communication*, 25(5), 447–465.

Haraway, D. (1991). *Simians, Cyborgs, and Women*. New York, NY: Routledge.

Ito, M., Matsuda, M., & Okabe, D. (2006). Introduction: Personal, Portable, Pedestrian. In M. Ito, M. Matsuda, & D. Okabe (Eds.), *Personal, Portable, and Pedestrian: Mobile Phones in Japanese Life*. Cambridge, MA: MIT Press.

Juul, J. (2010). *A Casual Revolution: Reinventing Video Games and their Players*. Cambridge, MA: MIT Press.

Kato, M. (2007, April). Space invaders. *Game Informer Magazine*, 40.

Kucklich, J. (2005). Precarious Playbour: Modders and the Digital Games Industry. *The Fibreculture Journal*, 5. Retrieved from http://five.fibreculturejournal.org/fcj-025-precarious-playbour-modders-and-the-digital-games-industry/

Lipkin, N. (2013). Examining Indie Independence: The Meaning of "indie" Games, the Politics of Production, and Mainstream Co-optation. *Loading... The Journal of the Canadaian Game Studies Association*, 7(11), 8–24.

Mangalindan, J.P. (2010, March 18). Is Casual Gaming Destroying the Traditional Gaming Market? *Fortune Magazine*. Retrieved December 16, 2019, from https://fortune.com/2010/03/18/is-casual-gaming-destroying-the-traditional-gaming-market/

McLuhan, M. (1994). *Understanding Media: The Extensions of Man* (Reprint). Cambridge, MA: MIT Press.

Taylor, T. L. (2006). *Play between Worlds*. Cambridge, MA; London: MIT Press.

Turkle, S. (1997). *Life on the Screen: Identity in the Age of the Internet*. New York, NY: Simon & Schuster.

Vanderhoef, J. (2013, June 1). *Casual Threats: The Feminization of Casual Video Games*. Retrieved July 7, 2013, from Ada: A Journal of Gender, New Media, and Technology website: http://adanewmedia.org/2013/06/issue2-vanderhoef/

Yee, N. (2017, January 19). *Beyond 50/50: Breaking Down the Percentage of Female Gamers by Genre*. Retrieved February 25, 2019, from Quantic Foundry website: https://quanticfoundry.com/2017/01/19/female-gamers-by-genre/

7   Hybrid play in edutainment

A media archaeology approach to *Math Blaster!*

Claire Carrington

Math Blaster!, developed by Davidson & Associates, was an early video game for the Apple II computer. It launched in 1983 as a form of entertaining education, or 'edutainment' (Rapeepisarn et al., 2006), with the intention of engaging elementary school students in the learning process. *Math Blaster!* was among the first of a large volume of video games[1] developed for the simultaneous purpose of captivating children's attentions and teaching a core subject matter, such as math or language arts. *Math Blaster!*, therefore, served as an important touchstone for developing this new genre of educational games. While these games offered a new technology-driven approach for teaching traditional subjects, they also provided students with a digital space to develop and refine their computer literacy skills by interacting with computer menus and programming. In the process, edutainment games allowed these student-users to be reconfigured by the computer as they learned to navigate digital spaces for the first time.

Math Blaster!, however, was not simply a practical way to teach both a core subject and computer literacy. Rather, it was intrinsically connected to powerful forms of control, as gameplay was leveraged to drive students toward achieving particular institutional outcomes. In particular, *Math Blaster!* served as a valuable instrument for instilling the values of a STEM education in United States elementary school classrooms in the context of the Reagan-era Cold War, in which concerns arose that the U.S. was falling behind in education compared to other countries. It additionally had significant power in shaping the everyday lives of the teachers who were required to implement these new technologies toward achieving improved student learning outcomes. In what follows, I detail the story of *Math Blaster!'s* integration in United States' classrooms, revealing critical threads of meaning around American cultural ideals. I examine the educational and political contexts surrounding the release of *Math Blaster!* to understand how this game became embedded within elementary classroom culture. In order to contextualize *Math Blaster!*, and its role in the 1980s classroom, I address the trajectory of computers in schools and edutainment gaming, along with emerging social imperatives that pushed American public education toward quantified standardized testing and quantified outcomes for a STEM education. I also explain how educational institutions co-opted gaming as part of an apparatus to quantify educational outcomes.

As these institutions co-opted and hybridized "entertainment" and "education" into edutainment, games like *Math Blaster!* established multiple hybridities through the merging of distinct contexts (de Souza e Silva & Sutko, 2008). First, *Math Blaster!* created a hybrid space by merging the physical space of the classroom and the digital interface of the game, in which play served the purposes of education. Further, it created another hybrid by merging education with a larger geopolitical context, in which play served the interests of the United States. Given this, we can understand *Math Blaster!* as engaging students in forms of play that, far from allowing spontaneity, whimsy, or frivolous activity, entangled them with larger power structures. As such, this begs the question, what does it mean to engage in forms of hybrid play when it's not willful but, instead, obligatory? And how can we reveal elements of power and control involved in playful uses of technologies?

To begin to answer these questions, I apply apparatus theory (Packer, 2013) to analyze *Math Blaster!* as a media instrument. Apparatus theory offers an approach to understanding how technologies contribute toward larger structures of power and, thus, can be applied to *Math Blaster!* to elucidate how the game served as part of an institutional suite of tools that reinforced governmental prescriptions for both students and teachers alike. In concert with apparatus theory, I utilize the media genealogical method (Huhtamo & Parikka, 2011) to describe *Math Blaster!* as a media instrument which subjectivized teachers and students while simultaneously encouraging a specific set of behaviors and practices around newly introduced classroom computers. As a subset of media archaeology, a media genealogical approach offers a deeper dive into complex, interconnected issues by following a specific thread of inquiry. In order to accomplish this, I combed through dozens of texts, explored the original media (*Math Blaster!* and its subsequent iterations), gathered historical information, and brought together a kaleidoscope of elements that, when viewed from a wider contextual lens, revealed crucial connections between the development of *Math Blaster!* and important sociocultural developments around it.

Examining media instruments and apparatus

According to Packer (2013), "Mediation is the process by which we come to know the world" (p. 12); therefore, it is critical to understand how certain elements of media came to exist in modern forms in order to provide a thorough understanding of how power works within a currently highly mediated world. Packer discusses the importance of investigating the instruments that mediate interactions, describing a media instrument as anything that functions to process the world into data as part of a relationship between technology and subjectification (p. 14). A media instrument in this case is something that transforms human experience into the quantifiable, measurable, or knowable. This description does not exclude the digital and, in a richly mediated society where software serves to transform human experience at all levels, it is crucial to place software like *Math Blaster!* under scrutiny as a media instrument. Although an instrument is typically considered to be an object designed with a concrete purpose in mind, media instruments can also be co-opted to function in ways that create and reinforce the boundaries of a media apparatus.

Apparatuses are institutions and activities meant to alter and/or capture human thought and behavior. A media apparatus is a network where many disparate elements converge, united by the function of supporting knowledge claims and the forces behind them. Instruments work together to bring an apparatus into existence. In addition, apparatuses are "strategically organized to address a perceived problem or urgency" (Packer, 2013, p. 12). An apparatus purports to provide the "solution" to a perceived social issue, and instruments such as *Math Blaster!* are an important thread of an apparatus, as they serve to produce and reinforce certain ways of thinking about the ostensible problem that an apparatus is meant to fix. In this case, *Math Blaster!* as a media instrument served to reinforce and uphold the belief that teaching students about mathematics was part of the solution to a social problem in 1983, namely that the U.S. was falling behind in education. Institutions saw the apparatus of quantifying education to measure learning outcomes as an answer to address this issue, placing teachers in a hybrid role as teacher-coders.

As a method, media archaeology most broadly provides a conceptualization of where and how disparate past technological threads converged to establish the present, in an often complex and nonlinear way (Monea & Packer, 2016). Media genealogy, as a subset of this method, performs this function while attending to Foucauldian (Foucault, 1996, 1972) elements of power. This method allows for a uniquely power-based construction of media history, while simultaneously drawing on unexpected and often nonlinear elements to illustrate how institutions functioned to steer the direction of media technologies. It allows for a more thorough and exhaustive understanding of how technologies came to exist in their modern forms, while troubling the notion that these media spontaneously occurred in a vacuum. As a media apparatus, *Math Blaster!* was developed as part of a trend of new computer technologies which attempted to address perceived sociocultural problems. To institutional powers, these problems indicated that the nation was at risk of falling behind its global competitors.

A nation at risk

The 1983 National Commission on Excellence in Education report, "Nation at Risk," was published during the same year that *Math Blaster!* was released. The report signaled a crucial turning point in education reform, and its subsequent impact led to the establishment of a media apparatus that sought to quantify education in order to prove that student scores and educational outcomes were improving measurably. Specifically, the report introduced the fear that America's science and tech innovation could not keep pace with other global competitors, and that the United States was slipping far behind in test scores (Cuban, 2001). Among the more hyperbolic claims, the report stated that the educational foundations were being "eroded by a rising tide of mediocrity that threaten[ed the US'] very future as a Nation and a people" (Cuban, 2001, p. 4). Such a claim represented a direct push for better educational outcomes in the classroom that would cater to proficiencies in subjects like mathematics with new forms of quantification. The "Nation at Risk" report led to calls for higher rigor in the classroom and for more quantitatively measurable standardized tests, directly resulting in administrators considering the addition of more science and math classes in the curriculum (Cuban, 2001, p. 7). Amid these calls for STEM education reform, *Math Blaster!* came to the fore as a privately outsourced solution.

The use of private outsourcing to solve educational problems, however, was not out of the ordinary. In 1983, other technology developers like Apple became involved in the educational outcomes of school reform, bringing a more capitalistic bottom-line-driven approach to school systems under the guise of keeping up with worldwide competitors (Apple2history.org, n.d.; Coburn & Tobey, 2014). The assumption, driving the United States' investment in technology and technology-driven edutainment games, was that this access would mean more classroom engagement, which would lead to better learning, and in the future, better outcomes for the United States' workforce (Cuban, 2001). Ultimately, this desire for better outcomes paved the way for the development of a series of educational games, that would supposedly improve educational outcomes through play. Math Blaster was among the first developed.

The race to space with the Blasternaut: contextualizing STEM education

There was an enormous societal stake for educators in 1983: The nation was at risk, allegedly failing in its efforts to keep up with other countries (e.g. the Soviet Union), and in a race to develop new technologies in order to be the first to achieve space-related goals. Educational institutions needed a way to prove that they were working toward helping students learn and grow in ways that would contribute to propelling the United States forward, especially as it seemed that the country was slipping behind not only in its classrooms, but in other crucial areas of technology. This context contributed to the establishment of *Math Blaster!* as a new apparatus that would quantify educational outcomes, in addition to reinforcing beliefs around the value of STEM education and its role in helping the U.S. move ahead in the space race.

Given that the space race was, above all, a race to demonstrate power and technological advancement amid Cold War tensions, it is not surprising that *Math Blaster!* featured the story of Blasternaut, a space-faring adventurer who taught children new math scores. Implicit within the inclusion of Blasternaut was the symbolic representation of the United States' goals through one of its means of achieving them, i.e. edutainment games. At the time of *Math Blaster!'s* release, the space race had reached a height in tensions between the United States and the Soviet Union. In March of 1983, the Reagan administration established the Strategic Defense Initiative, also known as "Star Wars" after the popular film franchise (The Cold War Museum, n.d.). This ambitious program aimed to produce missile systems to prevent attacks from the Soviet Union, and it aspired to create science fiction-like weapons like lasers and particle beams. Crucially, it may have provided a swell of inspiration for education reform in the name of preparing children for future careers focused on the new frontier of space. In an educational reform environment abuzz about the "Nation at Risk" report, efforts to improve students' quantifiable learning outcomes directly correlated with future jobs in technology industries that would ostensibly help the United States compete with its global rivals.

Developing *Math Blaster!*

Due to strong pushes from educational administrators for an improvement in quantified learning outcomes, especially in subjects like mathematics, edutainment game developers attempted to address the call for more engaging educational tools to captivate students and improve test scores. The Strong Museum of Play's online archive describes the original release of *Math Blaster!* as a part of *JumpStart*, a media series aimed at education for younger audiences in order to achieve better math scores and more engagement from these students. The archive states that the series began as a computer game simply entitled *Math Blaster!* which initially was centered solely around teaching mathematics skills. The game franchise grew over the next three decades through several iterations to encompass several subjects, such as language arts and history. However, the choice to focus on and develop mathematical proficiency first was indicative of prescriptions by governmental institutions around what should be most valued in education.

Just as edutainment began to emerge and shape the direction of play in the classroom in 1983, reviewers praised *Math Blaster!* for its seemingly endless options to improve math learning. These praises were based on reviews by adults, not the children playing the game, and predicated on the assumption that *Math Blaster!* would be a more effective tool for drilling math lessons than previous techniques. For instance, in the July 11, 1983 issue of *InfoWorld*, Doug Green and Denise Green (1983) reflected on the value of *Math Blaster!*, stating, "drill-and-practice isn't what it used to be. It's better!" (p. 55). This review and others like it helped push the notion that this game was accessible, easy to use, and inexpensive. To these reviewers, the game was a magic bullet of sorts, able to be molded and customized to suit any classroom situation in a fun and exciting way. With such high expectations for math education during a powerfully competitive time during the Cold War, *Math Blaster!* successfully entered classrooms *en masse,* both as a space-themed and ostensibly engaging video game that spoke to larger interests with space, as well as a new medium that offered to fill the need of quantifying education by saving and storing sets of math problems for students to solve.

However, to an overworked and underpaid teacher in 1983, such a complex and choice-driven game created specifically to engage one's students may have seemed like a gift (Associated Press, 1983). Teachers were increasingly blamed for falling test scores and depicted as underqualified (PBS Online, n.d.); to teachers facing such a quandary, using *Math Blaster!* ostensibly offered the possibility of improving test scores and achieving new goals while simultaneously freeing up teacher time to focus on lesson planning. This was unfortunately not the case.

Math puzzles and the puzzled teacher's work

Dusting chalk off the chartreuse board lining the front wall of the fourth-grade classroom, an elementary teacher in 1983 might have looked into the bored eyes of a classroom full of schoolchildren as he or she wrote out a new problem set with a worn-down chalk stick. To a teacher facing a room full of disinterested students, the newly introduced computer labs in schools boasting *Math Blaster!* must have seemed like a technological haven, filled with opportunities for attention-grabbing problem sets that would engage and amaze the children. There was also a computer in the corner of the teacher's classroom; one might have puzzled over how to use it during lessons, since there was only one. Would there be turn-taking? Would students argue over who got to play next?

However, as the teacher spent the evening reading the complex manual of problem sets and arrived at school early the next day to program lesson plan problem sets into *Math Blaster!*, he or she may have realized that this new technology brought with it an entirely new set of coding skills that would require mastery and the exhaustion that would come along with it. The InfoWorld article that the teacher read had said "neither teachers nor students need special computer skills to use this product," citing clear instructions and describing the main menu that appears upon start-up (Green & Green, 1983, p. 55). However, as he or she stared at the complicated manual of instructions, it would seem much like learning an entirely new language.

Although this game is an iconic, historically original member of the edutainment gaming category, *Math Blaster!* is an infamous example of the incorrect assumptions that more math will equal better math learning outcomes for students, along with less work for teachers. As in Young et al.'s (2012) study, there is still no solid evidence to support this idea. Becker (2017) describes *Math Blaster!*'s long history and use in the classroom, including its beginnings as a drill-and-practice game that was later bundled with a narrative in the 1987 version. She states, "*Math Blaster!* is one of the games that is commonly named by teachers and parents as an example of a good educational game, though rarely by the children who are to learn from it" (p. 193). It is repetitive, at times monotonous, and its actual in-game content is only peripherally connected with math, even in its space-based versions. According to Becker, *Math Blaster!* is even "used by professional game designers as a favorite example of a bad educational game" (p. 193). *Math Blaster!* has long served as an exemplar of perhaps the first widely available edutainment game, intended to captivate the attention of children in the classroom. However, its value as an educational tool remains questionable amid the distractions of seals bouncing balls, balloons floating up and down, and trash zooming across the screen in later versions. Indeed, the math problems almost seem like a distraction from the other attention-grabbing gameplay actions.

Although *Math Blaster!* did offer a new suite of tools for customizing and quantifying math-based play, it established a heavy burden of work for the teachers required to manage it. For instance, teachers needed to learn new rudimentary coding skills in order to customize the game to their classroom. Further, they needed to adapt to the strict criteria for entering lists of problems in the original 1983 Math Blaster Editor. This burdensome list of rules required the inclusion of at least five but no more than 25 questions, of no greater length than 18 characters, with answers at a maximum of six characters. The game only permitted two lines of problem instructions, with a max of 28 characters, which severely limited space for teachers to describe what students were supposed to do (Green & Green, 1983). No words were permitted in the problems themselves, only in the already-brief instructions, and the only symbols allowed for use were "+, -, # for division, * for multiplication, $ and %" (Green & Green, 1983). Although teachers could delete and insert lines, old numbers often remained on-screen. Reflecting on this frustration, Green and Green (1983) stated, "You can insert and delete characters. You can go to any line to edit, but you must retype the line to make any major changes" (p. 57). Thus, users could customize and create their own files but had to carefully work within the parameters of the game. If there were not at least five questions with different answers, the game simply crashed. As a result of these complicated instructions, teachers who used *Math Blaster!* in their classrooms would have inhabited a new hybrid role as teacher-coders, learning the complex language needed to properly use this new edutainment software for their classes. Although it may have been an unwilling role, this new hybrid role for teachers was primarily motivated by increasing pressures from educational higher-ups for students to attain higher test scores. Obligatory use of these new technologies meant that teachers were caught between drill-and-skill math exercises and new forms of digital media, and between their role as teachers and computer coders. This highlights that hybrid roles are not always something that someone willingly adopts. In some cases, hybridity (and even hybrid play) is thrust upon people by institutional powers as an obligation when new technologies are developed.

For a teacher who puzzled over how to use the new computer in the corner of his or her classroom, with its high-tech disk slots and blocky screen (see Figure 7.1), a game like this must have been—at best—a mixed bag of experiences. While there must have been teachers who took to *Math Blaster!* quickly and with great proficiency, becoming its early proponents and adaptors, there were undoubtedly also plenty of others who must have been perplexed and overwhelmed. The ostensible offerings of customizability, choice, and control via games like *Math Blaster!* became imperatives for teachers to spend more time learning how to be ambassadors for a new piece of technology that they were unfamiliar with, in a setting where it did not yet fit, with time they did not have. Yet, teachers who were resistant to this technology were deemed luddites, and those who presented new technologies with anything less than enthusiasm were chastised by administrators and policymakers in educational contexts (Bryson & de Castell, 1998).

While simultaneously creating more work for teachers who needed to learn how to work within this strict problem-set coding regime, *Math Blaster!* depended on instructors to spend even more of their already-limited

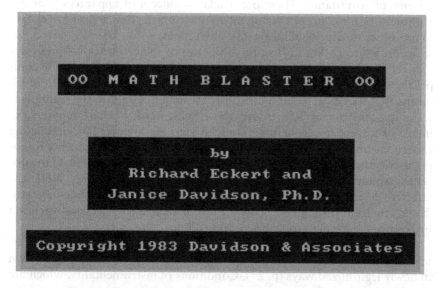

Figure 7.1 Home screen for the original *Math Blaster!* game. Copyright: Jumpstart Games, Inc.

time presenting the game to their classes. With limited characters for in-game instructions, teachers had to serve as the laborers to introduce and explain this new media instrument to their classrooms, with which they themselves had little or no familiarity. *Math Blaster!* failed at serving as an easy-to-use, effective STEM education tool. However, it did serve an important role as an introductory foray into computer use in the classroom. It introduced students to the newly available Apple II computers and began to familiarize both students and teachers with this powerful new technology.

Math Blaster! as a media instrument

Math Blaster! served a hybrid role as a media instrument. It was supposedly easy to use; yet, it had a complex set of instructions requiring a significant time investment for the teachers expected to use it. However, it contributed to an important emerging media apparatus: quantified STEM education. The media apparatus perspective, provided by Packer (2013), assists in establishing an understanding of how media instruments like *Math Blaster!* introduce and reproduce techniques of governance. In understanding the push for STEM education in the 1980s as an apparatus, media scholars can better theorize how edutainment games function within this apparatus to produce particular relationships between teachers, technologies, schools, and students. According to Packer, the concept of apparatus is a powerful way to conceptualize the relationships between media tools or instruments (like *Math Blaster!*) and the powerful institutions that rely on them to reify systems of governance. Therefore, Packer's concept of apparatus provides a framework for conceptualizing media instruments that served as vehicles to introduce institutional ideals into other areas.

According to Packer (2013), the processes of subjectification—processes that tell individuals how to organize themselves and others and/or compel them to do so—are "co-constitutive of the apparatus" (p. 27), which means that they help to simultaneously create and establish the technological apparatus' social hold. Along these lines, *Math Blaster!* conjures the image of a teacher shepherding students into a computer lab, organizing classroom time and space around the game, and ordering students to apply user settings (arguably a tool for freedom and customizability) to turn off the volume and quietly play the drill-and-skill math game. While the affective environment of quiet clicking helped to prescribe and manage students' attention through the game, it also managed the teacher's attention by requiring entering problem sets and coding.

Packer (2013) also discusses the "conditions of instrumentality and attendant epistemological stakes," which are how reality comes to be known in newly legitimized ways (p. 27). Conditions of instrumentality, which are the ways in which the apparatus becomes an instrument to serve a specific purpose, represent the direct material results of what the apparatus does.

The stakes relating to these results may include establishing new forms of institutional power and control. In the case of *Math Blaster!*, these conditions serve to translate the functional performance of students into data, and performance within the education system becomes known in a quantified digital form rather than existing within the physical realm. Ordinary paper mathematical data becomes digitized as quantified sets of on-screen math problems for students, changing the way that teachers used drill-and-practice work. As a result, these problem sets become new tools for the prescription of play and for controlling student activities, impacting the entire experience of the game: changing difficulty or sound, recalling previous problem sets, or shutting off the game entirely (see Figure 7.2). In addition to providing options for teachers and students, the functions of choosing and editing math problems within *Math Blaster!* organized and prescribed play in a rigid fashion akin to the drill-and-skill techniques that the game was attempting to teach. The settings for *Math Blaster!* allowed for custom math sets to be stored, as well as for students' scores to be directly quantified. *Math Blaster!* thus transformed math performance into a digitally encoded score, managed by the teacher and stored on data disks, but this game data was not yet harnessed to directly measure student scores on an institutional level; it merely provided teachers with a way to see how students in a particular class performed.

Media instruments serve to bring the elements of an apparatus together, or to converge very disparate objects for a specific purpose dictated by powerful institutions. This is fundamentally what complex programmable settings do and did within *Math Blaster!*, and what the game itself did for an increasingly quantified form of public education. They allowed the game to be used in and adapted for the institutional context of the American public elementary school; as a result, they allowed the government, technology industries, and other institutions to compel teachers and students to do work *for* these institutions. They also compelled a familiarity with new computer technology, both for teachers and students. The media instrument

Figure 7.2 (left) Initial user options for the original Math Blaster! game and (right) the original *Math Blaster!* game's options for gameplay, including the data disk, where teachers could manually enter problem sets. Copyright: Jumpstart Games, Inc.

Math Blaster! was one of many tools that pushed a generation toward the apparatus of quantifying education and valuing STEM careers above others. In the context of the space race and Cold War, STEM education would come to represent a solution to the pressure to push America ahead in budding technology industries. *Math Blaster!* reinforced these ideals, representing an opportunity to use new forms of media to bring students and teachers into the fold of computer technologies while simultaneously providing a "fun" way to data-fy math learning outcomes.

More importantly, media instruments tell subjects how to use media within existing apparatuses in order to create and reinforce those same apparatuses. While *Math Blaster!* and its array of options spoke to the institutional demands for new mathematical learning rigor, they also spoke to a greater demand for computer technologies to be used. The question of what games like *Math Blaster!* do *not* permit, despite all of these supposedly new and wonderful forms of control they *do* provide, leads to the answer that they do not permit an escape from the apparatus in which they function; on the contrary, they serve to reinforce subjects' obligatory use of their constituted apparatuses. They force various burdens on subjects who must then learn and adapt, with teachers required to learn how to code for *Math Blaster!* serving as an exemplar. Those who would choose not to partake in these instruments are labeled technophobes, who speak strongly to the sources of power in a world immersed in and functioning around these technologies. Teachers were given choices within games like *Math Blaster!*, but they were not given choices around whether to use computers and the new arrays of software that purported to give them technological (and curricular) legitimacy. Teachers' attempts to exercise agency to escape the confines of new computer technologies were regarded with disdain. After all, teachers were given a dazzling array of choices in order to carefully customize *Math Blaster!*, but they were given increasingly less choice in whether or not to use technologies like it. Edutainment games and the new forms of quantification that emerged around them were not optional tools, but culturally required new media instruments.

Hybrid roles in hybrid spaces

For teachers occupying this new hybrid role as teacher-coders, edutainment games like *Math Blaster!* attempted to harness the engaging nature of play to enforce new institutional ideals. Play and gaming, normally leisure activities set apart by ways of thinking and behaving (Huizinga, 1955) are now transformed into classroom work. Historical context plays a critical role in how play is perceived in an educational setting, whether as a frivolous waste of time or an important tool for transmitting cultural knowledge. Play is traditionally set apart from the repetition and drudgery of work; it is uniquely representational of fun and fantasy (Huizinga, 1955). However, in the case of edutainment games, play is shaped through the actions of companies like Apple and Davidson & Associates (the company that created the game), as well as education reformers into a tool to connect fun with the decidedly un-magical elementary classroom. This rise of edutainment neglected the role of choice and consent inherent to play (de Castell & Jenson, 2003), becoming another form of rigid lesson enforcement wherein the teacher became responsible for imparting specific knowledge rather than allowing for critical engagement with subject material.

In their 2012 study, Young et al. describe major trends for edutainment games, and importantly, their study found "little support for the academic value of video games in science and math" (p. 61). Studies like this show that edutainment games' attempts to breach Huizinga's "magic circle" (1955) to make classroom activities more game-like ultimately failed to achieve educators' initially prescribed goals. Young et al.'s meta-analysis finds that video games in classroom settings, specifically games about math, have contradictory results at best. For most edutainment games, there were no specifically measurable correlations between playing these games and improved test scores. In studies of edutainment games, academic value was measured by how students' numbers on other quantitative tests increased, or how their subject-specific (e.g. math) knowledge improved based on tests devised by researchers focused on measuring these valued topics.

However, these studies specifically describe positive learning outcomes as consistent increases in subject-specific test scores. Rather than direct content transfer, edutainment games develop a player's comfort and familiarity with the use of computational technologies as they work and play in hybrid learning/gaming spaces. The tools used to measure the learning outcomes of these games in classrooms suggest that either they are not quantifiable, or that computer-based education tools like *Math Blaster!* are outright failures. There is little evidence to support the idea that a game can directly teach a particular skill or transfer factual knowledge. Instead, using tools like computers in classrooms develops a way of thinking with and navigating technologies at work and at home, which builds toward a society that values proficiency in navigating computers that tread the line between the physical and the digital.

Overall, this game was a touchpoint of complexity in technological development that governed play in a way that other games before it did not, for both sets of hybrids: teachers/coders and gamers/students. These settings had the power to shape the affective learning environment through sound or difficulty and appeared to provide a modicum of choice for children (who *may* indeed have been given a choice in their play difficulty settings) and teachers (who had the ability to use their own problem sets, despite the significant investment of time and effort to program them). In this way, *Math Blaster!*'s options to program math problems represented a hallmark suite of ways to edit the game for the institutions using it (and possibly the players as an afterthought), but it was a paradox of an attempt to establish ease-of-use and complicated choices. *Math Blaster!* as a media instrument harnessed the idea that games could be fun and engaging, along with the desire of its audience (students) to play video games. Although it failed in its attempts to directly transmit math knowledge, *Math Blaster!* was nonetheless part of a complex arrangement of instruments that reinforced the value of quantified knowledge, and of STEM education more broadly. Rather than teaching drill-and-skill math, the game instead began to familiarize students with the skills necessary to navigate new hybrid physical/digital spaces in their daily lives.

Conclusion

Math Blaster! as a media instrument played a significant role in quantifying STEM education and compelling teachers to adopt a new hybrid teacher/coder role. One of the critical problems with edutainment games (and *Math Blaster!* in particular) was creating more work for teachers. Essentially, teachers needed to learn a new set of skills on top of balancing being classroom managers, hubs for social support, researchers, and a number of other roles. Rather than creating new work in the same realm of familiarity for many teachers, however, *Math Blaster!* and its suite of software produced a need for teachers to fill a new hybrid role as teachers and coders. Math teachers had to manage classrooms in new and innovative ways, and after the introduction of games requiring the navigation of a complex set of coding language, they were also subjectivized into newfound roles as edutainment gaming advocates—otherwise, they were branded as "luddites" and threatened with obsolescence. Teachers were responsible for serving as not only classroom managers, but hybrid technology users as they developed coding skills in an effort to utilize these new computer technologies and share them with coworkers.

There is an incredible value in studying such a powerful media instrument as *Math Blaster!* both as a touchpoint for the development of new media apparatuses, and for the digitization of quantified scores in the classroom. According to all measurable accounts, edutainment games fail at imparting subject-specific knowledge and improving quantifiably measurable learning outcomes. However, while STEM-based edutainment games may fail at teaching direct mathematical knowledge, they certainly did (and do) familiarize a new generation with a set of media tools in the form of computer use that would be critical for future participation in a hybrid world fulfilled with data. A continual effort to trace the histories of media instruments like *Math Blaster!* is necessary in order to understand the threads of power that run in and among computer technologies, on which this work has just begun to scratch the surface.

Note

1 Some other early edutainment games include *Donkey Kong Junior Math* (1983), *Math Rabbit* (1986), *JumpStart* Kindergarten (1994), and *Word Blaster* (1996).

References

1982–1985. (n.d.). Apple2history.org. Retrieved from https://apple2history.org/appendix/ahb/ahb3/.

Associated Press. (1983, October 3). As talks lag, Chicago teachers call for a strike. *The New York Times*. Retrieved from http://www.nytimes.com/1983/10/03/us/as-talks-lag-chicago-teachers-call-for-a-strike.html.

Becker, K. (2017). *Choosing and using digital games in the classroom: A practical guide*. Cham: Springer.

Bryson, M., & de Castell, S. (1998). New technologies and the cultural ecology of primary schooling: Imagining teachers as luddites in/deed. *Educational Policy, 12*(5), 542–567.

Coburn, D., & Tobey, K. (2014, May 19). From Apple II to Touchcast, the evolution of computers in the classroom. *The Washington Post*. Retrieved from https://www.washingtonpost.com/news/innovations/wp/2014/05/19/from-apple-ii-to-touchcast-the-evolution-of-computers-in-the-classroom/?utm_term=.cdfbb2cf603c.

Cuban, M. (2001). *Oversold and underused: Computers in the classroom*. Cambridge, MA: Harvard University Press.

De Castell, S., & Jenson, J. (2003). Serious play. *Journal of Curriculum Studies, 35*(6), 649–665.

de Souza e Silva, A., & Sutko, D. (2008). Playing life and living play: How hybrid reality games reframe space, play, and the ordinary. *Critical Studies in Media Communication, 25*(5), 447–465.

Foucault, M. (1972). *The archaeology of knowledge and the discourse on language* (A. M. S. Smith, Trans.). New York, NY: Pantheon Books. (Original work published 1969).

Foucault, M. (1996). The archaeology of knowledge (J. Johnston, Trans.). In S. Lotringer (Ed.), *Foucault live: Collected interviews, 1961–1984* (pp. 57–64). New York, NY: Semiotext(e).

Green, D., & Green, D. (1983, July 11). Math Blaster, for elementary-school-age children. *InfoWorld, 5*(28), 55–58.

Huhtamo, E., & Parikka, J. (2011). *Media archaeology: Approaches, applications, and implications*. Berkeley, CA: University of California Press.

Huizinga, J. (1955). *Homo Ludens: A study of the play-element in culture*. Boston, MA: The Beacon Press.

Monea, A., & Packer, J. (2016). Media genealogy and the politics of archaeology. *International Journal of Communication, 10*, 3141–3159.

Packer, J. (2013). The conditions of media's possibility: A Foucauldian approach to media history. In J. Nerone (ed.), *Media history and the foundations of media studies*. New York: Blackwell, pp. 1–34.

PBS Online: Only a teacher: Teaching timeline. (n.d.). Retrieved from http://www.pbs.org/onlyateacher/timeline.html.

Rapeepisarn, K., Wong, K. W., Fung, C. C., & Depickere, A. *Proceedings of the 3rd Australasian Conference on Interactive Entertainment*, 4–6 December 2006, Perth, W.A. 28–32.

Siddiqi, A. A. (2000). *Challenge to Apollo: The Soviet Union and the space race, 1945–1974* [Digital version]. Retrieved from https://history.nasa.gov/SP-4408pt1.pdf.

Squire, K. (2011). *Video games and learning: Teaching and participatory culture in the digital age.* New York: Teachers College Press.

Steinkuehler, C. (2010). Video games and digital literacies. *Journal of Adolescent & Adult Literacy, 54*(1), 61–63.

The Cold War Museum. (n.d.). *The Strategic Defense Initiative (SDI): Star Wars.* Retrieved from: http://www.coldwar.org/articles/80s/SDI-StarWars.asp.

Young, M., Slota, S., Cutter, A., Jalette, G., Mullin, G., Lai, B., Simeoni, Z., Tran, M., & Yukhymenko, M. (2012). Our princess is in another castle: A review of trends in serious gaming for education. *Review of Educational Research, 82*(1), 61–89. DOI: 10.3102/0034654312436980.

8 Subjectivation in the making

The hybrid logics of productivity and play in the university makerspace

Jessica Elam and Stephen B. Crofts Wiley

The maker movement, or maker culture, has roots in various hobbyist, do-it-yourself (DIY), and counterculture movements and communities that focus on innovation, collaboration, and experimentation with emerging technologies and traditional arts and crafts. Maker culture has been defined in a variety of ways, but at its heart is its commitment to the democratization of innovation. Given the increased accessibility and affordability of emerging technologies, along with a vast and growing online community that provides (typically free) access to resources, support, and skill-sharing (Anderson, 2012; Hatch, 2014), the maker movement has become a significant site for experimentation with communitarian and egalitarian approaches to technological development. Makerspaces are, for the most part, workshop-type community spaces with the tools, technologies, and materials to engage in "making" activities, which widely refer to a broad set of experimental material engagements for the purpose of learning and innovation. For example, makerspace users may create specific products for business or personal purposes, using emerging technologies like 3D printers, high-powered laser cutters, computer-aided design (CAD) programs, and a variety of other tools and technologies. Others visiting makerspaces come to develop skills in areas like electronics prototyping and coding, or to experiment with technologies such as Arduino circuit boards, sensors, and activators or Raspberry Pi open-source computers to generate ideas or solve specific problems.

As community makerspaces multiplied around the world and the maker movement became more visible in the past decade, makerspaces began to emerge in more institutionalized settings like universities, public libraries, and K-12 facilities. In addition, maker practices were being integrated into educational activities and pedagogical theory as new ways of "learning by doing" that might facilitate equity and creativity (Ratto, 2011; Sayers, 2011; Halverson & Sheridan, 2014). However, with its growing popularity, maker culture and makerspaces have been criticized for forfeiting their democratic potential as they are transformed by political and institutional authority (Morozov, 2014). Rather than fostering open-ended, playful experimentation, institutional makerspaces often entail a particular set of rules and standards that limit the potential for creative exploration to practices that are economically or educationally *productive*. Additionally, it has been pointed out that makers are actually *more* dependent on consumerism and corporations through the DIY ethos (Holman, 2014). Others have called attention to both maker culture and makerspaces as perpetuating their gendered social history, devaluing individual identity, and assigning a superiority to "making" over other forms of craft or labor when the former is more strictly defined as engaging with high-technology for the purpose of innovating a product (Bucholz et. al., 2014; Chachra, 2015). For example, crafting and sewing are historically labeled women's work and thus are de-valued in relation to the use of supposedly masculine technologies such as 3D printers, milling machines, or computer circuit boards. Further, the notion of losing individuality stems from the perceived pressure to identify as a member of the community at large and, as such, adhere to community-generated values and norms.

And yet, the makerspaces created within the institutional and pedagogical spaces of university libraries and laboratories are also open—at least partially—to logics of experimentation and technological play. Depending on a number of factors, such as the institutionally and culturally defined aims of the programs that fund these spaces, as well as the explicit and implicit rules and expectations that makerspace staff, faculty, event organizers, and sponsors communicate to participants in the makerspace, the range of practices and experiences that can develop there may be quite wide or quite narrow. At stake in the concrete arrangement and rules of the university makerspace is the degree of openness that will be permitted and encouraged—the extent to which such spaces will extend and develop the potential of the maker movement before it entered the institutional settings of higher education and corporate sponsorship. In other words, makerspaces may be sites of creative play, where experimentation is open-ended and not subjected to particular goals or evaluative criteria. Even more importantly for the current historical conjuncture, makerspaces have the potential to be sites of *hybrid* play—places where humans and nonhumans are mixed together (Johnson, 1988; Latour, 2005) and where new "cognitive assemblages" (Hayles, 2016) develop.[1] Our approach takes "hybridity" further by questioning the human–technology dichotomy that undergirds some approaches. In one sense, we are attempting to theorize what van der Meulen and Bruinsma have called "a hybrid human-data aggregate" (2018, p. 347); yet, even this conceptualization presumes an underlying ontological distinction of the organic (or the human) and the technical. Instead, by defining subjectivation in relation to the molecular, ontogenetic processes of desiring-production that precede any human/technology distinction, we reject the dichotomy and posit a radically technogenetic approach to the composition of subjects (Wiley & Elam, 2018). In this view, "hybridity" refers to *the mixture of logics intervening in what is already an organic-technical composition*. As we argue elsewhere (Wiley & Elam, 2018), makerspaces can then be seen as strategic sites for the discovery of new compositions that intertwine biological and sociotechnical elements, opening up new potentials and new modes of subjectivation—new ways of becoming "human" (Stiegler, 1998; Kittler, 1999; Siegert, 2013, 2015). For example, in the 1800s, a print- and reading-based "typographic man" emerged from innovations like the printing press and the typewriter and the practice of individual, silent reading (Kittler, 1999). In the late 1900s and early 2000s, this historically situated typographic mode of subjectivation gave way to a different kind of subject as computing and digital technologies became widespread. In the current historical conjuncture, the ubiquity of broadband connectivity and the proliferation of mobile digital devices are giving rise to new organic/technical compositions and new modes of subjectivation. While many present-day cultural techniques (Siegert, 2015) involve technological practices and data surveillance networks that produce predictable, standardized, and commodifiable subjects (Grandinetti, 2019), maker practices and the greater accessibility of open technologies make alternative modes of subjectivation possible (Sylvia, 2019). As such, the modes of play, the hybridity of logics, and the range of compositions that are allowed to develop are a critical issue, not just for the pedagogical mission of universities, but for our historical conjuncture generally.

As sites of hybrid play, university makerspaces are particularly important because they operate at the intersection of multiple contradictory logics, shaping contemporary processes of subjectivation. In the makerspace, subjectivation can go many ways and, depending on the combination of logics at work, certain capacities may be activated, while others are suppressed. In this chapter, we consider university makerspaces as sites where capitalist, institutional, and State logics dominate, but where playful experimentation, a multiplicity of logics, and the open-endedness of subjectivation may also lead to the emergence of more open, active, and unruly subjectivities. We put the concept of *synthetic subjectivation* (Wiley & Elam, 2018) to work in a comparative analysis of two different makerspace events: a corporate-sponsored, industry-focused "Make-A-Thon" competition organized by a university library; and an experimental play session carried out by one of us (Jessica) in which some of the same machines, materials, and bodies were arranged to make a very different composition. Drawing on participant-observation and autoethnographic data from these two experiences, we reflect on the differences between entrepreneurial logics (which combine educational and institutional norms with a corporate-capitalist understanding of innovation) and more playful, polyvocal logics (which maintain the openness and democratizing potential of the maker movement). We examine the complex articulation of these multiple logics in shaping the ways in which desiring-production (Deleuze & Guattari, 1972) is channeled in particular arrangements of the makerspace, either limiting the paths of subjectivation or opening up new potentials.

Synthetic subjectivation

Subjectivation is grounded in what Deleuze and Guattari call "desiring-production" (1983 [1972], p. 41). Desiring-production is the "machinic" constitution of reality through the synthesis of desire (p. 41). It is the process of nature making itself, *natura naturans* (Deleuze, 1988, p. 92). Desire—libido, labor power, or, more generally, energy—is invested directly into a natural and sociotechnical field, forming connections between bodies of all kinds, from molecular particles to large natural and sociotechnical aggregates such as a solar system or a society (Deleuze & Guattari, 1983 [1972], p. 29). Each body, no matter how large or small, and every aggregate body, no matter how simple or complex, is a machinic composition, a folding (a complication) of the forces of a social field.

Desiring-production involves three ontogenetic syntheses; the first two of these are the connective synthesis, which brings bodies into relation; and the disjunctive synthesis, which produces inscriptions and codings as an effect of embodied encounters (Deleuze & Guattari, 1983 [1972], pp. 39–44). Subjectivation—the formation of a temporary subject positioning—is the product of a third synthesis, the conjunctive synthesis (Deleuze & Guattari, 1983 [1972], pp. 17–18). Subjectivation is an event of the production of *sense*. According to Protevi, sense entails three aspects: "sensibility, signification, and direction" and produces a "body politic" (2009, p. 16).[2] We build on Protevi's definition of sense, but reformulate his three-part conceptualization. For us, subjectivation involves:

- *sensation*, an affective shift that is the product of an encounter between bodies and the sensual perception of that encounter (Deleuze, 2005 [1981]);
- *polysemiosis*, a coding according to multiple modes of inscription and semiosis (Guattari, 1984, 1995 [1992], 2000 [1989]; Langlois, 2011; Lazzarato, 2014); and
- *orientation*, a perceptual and epistemological positioning within a constellation of inscriptions and codes that is also an orientation toward action (Wiley & Elam, 2018, p. 208).

Sense, with its three dimensions—sensation, polysemiosis, and orientation—is an *event* with a particular duration and scope. It is both the product of the process of composition or arrangement to which it belongs and an active element of that composition, potentially (but not necessarily) with the autopoietic capacity to orient action by piloting desiring-production in future encounters.[3]

We further extend Deleuze and Guattari's conceptualization of desiring-production and subjectivation by incorporating the insights of materialist media theory (Kittler, 1990, 1999, 2010; Stiegler, 1998; Siegert, 2013). As Deleuze and Guattari argue, desire is invested directly in the social field; however, the social field must be understood as *sociotechnical* field, populated not only by organic bodies, social groups, and institutions, but also by sociotechnical machines, including media (Kittler, 1990, 1999, 2010; Stiegler, 1998; Packer and Wiley, 2013), a fact that is under-theorized both in Foucault and in Deleuze and Guattari (Kittler, 1999, 2010; Savat, 2012). Therefore, the technical must be seen as a constitutive element of the ontogenetic process of subjectivation. Subjectivation is synthetic subjectivation (Wiley & Elam, 2018, pp. 208–209).

Thus, "the human" as we understand it today is one particular historical production of subjectivity with a specific arrangement of *cultural techniques*—"a more or less complex actor-network that comprises technological objects as well as the operative chains they are part of and that configure or constitute them" (Siegert, 2013, p. 58). As Siegert notes, "Humans *as such* do not exist independently of cultural techniques of hominization" (2013, pp. 56–57). As synthetic subjects experimenting in the makerspace, we have the potential to explore and invent new cultural techniques and thus new ways of becoming "human." The ability to actively intervene in cultural techniques is critically important, as it is this capacity that characterizes *autopoietic* subjectivation—a process/event of subjectivation that alters the infrastructure of its own subjectivation and thus actively *pilots desire* in ways that raise its power. For example, the cultural technique known as *driving* involves specific investments of desire and energy, making connections between multiple components to form a complex arrangement or composition capable of certain kinds of perception and action. The cultural technique called driving produces a synthetic subject called a driver. While we follow Hayles (1999) in viewing this composition as a "cybernetic circuit" that leads to "a distributed cognitive system" (xiv), instead of thinking of the components in a dichotomous way, as "car" (technical body) and "driver" (human), we subtract the taken-for-granted molar identities (human and technical machine) and think in terms of molecular partial objects—that is, "parts" that are not defined a priori as parts of a molar whole (Deleuze and Guattari, 1983 [1972], pp. 36–45). It can be helpful to describe this complex composition by listing some of the components: hands, feet, muscles, bones, steering wheel, eyes, ears, windshield, road signs, dashboard, neural impulses, transmission, brakes, tires, pavement, money, gasoline, etc.[4] The investment of different sources of desire/energy (metabolism, desire for movement, petroleum combustion, highway construction, kinetic energy, etc.) forms a series of connections (eyes and dashboard, eyes and landscape, hands and steering wheel, feet and brake pedals, transmission and axle, tires and pavement, etc.) that assemble a complex *new* body—a moving automobile—and insert it into a sociotechnical field composed of roads, traffic signs, and other moving cars. As these connections are made, changes are recorded in various ways: Eyes see a red light, neurons recognize an iconic color and shape, muscles are activated by an electrical impulse, brakes sense pressure from a pedal, tires register the friction of the pavement, muscles and brain experience deceleration, etc.

Furthermore, feedback loops of various kinds *process* those recordings or inscriptions, thus turning connections into relations. Recursive processes work to maintain the coherence of the complex composition—or to alter it in some way, as when the engine is turned off and a different body occupies the driver's seat. And finally, a subject is formed: Out of the multiple connections, inscriptions, and recursive processing loops, an *event of sense* arises. The subject thus formed—a driver—is the product of the composition and all the capacities it has arranged. A driver is not a human subject; it is a particular historical capacity for perception and action—for sensation, semiosis, and orientation—that is produced by the arrangement of natural, organic, and technical components in a particular historical conjuncture.[5]

When we consider the university makerspace as a site of synthetic subjectivation, we consider the connections that become possible in this space as well as how these connections might be inscribed and coded—in habits, in polysemiotic embodied memory, in technical storage, and in databases. We additionally consider the subjectivitations that arise from these machinic compositions and the manner in which they pilot desire into particular modes of sensation, semiosis, and orientation to the sociotechnical field. From these considerations, we ask how and *why* the makerspace produces subjects in the context of its various institutional aims (university, broader maker movement).

The university makerspace

The makerspace in which the autoethnographic and participant observation that illustrate our case studies occurred is housed within the library of a large public university in the southeast of the United States. The experiences recounted occurred during the three years that one of us (Jessica) worked as the Makerspace Graduate Assistant. At the time of the observations, the space had been open for nearly three years and contained a wide variety of emerging technologies. The space is cordoned off from the rest of the library by a large glass wall on one side, giving it a fishbowl effect. Through the entryway is a small section designated as "visitor space"; the rest is designated "user space" and is only accessible to those who attend an orientation session—a student-built access control mechanism requires patrons to swipe their university ID card in order to enter.[6] Past the entryway, cabinets, drawers, and workbenches line the walls, providing storage space for tools and equipment. The majority of user space is occupied by large worktables, to which patrons bring equipment and materials taken from storage.

Beyond the physical layout, the makerspace has a set of guidelines and motivations that mirror those found in similar academic library makerspaces, including supporting learning, encouraging collaboration, and providing access (Burke, 2015). The space's espoused mission parallels the overall university libraries' mission: to provide access and cultivate literacies. Makerspace management and staff strive to cultivate an inclusive environment in which diverse patrons can enjoy a helpful, non-judgmental community that doesn't privilege expertise. Along these lines, the space is meant to be open to patrons pursuing a range of personal, academic, and/ or entrepreneurial projects. Though the makerspace is meant to provide an environment in which patrons can work on specific projects, it is also billed as open to more playful practices and experiences. Play, in this sense, encompasses activities undertaken without a defined goal or specific product in mind—to simply see where tinkering leads, or activities to enhance technological literacy. However, the majority of makerspace patrons' motivations fall under the following three categories:

1   *Making stuff for fun.* Students often enter out of curiosity, aware of the existence of certain emerging technologies (especially 3D printers, in the wave of increased accessibility and affordability of the technology) but without any hands-on experience. Many students learn to use the equipment through the production of vanity projects, often finding an existing 3D model on a community repository site like thingiverse.com. This approach allows them to learn how to operate the machine first, skipping the more complicated step of creating their own model. Once they become familiar with the functioning of the machine, some students continue to print vanity projects based on existing models rather than designing their own creations (for example, many students print Pokémon figurines or playing pieces for the game Dungeons & Dragons). Others move on to design their own models in 3D modeling programs, and while many continue to create or modify 3D models for their vanity projects, others see this "making for fun" as a steppingstone to pursue other motivations, two of which are described below.

2   *Making prototypes for entrepreneurial/institutional purposes.* Certain patrons enter the makerspace with curiosity, as described earlier, which eventually leads to an opening-up of new possibilities. However, in many cases, these possibilities become narrowed and defined, channeled through an entrepreneurial ethos in which the patrons focus on the space's potential to develop products specifically intended for commodification. For example, one student initially came into the space with the desire to learn 3D-printing skills. He began by downloading existing 3D models, and after printing several projects for fun, he decided to capitalize on the fidget-spinner craze by 3D printing the shells and assembling the final products with the makerspace's hand tools. He then began selling these on the Amazon Marketplace for a profit.

Additionally, many patrons initially entered the makerspace driven by the specific desire to channel its potential into their institutional pursuits, most often consisting of course projects or university events and competitions. For instance, during an annual institutional competition in the undergraduate engineering program, Engineering 101 students place increased demand on the Makerspace, with students forming wait-lines to access the space. Despite this temporary influx of Makerspace use, many students do not return after the annual event, suggesting that following the completion of their specific purpose, they retained no desire to channel the makerspace into creative endeavors outside of institutional requirements. Students from a variety of disciplines, such as textiles, art, and chemistry, have utilized the space in a less structured way in order to complete course-required projects that involved developing a product or model. Additionally, another form of makerspace utilization that often overlapped with institutional purposes is made distinct by its underlying motivation, which sets it apart from the specifically product-driven goal.

3   *Critical making.* As a research method or experimental practice, critical making combines material engagement with critical reflection (Ratto, 2011, p. 253). Further, as a form of social critique or activism, it encourages "explor[ing] what is possible with new technology, how we could change socio-technical conditions, [and] how we could re-imagine our social environmental situations" (Jeremijenko, 2015, np). Critical making is oriented toward the processes in these engagements rather than the products of the practice, although it's been suggested that objects resulting from critical making activities may also have an impactful effect (Hertz, 2015).

The most frequent use of the makerspace for critical making activities involved either open-enrollment workshops for department symposia and special events (e.g. the campus-wide Sustainability Week) or instructors bringing their classes in as part of a module in their given course. For instance, a variety of courses have used the space to engage students in critical thinking by solving a problem or exploring an idea via prototyping with often unfamiliar technologies and materials, necessitating ingenuity and creativity. In this sense, the "critical" aspect of making refers to an academic endeavor that channels the makerspace for answering or revealing some real-world issue or theoretical quandary. Such practices focus on the process of engaging with the material rather than beginning with a product in mind and, as such, there is often a tension between the subject as "critical" maker and the subject as budding entrepreneur, potentially leading to conflicts over the ethics of practice and questions about the place of critical making within the university (Galloway, 2015). In the next section, we consider a specific event that illustrates these tensions.

Case study 1: Make-A-Thon[7]

Make-A-Thon, an annual multi-day competition organized by various entities across the university and hosted by makerspace and libraries staff, asks student teams to prototype a technology for sustainability, and this was Build Day. The first two days were allotted to team formation, brainstorming, and blueprinting. On the third day, student teams built projects to be judged by a cadre of industry representatives. Mentors drawn from university faculty and industry volunteers floated around to offer advice and assistance, along with makerspace staff members on hand to provide technical support.

The Make-A-Thon is pitched as a challenge to innovate a creative sustainability solution through engagement with emerging technologies, but the atmosphere was rife with an entrepreneurial ethos. Even though the order of the day was to offer up proof of concept—a mock-up, diagram, or prototype—many students were intensely focused on making a *working* prototype. Several student groups stated this intention outright, believing that building a working product rather than simply engaging in experimentation for the sake of experimentation increased their chances of impressing the judges. They believed that its observable functionality would signal its value as the next potentially marketable, profitable merchandise. In addition, the entrepreneurial ethos was evident in the rewards, including a number of prizes funded by industry sponsors, along with the grand prize of a 3D printer for each group member and the opportunity to pitch their idea to the university's Resident Entrepreneur. Further, the team with the best social-media documentation of their four-day journey would win a smartphone bundle; the award for best use of one company's software was an assortment of high-end gadgets, and best incorporation of another company's component would be awarded with a cash prize.

During the Make-A-Thon event, while the Makerspace was available to students, space and ventilation requirements necessitated a temporary expansion into an adjacent library area to accommodate the upward of 100 student participants. Tools, technologies, and materials were made available in both spaces, and many were mobile, traveling between areas as the need arose, which suggests that makerspace is an *event* that may recur within the same physical place, but not necessarily. It is, rather, the composition of material, technological, and organic bodies under a particular regime of governing logics that constitutes the *makerspace*. The logics influencing processes of subjectivation during Make-A-Thon represent a composition we might call the *institutional* makerspace. Institutionalization is certainly not limited to this particular event; as a composition or arrangement, the university makerspace is often over-coded by logics of capitalism, institutional higher education, and the State, which stratify the event-space with hierarchical relations and prioritize entrepreneurial endeavors over open experimentation.

Though free play was encouraged as a process of gaining and nurturing technical literacies, playfulness was coded as a means to an end; creativity was a strategy for developing the technical literacies required to engage entrepreneurial flows of capital—deterritorialization for the sake of reterritorialization (Deleuze & Guattari, 1983). These logics place limits and shape the conditions of possibility for processes of subjectivation. The entrepreneurial ethos, the aesthetic focus, and the need to make *sense* of an object in a way that supports dominant logics are forces that shape how desire is channeled. As an event at the intersection of institutional (university) logics and the logics of entrepreneurial capital, the Make-A-Thon can be seen as part of an ongoing process that orients subjectivation, and the productive arrangements that produce subjects, toward commodification. An alternative to this mode of subjectivation would entail engagements without the expectation of capitalist entrepreneurial value and perhaps without the need for making sense at all. This would be a process of subjectivation via continual experimentation—one in which machinic connections proliferate without policing, the inscriptions and codifications that arise remain polyvocal, and the subject positions that take shape are flexible and resistant to apparatuses of discipline and control. Given the institutional overcoding of the makerspace, what subjectivations can emerge from this practice that are not already subjected to dominant logics?

Case study 2: experimental play session

From the perspective of a theory of synthetic subjectivation, alternative subjects can be made in the makerspace through creative experimentation with materials, tools, machines, and bodies by maintaining the openness of connections, the polyvocality of inscriptions and codings, and an agile, nomadic approach to the event of sense. The following narrative describes a spontaneous experimental play session that Jessica carried out in the university makerspace. While it was unplanned, it may still be considered a critical making activity, particularly given the reflection recorded following the session, and further reflection in the context of this chapter.

One weekday during the late afternoon, I was working as a staff member in the library makerspace. There were no patrons present, I was the only staff member on shift, and no equipment was running. It was an uncommon occurrence, as more often than not at least one 3D printer would be in operation (patrons weren't required to remain in the space for the duration of their 3D print job). While I knew a patron might come in at any time, I had no tasks before me in my role as a university employee and took the opportunity to play with the idea of experimentation. Something about the emptiness of the space made it feel unconstrained. With no eyes on me, I wouldn't be tempted to limit my experimentation for the sake of appearing to be engaged in an institutionally productive activity.

I walked around the space and selected tools and materials seemingly at random, ending up with a LilyPad Arduino microcontroller kit[8] (Figure 8.1), a sewing machine, and some scrap fabric. I randomly selected the pulse sensor as an input device (Figure 8.2). I didn't know where I was going with this, so I just set up the circuit to test the components. I watched as my pulse was translated into values on the Arduino IDE serial

Figure 8.1 Lilypad Arduino. Copyright: Jessica Elam.

Figure 8.2 The heart-rate sensor/orchestra conductor. Copyright: Jessica
Elam.

monitor and then the serial plotter.[9] *For some reason, it made
me think of music. I found some code on an internet maker
forum for the LilyPad MP3 player microcontroller and went
to a free music site where I downloaded a package of single
notes from the instruments of a full orchestra. I modified the
code to trigger random MP3s based on the range of values my
pulse generated, as detected and transduced by the sensor.
I sewed conductive thread into a piece of cloth to remake
the circuit away from the breadboard.*[10] *I tested it; I had to
make some modifications because I forgot a semicolon in the
code and needed to change out the power source (connecting
the board via USB to a laptop instead of using an external
battery pack). Then, I placed my device against my throat,
closed my eyes, sat back, and listened, wondering what my
vascular system would compose. Just random notes. A vio-
lin, I think. A cello. Flute. Cello again. Oboe or clarinet—I
don't know. More strings. Brass (a trumpet perhaps). I held
my breath to see what would happen. Not much difference.
I changed the parameters in the code, I looked around cautiously and did some jumping jacks in the back corner of the*

space, and then...this rapid succession, this amazing dishar-mony of notes, and I thought...I'm not making a song, it's an orchestra tuning up!

The sensation was one of joy in uncovering a capacity for ex-pression, a pulse inscribed onto a microcontroller transduced into aural output that, in the moment, didn't serve any pur-pose, as defined by the dominant logics organizing the university makerspace. It felt like a liberation or even an unleashing of a new composition that inspired something essentially euphoric. Several days later, while reflecting on this session, I realized the composition had activated sensations from previous inscrip-tions in the form of organically stored memories (that is to say, "my own" brain memories). First, I recalled that this experience wasn't the first time I'd associated data generation with music. The above line "for some reason it made me think of music" was recorded shortly after I ceased the free play/experimentation. Again, only upon reflection did I remember otherwise. On a few of occasions, while engaging with similar technologies, specifi-cally when I watched visualizations of data generation, I'd hear musical notes in my head and sometimes hummed in time with values appearing on the screen. Second, while I can't pinpoint the genesis of it, thinking back many years I recalled that the sound of an orchestra tuning up either in a live performance or playback of a recording has always instilled a sense of serenity in me. Perhaps part of my joy in the experimental play session was induced by the prior connection—the memory of orchestra tuning and the sensation of serenity—and was activated when I wasn't looking for it, when I didn't even consciously recognize it in the moment.

What made the processes of subjectivation in this scenario a different kind of subjectivation than others that occur more frequently in the makerspace? This scenario of play was an experimentation with dif-ferent transductions of the body and its processes, taking an organic inscription medium (the heartbeat) and altering it technically, which, in turn, altered the arrangement's capacities to process inscriptions. The heart registers affective states in the body and simultaneously responds—it's already inscriptive of desire. The pulse sensor regis-tered these interoceptive processes of the heart; the microcontroller transduced the pulse data into digital data and routed it through a speaker, producing sound. The moment in which the association was made between data and music was possibly induced by a connection to unconscious memories of previous play involving the processing of data as music. This initial connection created a subjectivation that led to second phase in which the composition was expanded through transduction into visible, readable data. The numerical readout of heart rate was an a-signifying subjectivation which led to new enjoyment of the arrangement, which, in turn, expanded the brain's capacity to consider other options.

Even though this case took place in the university makerspace, it resisted being over-coded or made to signify; it involved bringing things together without a plan and employing (and enjoying) them the "wrong way." A chain of institutional circumstances, relations, motivations, and logics may have led to the session; yet, it was also undertaken with an intention of disrupting the overarching, oft-present sentiment in the university makerspace of engaging with the equipment with a particular purpose, not even the encouraged literacy-gaining, as Jessica had been in composition with these elements before and was very much attuned. In fact, Jessica's deep learning of technical literacies leading up to this session was representative of training and disciplining in the "right way" to engage with the technologies, which begs the question of what capacities might have opened up without compositional attunement in any form.[11]

Hybrid logics at work and play

The Make-A-Thon engendered an entrepreneurial ethos: Student groups were prompted to prototype and subsequently pitch a product contributing to sustainability, and both the competition instructions and the judging criteria highlighted the feasibility of implementation, cost savings, and marketability. As such, participants were expected to have a plan to create a specific product prior to engaging with prototyping materials. With this in mind, we can point to various logics at play shaping processes of subjectivation during the event.

Entrepreneurial logics were apparent in the focus on creating a commodifiable product, its marketability, and the best integration of an existing commercial product. The teams were required to come up with a product that could serve a specific purpose, as outlined in the competition guidelines and judging criteria (Figure 8.3). While experimentation with equipment and materials was sometimes necessary during the prototyping process if an initial attempt failed to achieve a particular purpose, the experimentation was channeled toward the desired functionality of the designed product. Not only was the focus on creating a product, but also on its marketability as a commodity for businesses and/or consumer markets. The criteria included descriptors like innovative, useful, and cost-efficient.

Science-Fair Style Presentation Evaluation (0 to 33 points possible)	Very Strongly Agree *** Reserve this selection for exceptional work	Strongly Agree	Agree	Disagree
Problem Definition- A sustainability challenge was thoroughly explained	3	2	1	0
Problem Definition- Solution addresses an existing opportunity	3	2	1	0
Problem Definition- Resources needed were clearly identified	3	2	1	0
Problem Definition- Solution is original (e.g. never seen before)	3	2	1	0
Impact- Solution will have a large impact for the stated challenge scale (e.g. campus, community or world)	3	2	1	0
Feasibility- Solution is likely to be successful	3	2	1	0
Feasibility- Solution is based on clear and reasonable assumptions and/or research	3	2	1	0
Feasibility- Solution will effectively meet the sustainability needs	3	2	1	0
Feasibility- Team has thoroughly explained concept or implementation	3	2	1	0
Pitch- Team is prepared and persuasive in illustrating the benefits of this solution	3	2	1	0
Overall Showcase- Aesthetic components of this showcase are clear & compelling	3	2	1	0

Figure 8.3 Make-A-Thon Judging Criteria: Impact and Feasibility. Copyright: Jessica Elam.

MAKE-A-THON COMPETITION PROMPTS
Here's your specific Make-a-thon challenge:

How might we more sustainably use water, energy, waste, transportation or food?
... as individuals?   ... on campus?   ... in our community, country or world?

What solutions can we prototype using things like...
...data science?   ...entrepreneurship?   ...3D design & printing?   ...the Internet of Things?

Figure 8.4 Make-A-Thon Competition Prompt. Copyright: Jessica Elam.

Another component of the entrepreneurial logics evident in Make-a-Thon was the sponsorship and prize categories offered by businesses that asked groups to incorporate their existing product (e.g. IBM's Bluemix cloud platform, Autodesk's Fusion 360 design software).

Institutional logics stemmed from the competition prompt (Figure 8.4) and guidelines asking participants to develop a product to better serve the university or municipality. These logics came into play in the requirement that the product prototype must serve a purpose, specifically for sustainability initiatives on campus. While this was a worthy endeavor to promote environmental protection, most solutions simply emphasized cost-savings aspects (e.g. reducing costs associated with energy and water use, waste disposal processes).

Finally, *creative logics* influenced subjectivation processes, emphasized in the judging criteria centered on uniqueness of the product in the existing market—an "original" product that may not have an existing counterpart, or at least boasted significant "improvements" on an existing product (Figure 8.5).

"What We Made at Make-a-thon" Google Form Evaluation (0 to 24 points possible)	Very Strongly Agree *** Reserve this selection for exceptional work	Strongly Agree	Agree	Disagree
Problem Definition- The sustainability challenge was clearly stated stated	3	2	1	0
Problem Definition- The sustainability challenge represents an existing opportunity	3	2	1	0
Solution Description (Originality)- Solution is original (e.g. never seen before)	3	2	1	0
Solution Description (Impact)- Solution will have a large impact for the stated challenge scale (e.g. campus, community or world)	3	2	1	0
Solution Description (Feasibility)- Solution is based on reasonable assumptions	3	2	1	0
Solution Description (Feasibility)- Solution is likely to be successful	3	2	1	0
Solution Description (Benefit)- Solution will effectively meet sustainability needs	3	2	1	0
Solution Description (Implementation)- There is a reasonable implementation plan	3	2	1	0

Figure 8.5 Make-A-Thon Judging Criteria: Originality. Copyright: Jessica Elam.

By contrast, Jessica's experimental play session was undertaken with the desire to experience and embody our concept of synthetic subjectivation. As stated in the previous section, subsequent reflection on the encounter implies a more institutionalized encoding, but here we examine the logics influencing processes of subjectivation at the time of the event.

These logics include *technical logics*—that is, the design elements and potential capacities of technical devices such as sensors and circuit boards. In many ways, these were the same technical elements and logics as those present in the Make-A-Thon event; however, in the experimental session, these logics (the potentials of the LilyPad, pulse sensor, laptop, etc.) were discovered and engaged through *play* and thus shaped subjectivation via a *revelation of capacities or potentials*. By contrast, in the Make-A-Thon event, components were chosen and assembled based on their typical functions and on a pre-defined purpose. That is to say, by the time the Make-A-Thon teams began engaging with the materials and technologies of the makerspace, they had already decided exactly what each would be used to create. In the experimental play session, however, these technical logics were not already captured within another set of logics, and therefore were freer to pilot desire within the entire composition.

That said, *compositional logics* were at play in this session in that components of the composition (heart, hands, eyes, sensors, processors, data, speakers, sound, etc.) revealed or activated new capacities instead of being initially closed down by disciplinary overcodings in service of entrepreneurial logics. In other words, the ethos guiding the experimental session was not "how might I create a product and who might buy it?" but rather "what might enter into composition?" and "what might happen next?"

These *experimental logics* may seem similar to the creative logics promoted by the Make-A-Thon event. However, the experimental logics in Jessica's playful makerspace session were not centered on creating an original product for the market as a solution to a specific problem. Rather,

her experimental makerspace processes were guided by open exploration in response to new and unexpected capacities being activated—both technical capacities and the potentials of the organic body as medium. The event of subjectivation in this case was a joyful and unexpected set of connections and transductions leading to an orchestral tuning of a human heart—a temporary, nomadic subjectivation characterized by a sense of emergence and serving as a springboard for further exploration.

Conclusions

Connecting these logics to the shaping of subjectivation processes through sense and the body politic (Protevi, 2009) within our reframing as sensation, polysemiosis, and positioning or orientation to action, a series of questions emerged as a result of our analysis: (1) What new sensations are possible in this process/event of synthetic subjectivation? (2) How does Jessica make sense of it, how is it coded, if not based on entrepreneurial codes (the polyvocal logic of "and" at work during the process of fiddling with code and components)? and (3) How does the experience then reorient agency, with capacities to do something different from the dominant subject position in the makerspace?

The maker movement's nomadic subjectivation is characterized by deterritorialized flows of capital emerging from the miniaturization, accessibility, and un-black-boxed (open-source) technologies coupled with creative practice, inherent knowledge conferred within the "digital age," a resistance to the proprietary capture of invention, and a rejection of the concept of a single author in favor of a communitarian ethos. In tinkering or making practices where material engagements occur outside boundaries put in place by institutional authority and the requirements of entrepreneurial capitalism, subjectivation is not about a wholly constituted individual inventor and the merchandise they are building. Instead, it is about hands and eyes and ears and circuits and voltage and plastic and so on, entering into relation and becoming something new—becoming what Guattari (1995 [1992]) called an active, agential subject group, as opposed to a subjugated group.[12] However, as is the historical tendency with nomadic movements and resistance to dominant regimes, these practices have been continuously recaptured by the axiomatics of capital and the stratifications of State and institutional logics. There is a market for the "maker" products of entrepreneurial engineering. The practices, discourses, and material components that might otherwise be the elements of experimental composition and invention are instead made into an industry: Technologies become products and human bodies are made into market innovators and into customers in need of the latest goods and services. The imposition of this ordering and categorization onto what was a nomadic composition is like a pop band covering a punk song. What was once a discordant cacophony of disjointed melody and harmony and screeching, a-rhythmic instrumentals now follows the order and structure of convention. The affective encounter is no longer revolutionary; it is now *recognizable*.

An alternative to this mode of subjectivation would entail engagements without a predetermined end state or the influence of entrepreneurial logics—a mode of composition that played out in our experimental makerspace session. This session entailed a random gathering of materials and building something without concern for functionality or purpose. The result was a combination of a heart, a pulse sensor, and an Arduino microcontroller that triggered random musical notes with each input of heart-rate data. Unlike the material engagements within the Make-A-Thon, this free play enacted more polyvocal processes of subjectivation, resisting the tendency to cut off proliferating connections, limit potential inscriptions, and circumscribe conjunctions. Connections multiplied as a free play of body parts and technics in transduction, without a priori rules or goals. Connections and the affective shifts they caused were inscribed in auditory signals and synapses, in haptic sensors, and in digital data registries. Inscriptions were processed through polyvocal semiotic chains, including the asignifying semiotic processing of computer algorithms and the mixed-semiotic associations of embodied neural memory, and these entered into feedback loops of further polysemiotic codings, keeping semiosis open to new disjunctures, refusing to overcode the process with a biunivocal set of "meanings." And from these iterations of distributed inscription and processing, an event of sense arose, producing a synthetic subject with new capacities of sensation, new modes of semiosis, and a new orientation toward the future. The makerspace made a heart-music-machine and a new synthetic subject—a subject enjoying the cacophony of its data/body, actively intervening in its own infrastructure of subjectivation to multiply connections, making sense of the affective shifts underway, and raising its power of action through hybrid play.

From our case studies, we see that university makerspaces tend to impose certain logics on subjectivation. We are not suggesting that there is an institutional disapproval of experimental compositions in the makerspace, but rather that there is a continual channeling of these compositions into entrepreneurial and institutional/educational machines. While we do not wish to dismiss all maker activities undertaken with particular products in mind (as in the case of the Make-A-Thon), the ethics and politics of the grassroots maker movement must not be lost in institutionalization and commodification. This is not an all-or-nothing scenario: We can hold onto some of the open, revolutionary logics of the maker movement while recognizing the inevitable influence of institutional norms and the reality of corporate engagement with university makerspaces and their programs. Additionally, other programming and practices promote the library's evolution as a transitional space between "old" and "new" media, indicating that university makerspaces are indeed open to rearticulation.

Such rearticulation reflects a "legitimate" use of the three syntheses of desiring-production (Deleuze & Guattari, 1983 [1972]): a connective synthesis open to new connections; a disjunctive synthesis in which inscriptions and codings non-restrictive—not limited to this *or* that; and a conjunctive synthesis that invigorates nomadic subjectivations open to permutation and repositioning, not those locked into a State-maintained structure or the axiomatics of capitalism. Makerspaces can be spaces for experimental, nomadic subjectivations if they enable the multiplication of connections and the polyvocality of codings, rather than imposing particular pre-defined arrangements and meanings. We must also consider how the *composition* enjoys the processes—that is, how a synthetic subject experience is transformed by polyvocal event of sense. It is easy to take an anthropocentric view and point to the human enjoyment of the experience of producing musical notes with your heart. However, we aim to take a post-human approach, to think about that moment as synthetic, where nonhuman components participated in that enjoyment.

These two contrasting case studies illustrate the multiple and often conflicting logics (ludic, experimental, institutional, entrepreneurial, capitalist, surveillance, and control logics) that meet in makerspaces, shape maker projects, and inform maker subjectivities, piloting the investment of desire that is at play. In this context, the proliferation of discourses of hybridity may be seen as an index of a broader post-human condition that troubles received understandings of the "online" and "offline," "physical" and "digital," "human" and "nonhuman," etc. In this chapter, we demonstrated a different approach—one that examines the *genesis* of subjectivity through the molecular *processes* of synthesis—and does not rely on a priori categories that reproduce the human/technical dichotomy.

From this angle, the experience or perception of "hybridity" and hybrid play may be seen as an effect rather than a cause, the end result of a process in which discursive/linguistic categories that derive from an older media episteme—the typographic—are mobilized in an attempt to make sense of what is arguably a radically new media-epistemic context. In one sense, we have *always* been "hybrid" subjects because we have always been complex compositions of organic and technical elements: *homo habilis, homo scriptor, homo lector,* and *homo binarii codice.* In this sense, hybridity is the *characteristic* mode of ontogenesis—Spinoza's *natura naturans*—and the technogenesis of "human" subjects is just a variant on that process of nature making itself. This is hybridization not as the cyborg combination of two distinct modes of being (the technical machine and the human as organic body) or as two distinct types of space (the physical and the digital) but as the ontological condition of the so-called human. Hybrid play, from this point of view, would then be an affirmation of the radical openness of that ontogenetic process: a machinic becoming of organic and technical compositions that remains open to the potentials of connection, polysemiotic coding, and nomadic subjectivations.

Notes

1 As Hayles (2016) notes, "the resulting cognitive assemblages transform the contexts and conditions under which human cognition operates, ultimately affecting what it means to be human in developed societies" (p. 35).

2 Protevi (2009) develops a useful reading of Deleuze and Guattari drawing on recent work in complexity theory, neurophysiology, and distributed cognition. He makes the point that the body, for Deleuze and Guattari, is the product of a political physics (p. 187) that imposes exclusive disjunctions (codes and inscriptions) to organize desiring-production and form docile bodies for social reproduction and labor (p. 109). The "body politic" is not reducible to the organism but is in fact a bio-socio-technical body.

3 The concept of autopoiesis was initially developed by Maturana and Varela (1980 [1971]) and Varela et al. (1974) and taken up by Guattari (1995 [1992], pp. 7, 13, 2000 [1989], n. 74, pp. 100–102).

4 On the usefulness of lists for describing compositions or assemblages, see Fuller (2005, pp. 13–15).

5 Of course, this is a rather simplistic example. Present-day driving arrangements often involve more complex technical processing by the built-in computer components of an automobile (or add-on "safe-driver" monitoring systems); by various GPS-enabled devices and databases; and by the recursive relation between eyes, ears, screens, and computer voices.

6 The access control system was actually built by Jessica and the system uses a recording of her voice.

7 Participant-observation data gathered in 2017.

8 A microcontroller is essentially a small computer that can be programmed to carry out specific operations (usually one at a time, e.g., making a light blink, triggering a sound effect) when properly configured in circuits with components like LED lights, speakers, etc. The LilyPad Arduino is a brand of microcontroller designed specifically for integration with electronic textile projects. See the product page for more information: https://www.arduino.cc/en/Main/ArduinoBoardLilyPad/

9 Arduino IDE refers to the software used to write, edit, and upload code for certain microcontrollers. The serial monitor feature is a tool that allows the user to send commands to the microcontroller and also receive data readouts from the microcontroller. In this case, the serial monitor was reporting values from the pulse sensor. The serial plotter is another visualization tool that takes those incoming values and plots them in a line graph.

10 A breadboard is a device used in electronic prototyping that allows for non-permanent electrical connections to be made between a circuit's components.

11 Furthermore, even critical reflection on the process of experimentation—such as this essay's analysis of the association with an orchestra tuning up and the subsequent connection to personal experiences of feeling serene—might capture the arrangement in restrictive codes of meaning and channel further subjectivations. In this case, continued reflection channels it toward academic publishing as a bureaucratized and capitalized mode of knowledge production. For a time, however, the composition produced a nomadic, experimental subject.

12 For a more detailed discussion of subject groups as autopoietic compositions of agency, see Wiley and Elam (2018).

References

Anderson, C. (2012). *Makers: The new industrial revolution.* New York, NY: Crown Business.

Burke, J. (2015). Making sense: Can makerspaces work in academic libraries? Paper presented at ACRL 2015. Retrieved from http://www.ala.org/acrl/acrl/conferences/acrl2015/papers

Chachra, D. (2015, January 23). Why I am not a maker. *The Atlantic.* Retrieved from https://www.theatlantic.com/technology/archive/2015/01/why-i-am-not-a-maker/384767/

Deleuze, G. (1988). *Spinoza: Practical philosophy.* (R. Hurley, Trans.). San Francisco, CA: City Lights Books.

Deleuze, G. (2005 [1981]). *Francis Bacon: The logic of sensation.* (D. Smith, Trans.). London and New York, NY: Continuum.

Deleuze, G. & Guattari, F. (1983 [1972]). *Anti-oedipus: Capitalism and schizophrenia.* (R. Hurley, M. Seem, & H. Lane, Trans.). Minneapolis: University of Minnesota Press.

Fuller, M. (2005). *Media ecology: Materialist energies in art and technoculture.* Cambridge, MA: MIT Press.

Galloway, A. (2015). Critique and making. In *Conversations in Critical Making,* eds. Arthur and Marilouise Kroker. Victoria, BC: CTheory Books. Retrieved from http://ctheory.net/ctheory_wp/2729-2/

Grandinetti, J. J. (2019). *Streaming locality: Streaming media and the production of space and subjectivity.* Doctoral Dissertation. North Carolina State University. Retrieved from http://www.lib.ncsu.edu/resolver/1840.20/36510.

Guattari, F. (1984). *Molecular revolution: Psychiatry and politics.* New York, NY: Penguin.

Guattari, F. (1995 [1992]). *Chaosmosis: An ethico-aesthetic paradigm.* (P. Bains & J. Pefanis, Trans.). Bloomington and Indianapolis: Indiana University Press.

Guattari, F. (2000 [1989]). *The three ecologies.* (I. Pindar & P. Sutton, Trans.). London and New Brunswick, NJ: The Athlone Press.

Halverson, E. & Sheridan, K. (2014). The maker movement in education. *Harvard Educational Review, 84,* 495–504.

Hatch, M. (2014). *The maker movement manifesto: Rules for innovation in the new world of crafters, hackers, and tinkerers.* New York, NY: McGraw-Hill Education.

Hayles, N. K. (1999). *How we became posthuman.* Chicago: The University of Chicago Press.

Hayles, N. K. (2016). Cognitive assemblages: Technical agency and human interactions. *Critical Inquiry, 43,* 32–55.

Hertz, G. (2015). *Conversations in critical making.* Victoria, BC: CTheory Books.

Holman, W. (2014, December 31). The toaster paradox. *Medium.* Retrieved April 14, 2019, from https://medium.com/@objectguerilla/the-toaster-paradox-a289fe41eb50

Jeremijenko, N. (2015). Engineering anti-techno-fetishism. In *Conversations in Critical Making,* ed. Garnet Hertz. Victoria, BC: CTheory Books.

Johnson, J. (1988). Mixing humans and nonhumans together: The sociology of a door-closer. *Social Problems, 35*(3), 298–310.

Kittler, F. (1990). *Discourse network 1800/1900.* (M. Metteer & C. Cullens, Trans.). Stanford, CA: Stanford University Press.

Kittler, F. (1999). *Gramophone, film, typewriter.* (G. Winthrop-Young & M. Wutz, Trans.). Stanford, CA: Stanford University Press.

Kittler, F. (2010). *Optical media.* (A. Enns, Trans.). Cambridge, MA: Polity Press.

Langlois, G. (2011). Meaning, semiotechnologies and participatory media. *Culture Machine, 12,* 1–12.

Latour, B. (2005). *Reassembling the social: An introduction to Actor-Network Theory.* Oxford: Oxford University Press.

Lazzarato, M. (2014). *Signs and machines: Capitalism and the production of subjectivity.* (J. Jordan, Trans.). Cambridge, MA: Semiotext(e)/Foreign Agents.

Maturana, H. R. & Varela, F. J. (1980 [1971]). Autopoiesis: The organization of the living. In *Autopoiesis and cognition: The realization of the living,* ed. H. Maturana & F. Varela. Dordrecht; Boston; and London: D. Reidel Publishing.

Morozov, E. (2014, January 5). Making it. *The New Yorker.* Retrieved from https://www.newyorker.com/magazine/2014/01/13/making-it-2

Packer, J. & Wiley, S. B. C. (2013). *Communication matters: Materialist approaches to media, mobility, and networks.* London and New York: Routledge.

Protevi, J. (2009). *Political affect: Connecting the social and the somatic.* Minneapolis, MN and London: University of Minnesota Press.

Ratto, M. (2011). Critical making: Conceptual and material studies in technology and social life. *The Information Society, 27*(4), 252–260.

Savat, D. (2012). *Uncoding the digital: Technology, subjectivity and action in the control society.* London: Palgrave Macmillan.

Sayers, J. (2011). Tinker-centric pedagogy in literature and language classrooms. In *Collaborative Approaches to the Digital in English Studies,* ed. Laura McGrath. Logan, UT: Utah State University Press.

Siegert, B. (2013). Cultural techniques: Or the end of the intellectual postwar era in German media theory. *Theory, Culture & Society, 30*(6), 48–65.

Siegert, B. (2015). *Cultural techniques: Grids, filters, doors, and other articulations of the real.* (Geoffrey Winthrop-Young, Trans.). New York: Fordham University Press.

Stiegler, B. (1998). *Technics and time 1: The fault of epimetheus.* Stanford, CA: Stanford University Press.

Sylvia IV, J. J. (2019). From archaeology to genealogy: Adding processes of subjectivation and artistic intervention. *Communication+1, 7*(2), Article 3, 1–25.

van der Meulen, S. & Bruinsma, M. (2018). Man as 'aggregate of data:' What computers shouldn't do. *AI & Society.* Retrieved from https://doi.org/10.1007/s00146-018-0852-6

Varela, F., Maturana, H. & Uribe, R. (1974). Autopoiesis: The organization of living systems, its characterization and a model. *Biosystems, 5*(4), 187–196.

Wiley, S. B. C. & Elam, J. (2018). Synthetic subjectivation: Technical media and the composition of post-human subjects. *Subjectivity, 11*(3), 203–227.

Part III
Hybrid spaces

9 Haptic play

Understanding hybrid play through *Pokémon GO*

Larissa Hjorth, Ingrid Richardson, and Jordi Piera-Jimenez

As mobile devices become increasingly playful and entangled within our everyday lives, notions of hybrid play are recalibrated. Within this playful space, the digital is interwoven with material and social dimensions. Scholars such as Adriana de Souza e Silva (2006) have identified the texture of hybridity as movement and overlay between physical and digital worlds. Hybridity is, therefore, central in the mobile media experience in which overlays like AR (augmented reality) are integrated into quotidian cartographies. Since the phenomenal rise (and fall and semi-rise again) of the AR game *Pokémon GO*, we need to revisit our notions of hybridity and its various attendant overlays. In particular, the haptic affordances of the game highlight the need to develop vocabularies around haptic play and how it affords different multisensorial experiences and affects (Richardson & Hjorth, 2019).

In this chapter, we draw on ethnographic work conducted with *Pokémon GO* players after its "ludified perfect storm"—that is, when the initial novelty of a new media experience settles into the background of mundane old media practices. The ethnographic work involved participant observation, interviews and scenarios of use, and app walk throughs conducted in 2018–2019. The research was developed in response to participation in *Pokémon GO* playing in Badalona, Spain. We became particularly interested in the ways in which *Pokémon GO* was being adopted by health professionals as a form of digital health.

We argue that *Pokémon GO* represents a particular form of hybrid play that can be understood in terms of digital wayfaring and haptic play (Richardson & Hjorth, 2017). Digital wayfaring focuses on the embodied role of digital media in the material and social practices. It understands that the digital, material, and social are interwoven (Hjorth & Pink, 2014). Through overlays of the digital, material, and social, different techniques for world-building and place-making are created. In each specific cultural context, urban play functions differently. The haptic play of *Pokémon GO* can be seen to reflect ambient play—that is, the rhythms and routines of everyday life practices as they weave through and across digital, sensorial, and material worlds (Hjorth & Richardson, 2017; Richardson & Hjorth, 2019).

Haptic play acknowledges the importance of proprioception—the perception of the moving body and its material and sensory limits—as well as the significance of game "feel" in the ambient texture of play. In particular, through the *Pokémon GO* fieldwork, it became apparent that the role of mundane mobile media to offer inclusive and social ways in which to support older adults and non-normative body players. It is this particular phenomenon we would like to focus on in the chapter.

In order to explore the possibilities of *Pokémon GO* for older adults to play in the city, we begin with a discussion of *Pokémon GO* as an "old" media and how we can contextualize *Pokémon GO* as part of broader mobile game histories. We then reflect upon what it means to think about *Pokémon GO* in terms of quotidian health. Next, we discuss the role of haptic (touch screen) interfaces in allowing inclusive forms of play, especially by older adults or players with disabilities. This is followed by a discussion of the ethnographic fieldwork in which we focus on three key participants who bring different perspectives to understanding the possibilities of *Pokémon GO* as a vehicle for hybrid play and informal digital health.

Back to the future: old new media

In the streets of Badalona, north of Barcelona (Spain), it is not uncommon to see a digital wayfarer in the form of a *Pokémon GO* player. As a game, *Pokémon GO* does not discriminate across age groups—rather, as we find in our ethnographies with players, it was often deployed as a key intergenerational tool. Sometimes, as in the case of grandmother Sofia, a grandson teaches his older family members; other times, it is vice versa. *Pokémon GO* also generates new rhythms and textures of affect in the quotidian streets of Badalona; mundane trips to the market could make for a playful encounter with a fellow player. The play of *Pokémon GO* in 2019 is significantly different from the initial modes of play when it was released in 2016. It is more complicated in its intricacies of intergenerational care and mundane digital wayfaring. But first, to better understand these emergent complexities of hybrid play, we need to go "back to the future" when it was first launched.

Over the first weeks of July 2016, a strange phenomenon started to unfold in many parts of the world.[1] A mobile game went viral. Streets in cities like Barcelona, Melbourne, Singapore, and New York began to fill with groups of people engaged in choreographies of digital wayfaring as part of the AR game, *Pokémon GO*. The game popularized the digital overlay technique of AR in which real-time peripatetic movement converges with digital play. As de Souza e Silva (2016) notes, hybrid reality games "are not new" (p. 20), as their genealogy can be mapped back over two decades within art and research communities—epitomized by Blast Theory's *Can You See Me Now?* (2001). For de Souza e Silva, hybridity describes the movement between material and digital worlds.

In the first year, the rise and fall of *Pokémon GO* provided a critical lens allowing us to focus anew on the role of playful media as an important part of sociality (Hjorth & Richardson, 2017). The games cast a different light on various topics including darker debates around location-aware technologies in constructions of privacy (Coldewey, 2016; Cunningham, 2016), mobile media commodification (Evangelho, 2016), and risk and surveillance (Machkovech, 2016). It has also, conversely, provided insight into the expanding social, cultural, and creative dimensions of play (Isbister, 2016; Mäyrä, 2012).

The success of *Pokémon GO* lies in its coalescence of various technological and cultural trajectories emerging from the playful turn, or what Raessens' (2006) terms the ludification of culture. The craze was so prolific that *Pokémon GO* overtook porn as the most searched term on the internet globally. Over the first few weeks, media outlets everywhere scrambled to have their say on this playful phenomenon—encompassing a variety of perspectives including wellbeing (the fact that the game encouraged pedestrian movement with concomitant positive effects on mental and physical health) and the social dimensions of games (highlighting that games are fundamentally *social*), to the darker debates around safety, surveillance, racism (i.e. redlining), and risk.

These debates around mobile media are not new—rather, they can be understood as part of broader new media arguments that render technology the scapegoat for political polemics. As media scholars such as Wendy Chun (2016) remind us, understanding new media isn't about chasing the rapidly growing cycle of obsolescence. Rather, new media are most interesting when they recede from the spotlight and become absorbed as part of everyday and habitual rituals of mobility and communication.

And so, as the dust settled on the "ludified perfect storm" of *Pokémon GO* and it became forgotten as "old" media, a more compelling phenomenon began to emerge. Indeed, mobile games and apps become most interesting when they become mundane and part of everyday quotidian life. Of relevance to the discussion of *Pokémon GO* in this chapter, technologies like AR and Virtual Reality (VR) are increasingly being used to innovate in health solutions—especially to create multisensorial tools for aging well and ameliorating against the effects of dementia and phobia (Costa et al., 2014; Jakob & Collier, 2017). This unexpected use suggests that rather than developing new and untested mobile apps to deal with health issues, solutions can be found in the social and embodied affordances of "old" and more established media like *Pokémon GO*. That is, we can learn from the lived experiences as highlighted by ethnographic approaches.

The experience of digital wayfaring is further complicated within a hybrid reality game. In particular, sometimes the rules of the physical are not easily adapted into the game world and vice versa, and the game activity can defamiliarize the routine habits of urban mobility. In this context, there has been significant work within what has been called the New Games Movement by play design scholars (Pearce et al., 2007). Often referred to as the New Arcade (and sometimes the Modern Arcade, Indie Arcade, Neo Arcade, and DIY Arcade), it is a cultural movement that celebrates the locational gathering and playing of contemporary videogames in social and public contexts.

Urban games can be mapped through a variety of earlier manifestations such as the *flâneur* and the 1960s Situationist International (SI) techniques for reinventing the urban through the *dérive* (de Souza e Silva & Hjorth, 2009). In the 1970s and 1980s, the New Games Movement, currently experiencing a revival, sought to popularize cooperative and creative urban play, and deliberately challenged and disrupted the mundane and familiar by transforming public spaces into playful places. These games are often designed by independent makers and seek to highlight and challenge the collective and physical dimensions of game play.

However, as Miguel Sicart (2014) has highlighted, many of the festivals and events that feature such games often reveal the inequities of public playfulness, especially when players are required to challenge conventional ways of being in urban spaces. Here, it is important to highlight the uneven ways players come to the game space and the complexity of gameplay as it is interwoven with our cultural and corporeal "situatedness" in the world. Certain bodies have more latitude to deviate from normalized practices, while some—as Katie Salen Tekinbaş (2017) argues through the case study of *Pokémon GO*—don't. Salen turns to the potential disempowerment and marginalization that affects players of AR games and mobile location-based apps such as *Pokémon GO*. She asks, what can *Pokémon GO* teach us about mobility, accessibility, race, and privilege? For example, cities become effectively remapped via redlining techniques in which certain culturally diverse areas are less populated by virtual Pokémon than predominantly Anglo neighborhoods, making the game's objectives more difficult to achieve. It is also clearly more dangerous for some bodies to be in some places at certain times, and there is undoubtedly a hierarchy of risk at work that acts upon our bodies differently, depending on our age, gender, ethnicity, or social milieu.

Pokémon GO, therefore, requires users to explore and remake their (sub)urban environment as a mode of hybridized digital wayfaring, enacting a form of gameplay that is underscored by issues of racial inequity and the relative freedom people have to move playfully through their neighborhoods and cities. Sometimes, the inequities of our embodiment can be playfully resisted and subverted, while for others they reinforce existing boundaries and delimit our wayfaring practices in digital, actual, hybrid, and augmented realities. The rise of urban games, epitomized by *Pokémon GO*, can be contextualized through the last two decades of game and play design in which hybrid, layered, and multifaceted experiences of place, presence, and communication have emerged. But *Pokémon GO* also does something particular; it coalesces the possibilities for games to promote social change and health benefits as we discuss next.

Pokémon GO: quotidian digital health

The positive health dimensions of *Pokémon GO* are only now starting to emerge after three years since its launch. As Tim Althoff et al. (2016) note, games like *Pokémon GO* encourage physical activity as part of the game play. In the study, Althoff et al. were able to map ways in which exercise had increased in low activity participants. However, their study was conducted when *Pokémon GO* was first launched. They argued for the need of longitudinal understandings—something our study does through ethnography.

Pokémon GO has attracted many studies around its role as vehicle for intergenerational literacy, sharing, and informal health (Lindqvist et al., 2018; Militello et al., 2018). Hino et al. (2019) conducted a 10-month ethnographic study in Yokohama in Japan to explore the ways in which middle-aged and older adults were exercising with *Pokémon GO* (2019). In another clinical study in Japan, Kato et al. (2017) explored the role of *Pokémon GO* in encouraging to adventure outside for patients suffering the condition of *hikikomori* (a severe form of social isolation that can involve years of living in one room). Here, the game allows players to venture into a reconstituted world-as-playground mediated by the screen, engaging with familiar routines of gameplay in public places previously perceived as risky or strange. Yet while *Pokémon GO* can address the importance of exercise in dealing with mental health issues, it doesn't necessarily remedy the problem of social isolation within the culturally specific context of Japan, as people may play near one another without communicating. As one client noted in the Kato et al. study, "Most people are independently staring at their own individual screens in parks. We Japanese, unlike Westerners, don't chat with strangers!" (p. 75).

Hikikomori has often been associated with the negative effects of videogaming; the emergence of the condition occurred at the same time videogames became popular in Japan. It also emerged at the end of the economic downturn during the late 1980s, in which the salaried tradition of employment ceased to be a secure career option for men. And yet, as psychotherapists note, using AR videogames like *Pokémon GO* worked to encourage pedestrian adventures into the outside world through the familiar tropes of games and gameplay. However, as they note, such games must be employed in conjunction with other therapeutic techniques that foster sociality.

This study resonates with Jeanette Pols' (2012) findings about digital health in aged care—it only works when conducted in unison with face-to-face or co-located interaction. As Pols notes "care at a distance"—or the "closeness of technology"—needs to be centered around a diversity of prosocial practices. While Pols' study was conducted in formal care settings, the role of mobile media used in more informal contexts can be seen as an extension of "care at a distance." This echoes work in mobile communication fields that considers how networked media interfaces extend and enhance, rather than replace, co-located social interaction, such as studies on the informal uses of technologies enacted by families, in which intergenerational connections are enhanced through digital play (Sinanan & Hjorth, 2018).

In what follows, we explore the success of *Pokémon GO* further as a form of digital play that is both hybrid and ambient and which affords ways in which to rethink health and inclusion. We argue that *Pokémon GO* not only encourages for collative play and exercise but also an informal mode of care at a distance.

Haptic play for inclusive play

The uptake of *Pokémon GO* by elderly populations highlights the importance of taking haptic play seriously. The game demands particular haptic gestures (i.e. the flicking of the pokéball) that invite the knowing body to translate lived experience to the medium of the screen. As the experience of one participant in our study—a grandmother named Sofia—illustrated, once her grandson had taught her some basics about playing the game, she enjoyed the ways in which her corporeal experiences could be adapted into the world of *Pokémon GO* gameplay via the haptic screen; her phone would shudder when she came near Pokéstops—the game was literally "felt" through the body. Sofia offers just one example of intergenerational play and the affordances of touchscreen games for older users.

In fieldwork with participants in Badalona from 2018 to 2019, we explored the haptic engagements of *Pokémon GO* (Figure 9.1). Badalona has declining birth rates and growing aging populations (18% are aged +65) that are predominantly cared for by familial networks. It has been dubbed a "Silver City" for its innovative governance strategies for aged care and support. Badalona has pioneered and is recognized as one of the first integrated care delivery models organized through the city council and operationalized through a public organization called Badalona Serveis Assistencials (BSA).

BSA is an integrated health and social care organization with entirely public capital, whose unique holder is the City Council of Badalona. BSA manages seven Primary Care Centers, a 120-bed acute care Hospital ("Hospital Municipal de Badalona"), a 220-bed intermediate care Hospital ("Centre Sociosanitari el Carme"), an integrated Homecare Unit ("Servei d'Atenció Integral Domiciliària"), a Center for Sexual and Reproductive Health, two Community Mental Health Centers for children, two Community Mental Health for adults, one Center focused on addictions, and one Day Hospital for Mental Health issues. It provides care to a total population of 535,000 inhabitants in the most populated suburban area of Barcelona.

Figure 9.1 A *Pokémon GO* play session in Badalona, Spain. Copyright: Larissa Hjorth.

In order to develop a complex grasp of how *Pokémon GO* has been adopted in Badalona and elsewhere, we focus on the hybrid play of haptic media and the deployment of ethnographic methods such as walking interviews (following participants as they "walk and talk" their play practices), scenarios of use (modeling typical modalities of play), and haptic playability (interpreting the embodied dimensions of play).

Let's turn to 67-year-old widow and nurse Sofia[2] who has lived in the Catalonian town of Badalona in Spain for all her life. After losing her husband to cancer a decade ago, Sofia initially found it hard to overcome her grief and depression. Her daughters and grandchildren have helped in this transition. In particular, Sofia is especially close to her seven-year-old grandson, Diego. They do many activities together, constantly sharing intergenerational skills. It was Diego who first introduced Sofia to *Pokémon GO*. As they wandered the streets of Badalona together, he would show her the digital overlays and virtual objects perceived through the game, reinventing Sofia's everyday experiences of familiar and mundane spaces. He taught Sofia how to flick the haptic screen to capture Pokémon. After playing together in the beachside streets of Badalona, he asked her to collect them while he was at school. And, so, Sofia did.

Before long, Sofia began to enjoy collecting the pokéballs[3] herself, so she opened her own *Pokémon GO* account. She would wander the streets capturing Pokémon, and trips to the market or shops became *Pokémon GO* adventures in which she would navigate alternative routes to capture more of the virtual creatures. At first, she would fight in gym raids but, not knowing the strategy, would lose every time. Then, she started to notice other players at the sites where gyms were placed. She started talking to the players. They were young and old, male and female. They shared successful strategies. She learned how to fight collaboratively and win.

When she first began playing, Sofia felt shy meeting players. But then, over time and through the playful and social affordances of the game, she began to see regular players. They would stop and talk to share stories and adventures that wove the game play into everyday life. They would share stories about boss raids, and they would bond over their enjoyment of the game. At first, they shared stories and techniques and would organize meet-ups via WhatsApp.[4] However, the platform didn't accommodate the big groups (capped at 254 people) that were constantly changing, so they started using the Telegram app[5] to share stories and information about meet-ups. This allowed for thousands of players to coordinate meet-ups.

Sofia now has a *Pokémon GO* bracelet (called *Pokémon GO* Plus, see Figure 9.2) which allows her to collect Pokémon without needing to constantly attend to the mobile screen. In the mornings, she collects the balls and hatches eggs as she walks thousands of steps. In the afternoons, after a rest, Sofia ventures out for more social *Pokémon GO* meet-ups. She loves the way she has learned to master the technology and the way in which *Pokémon GO* brings different people together in a fun and playful way. She feels fit and socially engaged in her community, and she is an outstanding super-cool grandmother in the eyes of her grandson, Diego.

Sofia's story is not an exception. Rather, this is an increasingly common story, in which existing technologies are being incidentally repurposed and deployed to achieve digital health solutions. In Badalona, with its innovative and integrated healthcare system centralized through the city council, *Pokémon GO* is being recommended by social workers as a way for clients to enhance two key dimensions of aging well— *exercise* and *social inclusion*. Ethnographic exploration of these lived experiences highlights the need for digital health to focus more carefully on the social dimensions of aging well rather than just having a reactive solution in the form of yet another new-fangled app. Instead, we can learn a lot from "old" or established media experiences like *Pokémon GO* and how they can be reinvented, demonstrating the importance of understanding habitudes of social practice in designing for

Figure 9.2 Sofia getting ready to catch some *Pokémon GO*. Copyright: Piera Jimenez.

digital health solutions—especially in terms of aging well. Haptic games teach us about the possibilities of engaging various vulnerable agencies in different ways.

The power of *Pokémon GO* to connect generations and to provide alternative forms of social inclusion is not lost on 26-year-old social worker José. Over the period of the ethnography, we interviewed José numerous times for his insights as a social worker. José works at Badalona Servicios Asistenciales and is an avid *Pokémon GO* player. He has witnessed firsthand how the game can help support rehabilitation—so much so that he now recommends clients use the game to help foster social inclusion and regular exercise. We met José at one of the local *Pokémon GO* gym raids one early summer evening. *Pokémon GO* gym raids are coordinated through the Telegram app. Playing together means that players have greater strength and are more likely to win; therefore, collaboration is an active part of successful game play.

At the *Pokémon GO* gym gathering, we also met Mateo who was carrying two smartphones—one for his mom and one for him. Mateo and his mom use *Pokémon GO* as a way to stay connected in playful ways. Sometimes, they go to meet-ups together, but at other times, when his mom feels less mobile (she is in her seventies), Mateo takes both the phones out and plays for her. While much is written about "parallel play" in terms of early childhood development, there is something to be said for this activity in adult sociality—especially in terms of the ways in which mobile media encourage copresence. Here, copresence can be understood as the fostering of mediated intimacy via mobile media when physical co-location isn't possible. Matsuda (2009), for example, explores the concept of copresence in his investigation of the mobile phone as a "mom in the pocket."

The haptic affordances of *Pokémon GO* allow for different knowledges of the body to become integrated into our proprioceptive awareness. It is not by accident that haptic games like *Pokémon GO* are being taken up by a broad spectrum of players including the elderly, as the vibrating and haptic affordances effectively privilege embodied feelings of touch (rather than audiovisuality typical of many media interfaces), and the experience of playing becomes part of a "felt" and direct remaking of the urban environment and the new communicative possibilities of mobile play. By coalescing multisensorial feelings of the body, *Pokémon GO* illustrates the possibilities for haptic games to provide new ways of being in the world through touch-based screen cultures.

José is a long-time fan of *Pokémon GO*, having played various iterations of Pokémon across multiple platforms. However, what José especially enjoyed about the mobile AR version was that it enticed people out of their homes to the streets. For José, the group challenges of *Pokémon GO* such as gym raids helped to build collaboration and dialogue between players. The success of *Pokémon GO,* for José, is the fact that they have developed and enhanced the objectives beyond the initial goals of hunting Pokémon and completing the Pokédex. He notes that when *Pokémon GO* first started:

> ...the game was quite lonely but, now, after different updates, (it) has become a much more social game—a game that now requires more people to play especially if you want to get the strongest Pokémon of the game, which are basically obtained from legendary incursions. We have gone from a game where you were just by yourself, to a game that now involves team play.

We asked José why he first started thinking about deploying *Pokémon GO* in his social work. He indicated that it began by accident with one of José's clients, a boy with autism who had significant communication difficulties. The client's parents noticed that their son seemed able to express emotions and feelings more freely when watching cartoons at home. One day out of curiosity, José showed the child *Pokémon GO*, and observed an immediate change in his behavior and affective engagement. As José noted:

> You can quickly capture that spark of emotions, that spark in your eyes, that something had generated some kind of interest. People with autism tend to be quite apathetic, and it can be difficult to interact with them.

José talked with the parents about how well the child had responded when they played *Pokémon GO* together. The parents bought their son a mobile phone to play *Pokémon GO* and, the next time José met with them, things had changed dramatically. Each afternoon, the parents and child would go out to wander and hunt Pokémon, and their son reacted positively, expressing interest and enjoyment. José communicated the findings to his organization, Badalona Servicios Asistenciales, at a joint meeting with the diverse clinicians' group (which included all services including home care and palliative care teams). The various teams were interested in piloting how *Pokémon GO* could be used with other clients that experienced social isolation issues.

Badalona Servicios Asistenciales are known for technological innovation around health and social services. And so it made sense that, as an organization, they would be willing to test the possibilities of *Pokémon GO* as a way of enhancing dimensions of health and social care. As José observed:

> In our center, for example, there is a group of pediatricians who did a pediatric blog for many years now and have now made a mobile app. This already has more than 20,000 downloads and has won many awards. So in the center we experiment with the technology and how this can help us improve our way of working... It was not until later (long after the meeting in which the clinicians discussed *Pokémon GO*) where we had the opportunity to experiment with this technology in another type of situation. A colleague returned from another clinical session and began to talk about a patient who had been in the house for a long time because of depression due to the death of her husband... Her husband had died of cancer and the client was taking much longer than usual to get over the mourning process. They spent their time locked up in the house. The nurse felt that maybe *Pokémon GO* could be trialed but both the nurse and client did not use mobile technology very much and felt a bit confused by the process.

José assisted the nurse in learning how to play *Pokémon GO*, and she successfully instructed her client who began playing the game on a regular basis. José and his team then continued to explore how *Pokémon GO* might be incorporated as part of their general social services as a way to foster social inclusion. From those experiences, *Pokémon GO* became "a practice fully integrated into our DNA"—not just José's social services center but also the rest of the BAS primary care centers. BAS now have clinical sessions that incorporate *Pokémon GO* every afternoon for interested clients, where they provide assistance with technology use and the game's rules and mechanics. This allows people to gather together over a common interest and activity that emphasizes wellbeing and playful sociality rather than focusing on issues of health and isolation. As José notes:

> To (our) surprise, we learned of other center professionals who were also players of *Pokémon GO*, even some of them that had started to refer their patients to the game… For me personally, while I haven't kept track of the numbers, there are a lot of cases where the fact of playing this game has greatly favored the inclusion of people with difficulties relating socially in a safe way. The game allows you to fight against social exclusion or isolation. We also know about clients with depression who are very locked in at home but are forced to come to the streets and interact with people because of the *Pokémon GO* raids that are core to the game play… Increasingly we see elderly users with a mobile using *Pokémon GO or* even with the *Pokémon GO* bracelet out hunting the Pokémon… Currently there is a *Pokémon GO* Badalona group on Telegram which has almost 1000 people and many of these people did not know each other before they connected through the game. *Pokémon GO* encourages a collective resilience, in which people need to work together to succeed in the raids.

As cities continue to grow with aging populations that increasingly live alone, José is concerned with how people can be supported, particularly in terms of social inclusion. José talks about the BAS program "Neighbors by Neighbors"—a micro-activist initiative that seeks to empower community members to take care of each other. In the articulation of "Neighbors by Neighbors," *Pokémon GO* plays a key role, as elderly players can keep a friendly eye on each other. In this program, José and his colleagues have included two or three older people playing in the neighborhood, along with each of their primary care centers, to create an informal social system of careful surveillance (Hjorth et al., 2018). As José concludes:

> It is also a good system to share contact information because everyone is registered in Telegram. In this way, it is no longer the institutions that oversee these citizens, but the citizens who are vigilant and cared for by each other. We hope this program will become a bigger reality, and that we are able to move forward in innovative ways to develop social inclusion opportunities for all ages of society.

Another of our participants, 36-year-old male Santiago, lives with his mother, with whom he has a very close relationship, especially after Santiago's father left when Santiago was young. Santiago started to play *Pokémon GO* when it was first launched a few years ago and hasn't stopped since. Santiago and his mother have two dogs and they frequently take walks along the beach or on the mountain nearby. As *Pokémon GO* rewards walking (as a way to incubate Pokémon eggs—the more distance covered, the more Pokémon can be hatched and, thus, collected by the player), this dimension of the gameplay has become seamlessly integrated into their everyday life practices. As Santiago observes:

> My mother started playing *Pokémon GO* when she realized that it was a way to kill time. In addition to having the dogs to walk, she is a little overweight and it was fun exercise. She initially thought it was nonsense, since she is 70, but then she liked it more and we used it to stay out longer together. She accompanies me many times; even though she is in charge of the dogs in the mornings, the reality is that many evenings she comes with me and we play together.

These felicitous anecdotes of *Pokémon GO* play narrated by Sofia, José, and Santiago reveal an array of experiential play modalities that are enabled by the haptic, interactive, and locative capacities of mobile smartphone touchscreens. The beneficial social and corporeal effects of the game are authentic and potentially enduring precisely because of the way the gameplay fits comfortably and organically into the rhythms and patterns of daily life. Here, digital health, hybrid play, digital wayfaring, and haptics come together in ways that can provide inventive solutions for quotidian challenges.

Conclusion

In this chapter, we have argued that *Pokémon GO* represents a particular configuration of play, incorporating hybridity, touch, ambience, sociality, and digital wayfaring. As noted elsewhere, haptic technologies such as smartphones are impacting upon our sensorial experience of being-in-the-world, being-with-others, and being-with-media (Richardson & Hjorth, 2019). Informed by and informing this approach, many researchers are increasingly focusing on the intimate, social, and playful nature of mobile touchscreens.

The role of haptic and mobile technologies is especially significant when it comes to vulnerable agencies—in particular, as is the focus of this chapter, older adults and disabled. Mobile games that rely on touch-based interaction are fundamentally mimetic; that is, the mode of engagement calls upon our embodied memory of familiar actions (such as throwing a ball). In this way, such games do not require expert gameplay skills and are easily accommodated into our everyday corporeal schematics and sensorial knowledges.

Throughout our participants' stories of collaborative urban play practices, we can see how the AR game *Pokémon GO* effectively enables experiential modalities of hybridity (through the coalescence of digital, networked, and physical ways of knowing), digital wayfaring (as this hybrid experience generates a new kind of collective place-making), haptic play (through the tactile intimacy of the touchscreen and "feel" of the game), ambient play (as the game becomes diffused through the embodied routines of everyday life), and social play (via the embedment of collaborative action in the game's mechanics). Understanding and interpreting the significance of mobile games, and location-based AR games in particular, require a robust grasp of these complex and intervolved affordances.

Notes

1 In the US alone, it has been estimated there has been 7.5 million downloads since its July 6 release, which Bliss (2016) argues constitutes a "bonafide" craze.
2 Please note that all names are pseudonyms.
3 Pokéballs are used to catch Pokémon; they can be collected at Pokéstops (virtual places located in the real world), or purchased from the in-game store with Pokécoins. Pokémon Gyms (also located at points of interest on the game's map) can be captured by battling in collaboration with other players. Players are also alerted to nearby raid battles that take place at Gyms, and involve defeating a powerful raid boss; you can either play solo or join a raid with other players.
4 WhatsApp is an SMS app that allows users to text message, voice message, group chat, send photos and videos, and share one's location with other users.
5 Telegram is a cloud-based instant messaging and VOIP service with over 100 million users. Users can send messages and exchange photos, videos, stickers, audio, and files of any type.

References

Althoff, T., White R. W., & Horvitz, E. (2016). Influence of Pokémon Go on physical activity: Study and implications. *Journal of Medical Internet Research*, 18(12), e315. URL: http://www.jmir.org/2016/12/e315/

Bliss, L. (2016). Pokémon GO has created a New Kind of Flâneur. *City Lab*, July 12. https://www.citylab.com/life/2016/07/pokemon-go-flaneur-baudelaire/490796/. Accessed 10 June 2019.

Chun, W. (2016). *Updating to remain the same*. Cambridge, MA: MIT Press.

Coldewey, D. (2016). *Sen. Al Franken questions Niantic over Poké privacy policy*. Retrieved from https://techcrunch.com/2016/07/12/sen-al-franken-questions-niantic-over-pokeprivacy-policy/

Costa, C., Carmenates, S., Madeira, L., & Stanghellini, G. (2014). Phenomenology of atmospheres. The felt meanings of clinical encounters. *Journal of Psychopathology*, 20(4), 351–357.

Cunningham, A. (2016). *iOS version of Pokémon GO is a possible privacy trainwreck (Updated)*. Retrieved from http://arstechnica.com/gaming/2016/07/pokemon-go-on-ios-gets-full-access-to-your-google-account/

de Souza e Silva, A. (2006). From cyber to hybrid: Mobile technologies as interfaces of hybrid spaces. *Space and Culture*, 9(3), 261–278.

de Souza e Silva, A. (2016). *Pokémon GO as an HRG*: Mobility, sociability, and surveillance in hybrid spaces. *Mobile Media & Communication*, 5(1), 20–23.

de Souza e Silva, A., & Hjorth, L. (2009). Urban spaces as playful spaces: A historical approach to mobile urban games. *Simulation and & Gaming*, 40(5), 602–625.

Evangelho, J. (2016, July 10). "*Pokémon GO*" is about to surpass Twitter in daily active users on Android. *Forbes*. Retrieved from https://www.forbes.com/sites/jasonevangelho/2016/07/10/pokemon-go-about-to-surpass-twitter-in-daily-active-users/#8adbe735d3ec

Hino, K., Asami, Y., & Lee, J. S. (2019). Step counts of middle-aged and elderly adults for 10 months before and after the release of *Pokémon GO* in Yokohama, Japan. *Journal of Medical Internet Research*, 21(2), e10724. DOI: 10.2196/10724.

Hjorth, L., & Pink, S. (2014). New visualities and the digital wayfarer: Reconceptualizing camera phone photography. In: G. Goggin & L. Hjorth (Eds.), *The Routledge companion to mobile media* (pp. 488–498). New York: Routledge.

Hjorth, L., & Richardson, I. (2017). Pokémon GO: Mobile media play, place-making and digital wayfaring. *Mobile Media & Communication*, 5(1), 3–14. DOI: 10.1177/2050157916680015.

Hjorth, L., Horst, H., & Pink, S. (2018) Privacy at the margins. *International Journal of Communication*, 12.

Isbister, K. (2016, July 16). Why Pokémon GO became an instant phenomenon. *The Conversation*. Retrieved from http://the-conversation.com/why-pokemon-go-became-an-instant-phenomenon-62412.

Jakob, A., & Collier, L. (2017). Sensory enrichment for people living with dementia: increasing the benefits of multisensory environments in dementia care through design. *Design for Health*, 1(1), 115–133, DOI: 10.1080/24735132.2017.1296274.

Kato, T. A, Teo, A. R., Tateno, M., Watabe, M., Kubo, H., & Kanba, S. (2017). Can Pokémon GO rescue shut-ins (hikikomori) from their isolated world? *Psychiatry and Clinical Neurosciences*, 71(1), 75–76. DOI: 10.1111/pcn.12481.

Lindqvist, A. K., Castelli, D., Hallberg, J., & Rutberg, S. (2018). The praise and price of Pokémon GO: A qualitative study of children's and parents' experiences. *Journal of Medical Internet Research: Serious Games*, 6(1), e1. DOI: 10.2196/games.8979.

Machkovech, S. (2016, November 7). Armed muggers use Pokémon GO to find victims. *Ars Technica*. Retrieved from http://arstechnica.com/gaming/2016/07/armed-muggers-use-pokemon-go-to-find-victims/

Matsuda, M. (2009). Mobile media and the transformation of family. In: G. Goggin & L. Hjorth (Eds.), *Mobile Technologies*. London: Routledge. DOI: 10.4324/9780203884317.

Mäyrä, F. (2012). Playful mobile communication: Services supporting the culture of play. *Interactions: Studies in Communication & Culture*, 3(1), 55–70.

Militello, L. K., Hanna, N., & Nigg, C. R. (2018). Pokémon GO within the context of family health: Retrospective study. *Journal of Medical Internet Research: Pediatrics and Parenting*, 1(2), e10679. DOI: 10.2196/10679.

Pearce, C., Fullerton, T., Fron, J., & Morie, J. F. (2007). Sustainable play: Toward a new games movement for the digital age. *Games and Culture*, 2(3), 261–278.

Pols, J. (2012). *Care at a distance*. Amsterdam: Amsterdam University Press.

Raessens, J. (2006). Playful identities, or the ludification of culture. *Games and Culture*, 1(1), 52–57.

Richardson, I., & Hjorth, L. (2017). Mobile media, domestic play and haptic ethnography. *New Media & Society*, 19(10), 1653–1667, http://journals.sagepub.com/doi/full/10.1177/1461444817717516

Richardson, I., & Hjorth, L. (2019). Haptic play: Rethinking media cultures and practices. *Convergence*, 25(1), 3–5. DOI: 10.1177/1354856518815275.

Sicart, M. (2014). *Play matters.* Cambridge, MA: MIT Press.

Sinanan, J., & Hjorth, L. (2018). Careful families and care as 'kinwork': An intergenerational study of families and digital media use in Melbourne. In: B. Neves & C. Casimiro (Eds.), *Connecting families? Information & communication technologies in a life course perspective* (pp. 181–200). Bristol: Policy Press.

Salen Tekinbaş, K. (2017). Afraid to roam: The unlevel playing field of Pokémon Go. *Mobile Media & Communication.* DOI: 10.1177/2050157916677865.

10 How we deal with dark souls
The aesthetic category as a method

Cameron Kunzelman

In an interview about game design, David S. Heineman (2015) asks Eugene Jarvis, the creator of 1981's influential game *Defender*, about the craft of game design. In the middle of the interview, the idea of fine-grained design to maintain player interest comes up, and Heineman formulates a question about how a designer can tweak a game to constantly generate tension in the player. Jarvis says, "When I sit down to a game, I want to play it intuitively. This is like the Steve Jobs school of gaming where the point should be obvious; the creators should never have to tell you anything" (Heineman, 2015, p. 66). Later, Jarvis declares: "It's funny how the social environment of the era is also expressed in game design. If you're in the age of self-esteem, then everyone gets a trophy and it's wonderful" (p. 66). While these two positions are clearly part of the same train of thought, their juxtaposition should give us pause. Which one is it? If the best games are immediately accessible and transparent to players, then how is it possible for particular social relations to be fully immanent to them? The former claim implies that games can be eternal and transcendent, while the latter claim suggests that a transcendence is always overwhelmed by the culture a game emerged from.

The paradox I am pointing to in Jarvis has a parallel within games culture more broadly. Are games eternally able to communicate their content through universal mechanics, or are they so embedded in their cultural context that they cannot be extracted from them? In this chapter, I approach this question via Sianne Ngai's (2012) concept of "aesthetic categories" to discuss how modulations of aesthetics, and the attending game design ideas within those aesthetics, are used to generate subjectivities under particular commanding regimes. In this model, players are caught in a web of assumptions and normalized behaviors that stretch out beyond any single relationship with a given game and extend through a field of relations that encompass sets of mechanics, genre formations, control mechanisms, and a number of other shared qualities between different specific games. Further, I argue that Ngai's aesthetic categories are similar in operation to the concept of the diagram put forward by philosopher Gilles Deleuze. Aesthetic categories and diagrams provide an explanatory path beyond traditional theoretical and applied work around games, and also provide a way of understanding games as cutting across social and personal interactions. Their hybridity is such that they are not merely objects that operate on subjects, but instead they are shifting relational things that operate within broader categories of aesthetic experience. For this chapter, this hybridity is taken as a given, and the work of game studies is that of attempting to best demonstrate the already-hybrid of all modes of play. Aesthetic category theory allows us to better discuss that hybridity and to understand the ways that games, and their culture, normalize and standardize how players see themselves in relation to the games they play.

I present a case study in the form of the "soulsborne" genre, which emerges from the *Dark Souls* franchise and the game *Bloodborne* to consider how aesthetic categories cohere, shift, and then alter in order to encompass new developments in aesthetic production. The soulsborne is characterized by several factors: deliberate controls and an above-average difficulty derived from those controls, an ability to constantly re-attempt these difficult moments, and punishing battles that make every moment of progress something that is won from the machine. They are also characterized as having opaque narratives that must be puzzled together by players. As many reviews that I will analyze later remark upon, it is a genre that allows players to valorize their own actions in relationship to the game, media, and social context around soulsborne games. As I discuss, this interfaces with the social and technical aspects of games, which necessitates a broader understanding of what this game genre might be. If *Dark Souls* and its attending genre of the soulsborne operate as an aesthetic category that normalizes certain things in the design and reception of video games, then what is the mechanism through which it appears and begins to proliferate? Diagrams can help us here. This operates in strong distinction to many of the historical assumptions in the field of game studies that see games as a finite set of inputs emanating from objects that produce outputs in the form of their players (Galloway, 2006; Bogost, 2007; Gee, 2007). In sum, this chapter offers an analytic that looks to aesthetics and tropes of game design in order to argue for game types and game genres as modes of arrangement and discipline that will fundamentally give us better access to descriptions of games, how we become players, and what that play is in service to.

Aesthetic categories

Aesthetic categories are specific modes of aesthetics that encourage certain worldviews and ways of understanding the self in relation to media and the world of that media. In *Our Aesthetic Categories*, Ngai (2012) claims that the zany, the cute, and the interesting "are the [categories] best suited for grasping how aesthetic experience has been transformed by the hyper-commodified, information-saturated, performance-driven conditions of late capitalism" (Ngai, 2012, p. 1). Since these three categories "index …

the system's most socially binding processes" (Ngai, 2012, p. 1), they provide Ngai with the most fruitful way of tracing lines of alliance between aesthetics and subjectivation under capitalism. In Ngai's work on aesthetic categories, she continually makes the claim that particular aesthetics are ways of positioning oneself in the world and in relationship to other processes.

When Ngai writes about the zany, she invokes Lucille Ball's famous physical and exhaustive routines from *I Love Lucy* as being emblematic of the aesthetic category. The structure of *I Love Lucy* exists, Ngai argues, in order to "get zany" (Ngai, 2012, p. 175) and create a context in which Ball must put on new outfits and take on new roles "as if to suggest a new instability in the postindustrial United States between the activities of performing a role and working a job" (Ngai, 2012, p. 178). While Ngai dedicates a substantial chapter to this analysis, what I am interested in here is the relationship between the show *I Love Lucy* and the aesthetic category of the zany. The characters, their actions, and the expectations around them create conditions that wrap the viewer up in a particular aesthetic regime that normalizes certain behaviors. It is for this exact reason that I find aesthetic category analysis to be a fruitful method for game studies to adopt. If the zany, for example, directly correlates to a subject position under capitalism and a demand for a viewer to understand themselves in a certain way via an alliance with Lucy, then other mass media objects must also have attending aesthetic categories. Or, to take the claim further, certain aesthetic categories could be so singular in their eruption into the aesthetic field that they could ground an aesthetic category all on their own.

Gilles Deleuze's (1988) concept of the diagram is an important attending philosophical concept that makes Ngai's aesthetic category theory more robust as a method.[1] The Deleuzian diagram, as explained in the next section, offers a clear theory for understanding the mechanisms through which players are constructed *for* games and how video games as a discipline are constructed by a large assemblage of recognition from their players. From this position, we then begin to see the player not as a node for output or a mere actor that strives for entertainment. Instead, the diagram offers us the ability to render sensible the ways that games set the parameters of existence for players.

Assemblage theory and the Deleuzian diagram

If aesthetic categories are particular modes through which we engage with games, or understand our engagement with games, then diagrams offer the best mechanistic explanation for how these aesthetic categories come to ground themselves in our lives and proliferate through the world. My particular lineage of diagrams is indebted to Deleuzian assemblage theory, so it will be productive to begin with the idea of the assemblage and build from there. The most well known in game studies is T.L. Taylor's (2009) call for a generic assemblage theory in "The Assemblage of Play." I use the word "generic" not to suggest that it is somehow incomplete or imprecise, but rather to denote that Taylor herself is evoking the varied history of the term and its use in the "work of science and technology scholars, sometimes tied to the work of Deleuze and Guattari, sometimes grounded in a particular form of artistic practice" (Taylor, 2009, p. 336). For Taylor, the value of assemblage thinking as a methodology is in making sure that we do not reduce the complexity of relations down into easy, given categories. She explains this position by stating that the "notion of assemblage is then deeply interwoven with the contextual analysis of games and play, one which situates them in their specific interrelations and practices" and extols the virtue of the method because it allows us to explore "the everyday, the mundane, [and] the 'found objects' that construct it" (Taylor, 2009, p. 333). Within Taylor's application, assemblage theory is as much a sensibility as it is a method.

Taylor's (2009) piece is in the minority when it comes to attempting to use assemblage theory as a method that messily works through relations between players and games alone. More common is the evocation of assemblage as a way to supplement issues of political economy in the largest scales of game, player, and market analyses. For example, Daniel Joseph (2013) applies Manuel DeLanda's (2010) version of assemblage theory as a contrastable method to the immaterial labor position put forth in Nick Dyer-Witheford and Greig de Peuter's *Games of Empire* (Joseph, 2013, p. 92). Felan Parker (2013), writing on the art world of the indie game, finds a similar value in DeLanda's interpretation of assemblage theory, suggesting that assemblage theory is able to capture the shifting nature of art worlds in a more accurate way due to its focus on how social organization of components alters over time. For my own part, I have presented assemblage theory as a way of working through philosophical games like *Bioshock 2* (Kunzelman, 2018) and video game adaptations of films (Kunzelman, 2016), arguing in both that we need to look to how game spaces arrange themselves in relation to players to actually speak to the specificity of those games.

Assemblage theory is good for describing the relation of games, but an important question for methods is asking why it is good. One reason is that assemblage theory is fundamentally attached to diagrammatics, the process through which materials transform into different shapes. Operating as a kind of metaphysics, assemblage theory is a distinct form of materialism that attempts to map isomorphic structures across different domains, and so it needs an explanation of how things such as eggs, video games, and volcanoes come into the recognizable and dynamic forms that we see them in. If all things in existence are responsible to the same basic organizing principles, then we need a robust explanatory apparatus about how the process of the world differentiates itself. Being content-agnostic, assemblage theory needs the diagram to explain shared forms and processes across discrete latter. My interest in pursuing diagrams here is as an explanatory device for aesthetic category theory.

The diagram as a concept within assemblage theory is most clearly described by Deleuze (1988) in his book *Foucault*. Highlighting a change in Foucault's thought over time, Deleuze remarks that the former's *Discipline and Punish* (1977) "marks a new stage" in which "a 'thing' like a prison is seen as an environmental formation" (p. 31). *Discipline and Punish* is both constructed from and demands attention toward the material realm. The book is undeniably about the materially *real* prison, but Deleuze suggests that the theorization extends further than an analysis of those composited materials. The shift in Foucault's thought that Deleuze attends to here is the differential between the *thing* of the material prison and the environmental function of that prison.

In Deleuze's reading, the prison does not merely function as a set of material boundaries operating on bodies, but instead as an "arrangement" that operates "abstractly as a machine that not only affects visible matter in general (a workshop, barracks, school or hospital as much as a prison) but also in general passes through every articulable function" (Deleuze, 1988, p. 34). Within this reading, a concept like Panopticism, or the self-discipline of people under the assumption that an authority will police them if they do not, is understood as a generalized effect that is concerned with "impos[ing] a particular conduct on a particular human multiplicity" (Deleuze, 1988, p. 34). This process that is "always concerned with unformed and unorganized matter and unformalized, unfinalized functions" is given the name of diagram (Deleuze, 1988, p. 34). For Deleuze, a diagram is "a map, a cartography that is coextensive with the whole social field. It is an abstract machine. [...] It is a machine that is almost blind and mute, even though it makes others see and speak" (Deleuze, 1988, p. 34). In the passage Deleuze refers to in order to build out his theory of the diagram, Foucault is clear that the Panopticon, the diagram he's outlining, "is not a dream building: it is the diagram of a mechanism [...] a figure of political technology that may and must be detached from a specific use" (Foucault, 1977, p. 205).

All of this builds to the striking idea that the diagram is a way of understanding how a material system can create abstractions of itself that continue beyond the initial emergence of that system. A thing exists, writes the pattern of its existence into a set of potentials, and that pattern goes on to process other material objects agnostic of their similarity or difference to the material relations that produced it. The prison becomes a mode of organization, of structuring life, and that structure becomes abstracted from its initial use and can then be implanted into contexts where it might not have originated. The work camp, the military base, places of education, and all manner of 18th- and 19th-century locations begin to look and feel like one another not because of a nefarious scheme toward order and organization by a shadowy cabal; instead, it is merely the process of these patterns landing in different zones where they can operate on the human body.

Ngai's (2012) aesthetic category theory and Deleuze's (1988) diagrams operate in tandem with one another. Diagrammatics allows us to properly think about how something like a "soulsborne" can be created: It is a set of mechanics, modes of storytelling, and player expectations that branch out and proliferate from the original object. Diagrams allow us to identify *which* of these is being transported from one game to another. Aesthetic category theory then gives us the tools to discuss how the aesthetic packaging, or the communicatory potential, of this free-floating diagram actually mediates a relationship between players and broader systems beyond mere games and gaming. With these two methodological ideas on our toolbelt, we can now talk about *Dark Souls* and the soulsborne genre.

How to understand the soulsborne

Dark Souls is a part of a long lineage of video games that have been released from development studio FromSoftware. The same company's *King's Field* franchise, which began with the Japanese-only *King's Field* released in 1994 for the PlayStation, is similarly a dark fantasy tale with the same obscure mechanics and opaque story that *Dark Souls* has become known for.[2] It was precisely these qualities that *Dark Souls* became famous for during its worldwide release. As Keza MacDonald and Jason Killingsworth (2016) note in their *You Died: The Dark Souls Companion*, the first people to key into the uniqueness of *Dark Souls* against the field of other games at the time were game reviewers. Upon receiving their review copies, quite a few writers hooked themselves into a group email that MacDonald named "The Chain of Pain" (MacDonald & Killingsworth, 2016, p. 38). While the world of *Dark Souls* has been wholly mapped and analyzed since 2011, the time before a wide release was a moment in which people had to swap stories and anecdotes with one another to piece together strategies and tactics for completing the game.

The game comprises two major sections, and both have multiple possible pathways to completion. In the first portion of the game, players need to make their way to two Bells of Awakening. One is on the top of a chapel at the summit of this part of the game, and the other is in a spider's nest hidden under a poison swamp. After ringing both bells, players traverse the trap-filled Sen's Fortress and are transported to Anor Londo, the city of the gods. From there, they receive an item called the Lordvessel, are tasked with destroying several powerful creatures, and then must defeat the game's final boss Lord Gwyn. To write it this way makes it seem very uncomplicated, but there are dozens of frustrating and obscure pathways and mechanics that make the journey a difficult and arduous one. Simply finding the route to the next area can be an adventure in frustration.

Reviews from the game's release in 2011 remarked heavily on the game's difference from what was then-popular. Simon Parkin (2011) wrote in *The Telegraph* that it "runs contrary to prevailing fashion" (np) in that it rewarded radically different things than contemporaries. Oli Welsh (2011) wrote that *Dark Souls* has "a stubborn unwillingness to explain itself that, when it comes to discovering the game's many secret techniques and subtleties, is a great part of its appeal." After highlighting many of the strange and mysterious mechanics of the game, Kevin Van Ord (2011) at

GameSpot said that the game was "a methodical journey into the frightening unknown. And that's what makes it so riveting" (np). These reviews are representative of the reception of the game in a general sense, but also in a very specific way. A cursory glance across an array of reviews of *Dark Souls*, *Dark Souls 2*, *Dark Souls 3*, and *Bloodborne* would reveal to any reader a tendency for players to make a claim that is perhaps embodied best by Parkin (2011) in his review of the game. He writes:

> [*Dark Souls*] is a game in which you must improve yourself before progress can be won. In that sense, it is as orthodox as the earliest arcade games and yet, in sticking fast to this fundamental, feels like the freshest game of the year. It's a game that asks you to look before you leap, to learn enemy attack patterns before launching your own offensives, to observe (np).

The idea that is central to all of these reviews, and indeed to the general reception of *Dark Souls* in games culture, is that it requires an intense amount of self-discipline to succeed at them. One needs to work on *oneself*, whether that means through absorbing knowledge or by practicing strategies of brain-hand-controller alignment, to succeed at this game. A player has to become *better*; they cannot merely persevere.

While the reviewers of *Dark Souls* came to this point via the empirical act of play, Robert Boyd (2012) has persuasively argued that this focus on the discipline of the self is pervasive across the spectrum of ways players can encounter *Dark Souls* including a website name that goads players (PrepareToDie.com), an "open" world that is fairly delimited in how you can approach it, and a wide range of possible ways to play the game. By allowing a player to tackle the game in their own way, on their own terms, but knowing that the game is specifically meant to be difficult, the total package of *Dark Souls* makes it clear that success and failure are all up to that player. It's just the player, their brain, and some buttons. In other words, it is a hybrid relationship between all of these elements, the assemblage, that allows *Dark Souls* and its attending diagram of the soulsborne to proliferate across the world of video games. The game's design was specifically crafted to afford this relationship between the friction of difficulty and the smooth, freeing feeling of finally overcoming adversity. When a player in *Dark Souls* dies, they are resurrected at a nearby bonfire, and they can simply tackle the same challenge with a little more knowledge than they had before. Death is never the end, but instead it is a gateway to another attempt and more chances at success. "The key to success does not lie in the player's agility or virtuosity with the controls," David Mecheri and Sylvain Romieu (2017) argue, "but rather in their sense of observation, strategy and self-control" (p. 23). It might be productive to amend this statement to say "already-attained agility or virtuosity," but this statement rings true for many players of and writers about the game. This is the kind of self-discipline that leads Keza MacDonald to call *Dark Soul*'s design philosophy one of "death as education" (MacDonald & Killingsworth, 2016, p. 187). Failing at the game is the impetus that one needs to get back up and try one more time.

This is precisely what demands the introduction of aesthetic category theory as a method for game studies. Death as education, or death as an opportunity for the improvement of the *player* rather than improvement of a *character*, is largely what comprises the design of the "soulsborne" genre of games.[3] Sometimes simply known as a "Souls" or "Soulslike" or "Souls-like" game, the genre has substantially deepened in the almost-decade since *Dark Souls*' release. Fans have created a tag on the PC gaming platform Steam for "souls-like" on that platform, creating a kind of *ad hoc* categorization of games that follow the design goals or mimic some of the mechanics of FromSoftware's series (Souls-Like, 2019, np). Games like *Nioh* (Koei Tecmo, 2017), *The Surge* (Deck13, 2017), and *Lords of the Fallen* (CI Games, 2014) are all identifiably from the same mold as *Dark Souls*. These are third-person action games with difficult encounters, complicated boss fights, a focus on exploration of a delimited environment, and very little forgiveness when it comes to canceling animations or exposing weakness. From a narrative point of view, none are even remotely as opaque as *Dark Souls*, and it is clear from these games that a soulsborne can be crafted from mechanical similarity. Writing for *PC Gamer*, Austin Wood (2017) decried the overuse of the souls-like label as a problem for the industry. Naming the aforementioned games alongside several others like *Titan Souls* (Acid Nerve, 2015) and *Dead Cells* (Motion Twin, 2018), Wood declares that "these games offer an absurd range of experiences" and that "[t]hese labels blindly hone in on a few specific traits, and consequently clump way too many different games together" (Wood, 2017, np). I agree with Wood that the creation of this coherent genre is imprecise, but it is also readily apparent that *all* genre discussion fundamentally operates as a way of talking about the broad similarities between media objects. After all, *The Shining* (Kubrick, 1980) and *Friday the 13th* (Cunningham, 1980) are both horror films, but we don't have any problem as a culture with understanding them as films that access different parts of that genre.

At the same time, I think that Wood is fundamentally correct in identifying a problem in the genre. These games *are* all different, and they *do* offer different kinds of experiences. They are not all dark fantasy games. The souls-like genre seems able to contain many different perspectives as well, from top-down 2D to side-scroller to *Dark Souls*' third-person action gameplay. What unifies them is an understanding of the player and the player's relationship to the world. Consequently, a more precise analytic of this issue is also what diagrammatics and aesthetic category analysis can offer video game studies.

The aesthetic category of Dark Souls

Ngai (2012) writes that her three aesthetic categories are able to, in the most broad and abstract way, best provide an analytic for understanding the relationship between subjects and aesthetics under late capitalism. These are "certainly not the only noteworthy ones in a postmodern culture marked by a stunning variety of aesthetic styles and terms, but they are the ones that [she] would argue offer the most traction for grasping its aesthetic situation as a whole" (Ngai, 2012, p. 233). Subgroupings of aesthetic experience like video games, due to qualitative differences in their affordances for the people who interact with them, *must* have different aesthetic categories that have a privileged relationship to explanatory capacity. In other words, while Ngai's categories might be the best in the broadest circumstances, there must also be specialized aesthetic categories that offer a better angle on specific media.

To argue that the soulsborne has transcended a genre label and become an aesthetic category is to, in some sense, make a heretical claim about the method I am arguing is so profound here. At the same time, while "the cute" is certainly a mode (cuteness can be everywhere), it is also a "genre" to some degree. *Hello Kitty* and its pretenders constitute an entire genre of visual culture. Animal friendship photographs and their attending memes are an entire genre of internet imagery, so much that websites such as *The Dodo* have sprung up to facilitate and monetize their distribution. A genre trips over into a generalized aesthetic category when the aesthetics, the mode of engagement, become attached to a program of subjectivation. Things are no longer simply cute; instead, a person experiences and performs certain affects, acts a certain way, and has a disposition toward the cute.

To bring together the various threads from earlier in this chapter, what we get from an analysis of the soulsborne, as an aesthetic category, is an attending set of claims. First, it unifies the claims of game scholars who see games as an act of discipline with a way of understanding subjectivation beyond a simple input and output model (Chess, 2017; Anable, 2018). Games do things to their players, certainly, but that process is part of a broader system of management of a player's identity across multiple play experiences. Second, a diagrammatic understanding of the soulsborne means that we can track its transformations and the modulating demands that it makes on its players, particularly in the world of design. Aesthetic category analysis might seem on face to be a static container, but assemblage theory allows us to track it across different instances. Finally, it allows us to make attending claims about the broader purpose of the discipline. Aesthetic categories manage a relation, and like Ngai I feel that one of the most operative ones is between the player and the system of capitalism that surrounds them. If, as I stated earlier, hybridity is a given in this system, then this entire methodology is merely a mode of addressing hybridity without the obfuscation of the term. Aesthetic category theory and its diagrammatic components are how hybridity gets to work on its various elements.

How diagrams and aesthetic categories operate in the soulsborne

When game scholars (Bogost, 2007; Chess, 2017) argue that games fundamentally operate on how we exist in the world, they find themselves in the company of most major claims about media objects since the onset of modernity. From Mary Wollstonecraft's arguments that romance novels are bad for women in 1792's *A Vindication of the Rights of Woman* to Neil Postman's media culture critique *Amusing Ourselves to Death* in 1985 to the video game violence debates of the 1990s (Donovan, 2010), we can draw a fairly easy line from media form to media form and claims that interacting with those media fundamentally affects us in some way. What distinguishes the game scholars from these previous claims (and this is probably impacted by their being in response to video game violence debates) is that they claim that interacting with video games can produce something more politically ambiguous (Bogost, 2007; Galloway, 2007). Interacting with games can generate a particular kind of interacting subject who embodies a mode of thinking about the world. In this framework, the existence of the soulsborne makes sense. The soulsborne is a mode of recognition that is developed in a player as the output of extensive play in the FromSoftware universe, and aesthetic category theory gives us a theoretical ground from which to understand these claims.

Additionally, Shira Chess' (2017) idea of "designed identity" is extremely helpful in parsing how *Dark Souls* subjectivizes particular players. In her *Ready Player Two*, Chess argues that the way women are understood by the industry has a significant impact on how they are positioned as players. When they are "constructed, designed, and managed by the video game industry," they are interacting with designed identity, which Chess writes is a "by-product—an unintended consequence of the repurposing of women's leisure practices into digital play, and the result of industrial practices that idealize specific (lucrative) audiences" (p. 5). While Chess focuses specifically on how designed identities work on women who play games, she is also naming a system, a mode of subjectivation that operates as a diagram that produces outputs in the form of specific kinds of players. When players are brought into "constructed identities suggested within game design, advertising, and narrative," they are being mediated through those identities (Chess, 2017, p. 6). The language of soulslike is a kind of mirror of recognition for these players, allowing them to see a game like *The Surge* and consider it as *for* them, despite being a game that is abstracted away from *Dark Souls* and developed by another company.

Considering assemblage theory and its concept of the diagram as the beating heart of aesthetic category theory also allows us to talk more robustly about shifts that happen within games. A term like "soulsborne," our "souls-like" is a discursive indicator of such a shift, since if a game was a *Dark Souls* game developed by FromSoftware, it would not need a more generic identifier. But aesthetic category theory and its attending diagram give us some additional purchase on this due to the mode of analysis that we have to undertake to understand how an aesthetic category like soulsborne, with its specific affordances, allows us to make the analytical leap from the object itself to an aesthetic category. One way of doing that is by looking to all of the shared properties of soulsborne games: A focus on combat, being unable to cancel animations and being forced to "go through" with every input, interconnected level design, a third-person perspective, and a general design that is focused on completing sections of the game and defeating large bosses at the ends of those sections. All of this has a somber tone and an oblique story that needs to be put together by the player community.

Diagrams give us the ability to speak about transformations within the broader set of qualities that soulsborne games have in common. What does it *mean* when the magic meter transforms from a use-based system in *Dark Souls* to a meter-based system in *Dark Souls 3*? What are the qualitative differences between magic and the mechanical artifice of a game like *The Surge*? What happens when the crunchy combat of *Dark Souls* gets transported into a linear, bonecrunching hard game like *Angvik*, which shares almost none of the qualities of *Dark Souls* and yet somehow *feels* like it does? These transformative questions are best addressed holistically as a shifting diagram rather than as free-floating qualities that appear and disappear at random in different game designs. Naming the soulsborne, and considering it as a constructive force within game design and criticism, allows us to speak from a position of an operating structure rather than one of discrete mechanics or modes of engagement.

Working on the self

The final opportunity available to game scholars via the aesthetic category method is one that draws a line between video games and capitalism itself. Ngai (2012) hinges all of *Our Aesthetic Categories* on the link between media objects and capitalism, and she crucially dodges questions of political economy to get at other, similarly fundamental ways of understanding the intersection between economics and aesthetics. She, nor I, discount that approach. At the same time, capitalism is as much in the production of commodities and accumulation of capital as it is in managing the relationships between humans, those commodities, and that capital. As Ngai argues, this happens via aesthetic categories because aesthetics modulate the relationship between abstracted capital and the individual's role in that system. We know to be available, energetic, and adaptable because we see it modeled for us on *I Love Lucy*.

Video games take it a step further because, as game scholars have noted, you actually need to plug yourself into the system to make it work (Galloway, 2007). You perform *actions* while playing a game. It is a more intensive form of subjectivation that is occurring in a more specific way. This argument morphs slightly more when we take seriously that *Dark Souls* and its genre-fied soulsborne existence can come to operate as an aesthetic category under capitalism. When the soulsborne begins to operate as a *category*, it modulates the relationship between the individual player and capitalism. If *I Love Lucy* makes viewers identify with Lucy and valorize zaniness, or the mutability of the subject under capitalism, then what does the soulsborne valorize?

We already have the answer in the game reviews quoted earlier. The constant focus on self-improvement and betterment due to extended and repeatable effort evokes a stance toward the subject that dovetails almost completely with the core tenets of neoliberalism. This is no mere Lucy working several jobs. Instead, the player of a soulsborne game becomes embroiled in a system that does not only demand that they identify with a malleable hero under capital, but instead that they *be* one. The entirety of the system of gameplay, marketing lingo, and genre constraints collapse down into them, highlighting the hybrid nature of this play. It becomes difficult at this point to say where the game or even the player's desire begin and end. As Parkin (2011) so eloquently puts it, "you must improve yourself." While grinding levels and becoming more powerful in the role-playing game sense of increased in-game stats and abilities is important, it is the fundamental trial-and-error discipline of gameplay that so many reviewers have used to distinguish these games from others.

This form of augmentation to meet the framework of the video game is something that has been commented on within the field of game studies, but mostly in the direct relationship to capitalism. Games require certain stances and modes of engagement from the human body, and as Chess (2017) writes, "when I play *Kim Kardashian: Hollywood*, my body is fixed in very specific ways to respond best to the small screen and maximize my playtime" (p. 155). In other words, as she puts it, "game controllers bind bodies to screens" (Chess, 2017, p. 161). In the case of mobile games, this mode of bodily management has to do with monetizable time via microtransactions, ad clicks, and ad views, but other games do similar work. Greig de Peuter and Noah Wardrip-Fruin (2009) note in their *Games of Empire* that games under capitalism are fundamentally composed of "in-game identities [that] are never entirely separated from the options provided by the actual social formations in which the games are set, from which their virtualities derive and into which they flow back" (Dyer-Witheford & de Peuter, 2009, p. 192). These claims are also prefigured by C.L.R. James' work *Beyond A Boundary*, his 1963 biography that points to the fundamental relationship between colonialism, sport, and the imperial center.

The situation that these works describe in specific detail, alongside the more general theories of games as training tools that emerged in the early 2000s in both game studies and game design, creates a theoretical terrain around the soulsborne genre. These are games in which the player can always pick themselves up again; there are no fundamental structural barriers to their success other than their willpower; they can solve this world with force, trial-and-error, and enough attempts. As critic amr al-asser (2016) notes in an essay on the design of *Dark Souls II*, the act of playing these games is much like wage labor: "There's an insecurity to your resources that induces a similar mindset. There's a drive to immediately spend resources on something more 'permanent,' be it self-improvement or possessions, even if you'd be better served in the long term by saving for more expensive things that would improve your quality of life" (al-asser, 2016). al-asser continues by asserting that the true attachment of the game to labor under capitalism, however, is not simply *performing* the labor, but the discourse around the labor itself. The constant call of the fan community is "all you need to do it work hard enough" due to the fact that game design appears to be interpellating all bodies equally; the game "exists in a structure that is perceived to be equally taxing on everyone" (al-asser, 2016). The soulsborne genre carries within it an expectation of a certain type of labor under a certain regime where an individual must rise to a meritocratic baseline in order to be valorized within the social. In game scholar Chris Paul's (2018) terminology, this is "meritocratic game design," which "teaches players that the only way to succeed is based on their own talent and effort, eliminating concerns about the structural issues surrounding access" (p. 61). To follow through on al-asser's analysis in conjunction with the game studies scholars I've mentioned so far, defeating a boss in a soulsborne game is like hitting a certain credit score or securing a loan. It is a marker of success in an arbitrary market that nonetheless demands that you evaluate yourself via that arbitrariness. To be a good soulsborne player is to be a good worker within the day-to-day operations of global capitalism.

Conclusion

What aesthetic categories offer us as a method for game studies is a way of drawing these relations. The soulsborne genre, its reviewers, its discourse, and its players and their assumptions and assertions about the game are not mere additional details that inform our ideas about the text. Instead, they are crucial to understanding the relationship between the video game, the aesthetics that we experience through and with it, and what those aesthetics do to us as subjects. More than this, video games are totalizing in the way that they bring us into the aesthetic fold. They contain audio and visual content, and they also ask us to produce *actions* and behaviors. If watching Lucy work jobs makes us a better labor pool under capitalism, then actually *doing* that labor must necessarily be a more intensive and extreme version of that same process. Ngai (2012) phrases this as "the 'putting to work' of affect and subjectivity" (p. 188). In the case of the soulsborne's valorization of labor and the demand that you always try again, no matter what, it might be appropriate to augment this into a moment of *doing* the work of subjectivity. The method of aesthetic category theory combined with diagrammatics allows us better access to this analysis, and grounds it in a mechanistic analysis of the always-existing hybridity that shoots across games culture. The soulsborne presents us with a useful case, but the reality is that this is a process that lives anywhere and everywhere, and tracking its mobility and how it morphs in particular use cases is what makes aesthetic category theory so useful for us here. It is now the work of game studies to find its diagrams and ruthlessly interrogate their shifting forms.

Notes

1 For an extensive argument on the philosophical trajectories that unify these two seemingly separate arguments, you can see my dissertation *Assembling An End* (2019). For now, maybe just trust me.
2 I am not discussing 2009's *Demons' Souls* in this piece due to space constraints, but it is obviously a clear building block of the "soulsborne" genre. *Dark Souls* shares enough DNA with it, including its third-person camera, combat mechanics, and director that an entire chapter could be written about the conceptual differences for the two. I hope to pursue this in future work.
3 Soulsborne is a portmanteau of *Dark Souls* and *Bloodborne*, two FromSoftware games directed by Hidetaka Miyazaki that share a design sensibility. The word "souls-like" is often used as well. I simply like soulsborne more.

References

al-asser, amr. (2016, April 11). "A Majula State of Mind: Dark Souls II & The Struggle." Retrieved from: https://medium.com/@siegarettes/a-majula-state-of-mind-dark-souls-ii-the-struggle-acbd5fd1874e

Anable, A. (2018). *Playing with Feelings: Video Games and Affect*. Minneapolis: The University of Minnesota Press.

Bogost, I. (2007). *Persuasive Games*. Cambridge, MA: The MIT Press.

Boyd, R. (2012, September 26). "Deep Dungeon: Exploring the Design of Dark Souls." *Gamasutra*. Retrieved from: http://www.gamasutra.com/view/feature/178262/deep_dungeon_exploring_the_design_.php?page=3

Chess, S. (2017). *Ready Player Two: Women Gamers and Designed Identity*. Minneapolis: University of Minnesota Press.

Cunningham, S. (1980). *Friday the 13th* [Motion Picture]. USA: Paramount Studios.

DeLanda, M. (2010). *Deleuze: History and Science*. New York: Atropos.

Deleuze, G. (1988). *Foucault*. Minneapolis: University of Minnesota Press.

Donovan, T. (2010). *Replay: The History of Video Games*. East Sussex: Yellow Ant Press.

Dyer-Witheford, N. & de Peuter, G. (2009). *Games of Empire: Global Capitalism and Video Games*. Minneapolis: University of Minnesota Press.

Foucault, M. (1977). *Discipline and Punish: The Birth of the Prison*. New York: Vintage.

Galloway, A. (2006). *Gaming: Essays in Algorithmic Culture*. Minneapolis: University of Minnesota Press.

Gee, J. (2007). *What Video Games Have to Teach Us About Learning and Literacy*. New York: Palgrave Macmillan.

Heineman, D. (2015). *Thinking about Video Games: Interviews with the Experts*. Bloomington: Indiana University Press.

James, C.L.R. (1963). *Beyond a Boundary*. Durham, NC: Duke University Press.

Joseph, D. (2013). "The Toronto Indies: Some Assemblage Required." *Loading... Journal of the Canadian Game Studies Association*, 11, 92–105.

Kubrick, S. (1980). *The Shining* [Motion Picture]. Burbank, CA: Warner Bros.

Kunzelman, C. (2016). "Subjective and Affective Adaptations: Remediation and the Playstation 2 Video Game." *Widescreen*, 6, 1.

Kunzelman, C. (2018). "Decaying Bioshock 2: Videogames, Assemblages, Rot." In: F. Parker & J. Aldred (Eds.), *Beyond the Sea: Navigating Bioshock*. Montreal: McGill-Queen's University Press.

Kunzelman, C. (2019). *Assembling an End*. (Unpublished doctoral dissertation). Georgia State University, Atlanta, GA.

MacDonald, K. & Killingsworth, J. (2016). *You Died: A Dark Souls Companion*. BackPage Press.

Mecheri, D. & Romieu, S. (2017). *Dark Souls: Beyond the Grave, Volume 1*. Third Editions.

Ngai, S. (2012). *Our Aesthetic Categories: Zany, Cute, Interesting*. Cambridge, MA: Harvard University Press.

Parker, F. (2013). "An Art World for Art Games." *Loading...Journal of the Canadian Games Studies Association*, 11, 41–60.

Parkin, S. (2011). "Dark Souls Review." *The Telegraph*, October 3, 2011. https://www.telegraph.co.uk/technology/video-games/video-game-reviews/8803351/Dark-Souls-review.html

Paul, C. (2018). *The Toxic Meritocracy of Video Games: Why Gaming Culture is the Worst*. Minneapolis: University of Minnesota Press.

Postman, N. (1985). *Amusing Ourselves to Death: Public Discourse in the Age of Showbusiness*. New York: Viking.

Taylor, T. (2009). "The Assemblage of Play." *Games and Culture*, 4, 331–339.

Van Ord, K. (2011). "Dark Souls Review." *Gamespot*. October 3, 2011. https://www.gamespot.com/reviews/dark-souls-review/1900-6337621/

Welsh, O. (2011). "Dark Souls." *Eurogamer*. October 3, 2011. https://www.eurogamer.net/articles/2011-10-03-dark-souls-review

Wollstonecraft, M. (2009). *A Vindication of the Rights of Women*. Oxford: Oxford University Press.

Wood, A. (2017). "The 'Souls-like' Label Needs to Die." *PC Gamer*. August 19, 2017. https://www.pcgamer.com/the-souls-like-label-needs-to-die/

11 #HushHarbors

Get Out, memes, and Twitter

Katreena E. Alder

On Sunday, March 4, 2018, Jordan Peele became the first black[1] individual to win an Academy Award for Best Original Screenplay for his 2017 directorial debut, *Get Out* (Desta, 2018). On the surface, *Get Out* appears to be a film that simply follows an interracial couple, Chris (Daniel Kaluuya) and Rose (Allison Williams), as they embark upon a visit to Rose's home to meet her parents. However, a major part of the story focuses on Chris' concerns about how he will be received by her family because he is black and she is white. In a memorable scene, Chris is sitting with Rose's mother (Missy) and, after answering a series of probing questions, he finds himself talking about the night his mother died. Missy is drinking tea and repetitively tapping her spoon inside her teacup. Unbeknownst to Chris, Missy is actually hypnotizing him with the repetitive tapping. We later learn that she is hypnotizing Chris so that he loses his personal autonomy. Because of the hypnosis, Chris becomes immobilized, both hands pressing into the arms of a large leather chair, tears rolling down his face (Sims, 2017). While he sits there, he sees himself falling into what looks like a black void with [presumably] no bottom or way to get out. While he falls, we see what he sees from a first-person perspective and look upon him falling. Everything that he can see becomes increasingly distant and, although he can hear things, he silently screams, unheard and trapped in the black void. The sound of Missy's voice tells him, "now you're in the sunken place." While it becomes clear, during the film, that being in the sunken place is a terrifying experience of being trapped in one's own mind, unable to move and react, the film's writer and director, Jordan Peele (2017), clarified, via a tweet, that the sunken place is also a metaphor for the experiences of marginalized individuals, who often feel trapped in silence when they see what is happening around them but are powerless [or feel powerless] to stop it. Given this, *Get Out* operates beyond the tropes of the horror genre, evoking a powerful commentary on society and provoking powerful response within it.

Since *Get Out*'s release, the "sunken place" scene has been used as the backdrop to many conversations on social media (Rayner, 2018). In particular, the film reached heightened levels of discussion on Twitter. In an article on inverse.com, Lauren Serner (2017) stated, "Unlike a typical horror movie—where the Twitter response would be exclamations over its craziest moments—the number one reaction was earnest appreciation for the film's centering of the Black American experience." Implicit within Serner's statement is an understanding of the film's cultural significance, yet it additionally alludes to using social networking sites (SNSs) as venues for gauging reception. Often, such reception is measured by considering the use of hashtags, tags, or algorithmically determined "trending topics." Interestingly, however, Hennig-Thurau, Wiertz, and Feldhaus (2015) suggest that the conversations happening on an SNS may actually shape the discourse—by which they refer to the possibilities for conversations occurring on an SNS to drive impressions and shape the discourse in a cyclic effect. Given this, we might look at SNS as meaning-making spaces that offer valuable insights about how a particular culture distills ideas and creates coherence in the world around them.

In this chapter, I consider one particular SNS—Twitter—as a meaning-making space for black Americans, amid the release of the film *Get Out*. I specifically look at Twitter because of its importance to black Americans as a space for expression (Brock, 2012). Following *Get Out*'s release, Twitter users employed GIFs, memes, and text to engage with some of the film's provocations about the black experience, using the hashtag #sunkenplace to organize their conversation. Importantly, though, by considering Twitter as a hybrid space, I am careful to avoid suggesting that the conversations occurring in this space were solely online conversations. Quite the contrary, I follow the lead of scholars who have suggested that online and offline spaces are necessarily entangled (de Souza e Silva & Sutko, 2008; Nakamura & Chow-White, 2011; Pink et al., 2018; Saker & Evans, 2016). As such, the conversations mobilized on Twitter are intrinsically entwined with the embodied, lived experiences of black Americans. For this reason, I argue that the concept of "hybrid space" offers a productive intervention for understanding the significance of these conversations. As a concept, hybrid space suggests that the digital and physical are fundamentally connected, whereby that which occurs in one of these contexts impacts the other (de Souza e Silva, 2006). From this perspective, understanding Twitter as a hybrid space recognizes that the conversations occurring on Twitter are shaped by the physical world that black Americans inhabit and, vice versa, that the physical world that black Americans inhabit is shaped by the conversations occurring on Twitter. In addition, Twitter's capacity to allow for playful behavior (by circulating memes, GIFs, and other content) seemingly lowers the stakes of entering into a conversation, while also shaping the conversation taking place. It allows users to experiment with meaning-making and to draw from layers of cultural meaning in order to "get at" the heart of issues that are often difficult to discuss. Viewed in this way, it is the capacity to play that productively mobilizes the discussion.

To this point, many scholars have already offered insights about Twitter as a communicative platform, capable of community building, social/

political action, and identity exploration. For instance, Twitter has been discussed as a catalyst to social justice (Blevins et al., 2019; Bonilla & Rosa, 2015; Kuo, 2018; Lu & Steele, 2019); as a space for black expression (Brock, 2012; Graham & Smith, 2016; Manjoo, 2010; Walls, 2017); and as a space for identity performance (Florini, 2014; Maragh, 2018). Specifically, Bonilla and Rosa (2015) suggest that Twitter holds a transformative power for digital activism and that being online can widen access to a larger community and, therefore, "create a unique feeling of direct participation" (Bonilla & Rosa, 2015, p. 7). Further, Walls (2017) demonstrates how Twitter is used by black individuals to interact with specific communities and to discuss issues important to them. In this chapter, I build on these discussions to understand black expression on Twitter as historically situated practices renegotiated through hybrid spaces. Without discounting the "transformative potential" of Twitter for black Americans, I follow Walls (2017) in considering Twitter as a contemporary iteration of the longstanding practice of creating African American Hush Harbors (AAHHs)—that is, Twitter, like other AAHHs, offers a space in which black Americans can discuss ideas, share experiences, and even playfully engage in social and cultural expressions. In doing so, however, I consider how the hybrid space of Twitter shifts the locale of the AAHH, allowing the discourse contained therein to unfold across spaces: physical/digital and local/distant. I additionally argue that it is through this hybridity that this "transformative potential" is unlocked.

To make this argument, I offer a case study of a contemporary AAHH that developed through the use of the hashtag #sunkenplace on Twitter following the release of the film, *Get Out*. The use of hashtags by the black community following the release of *Get Out* cultivated a seemingly safe space where African Americans could discuss aspects of their black experience. The cultivation of this space, via Twitter, resembles the cultivation of traditional AAHHs insofar as AAHHs were semi-private spaces where Black individuals could freely participate or discuss aspects of their Black experience(s), using AAHH rhetoric. As Vorris Nunley (2011) explains, AAHH rhetoric includes the use of nommo ("the power of word"), parrhesia ("fearless, dangerous speech"), and phronesis ("practical wisdom, intellect, and virtue") (pp. 44–47). As such, I use these terms as analytical categories for my study of the Twitter AAHH hybrid space created by #sunkenplace.

I proceed by addressing the following questions: (1) Does African American Hush Harbor rhetoric appear in the tweets surrounding the release of *Get Out*? (2) If so, how does this shape our understanding of the affordances of Twitter as a hybrid space for producing forms of community? To answer these questions, I collected 102 tweets with the hashtag #sunkenplace between February 17, 2017 and June 2, 2017. To analyze this data, I used a mixed-method approach including critical and qualitative content analysis and elements of Critical Technodiscourse Analysis.

This mixed-method approach helped me to unfold how meaning is created through information and communication technology practices and to understand how marginalized groups, whose voices are typically obscured, find "safe" places for interaction (Brock, 2009).

In what follows, I situate Twitter as a hybrid space (de Souza e Silva, 2006) to understand its affordances as a space for cultural exchange. Following this, I discuss the historical practices of creating AAHHs to argue for how the hybrid nature of Twitter allows for contemporary iterations of these practices to form. I apply this understanding through my study of #sunkenplace as a contemporary AAHH that demonstrates the presence of African American rhetorics. I argue that the hybrid space of Twitter offers the conditions for the practice of African American rhetorics, but that these rhetorics are re-shaped through the affordances of Twitter, which allow for sharing memes and GIFs as well as connecting with others who do not occupy the same time and space.

Twitter: blurring the lines

To understand Twitter's affordances requires, in part, to situate it within the affordances of social networking platforms more generally. Blank and Reisdorf (2012) suggest that platforms allow for network effects to emerge (p. 539). In making this claim they suggest that, through platforms, individuals can participate and communicate with each other to generate substantive action. As a platform, Twitter is remarkably able to grow given its scalability, and it is also able to maintain user engagement, particularly since it allows users to respond creatively through tweets and retweets that engage a variety of media.

Twitter boasts that it "is what's happening in the world and what people are talking about right now" (about Twitter, 2019). Twitter is a resource for people to "communicate and stay connected through the exchange of quick, frequent messages" (New user FAQ, 2019). People can read, communicate, connect, and exchange messages on Twitter; however, hashtags (#) help to organize and circulate content across the platform. When a person clicks on or searches for a hashtag, they see other tweets that use the same hashtag. By the same logic, using a hashtag means that one's tweet will appear with other tweets employing the same phrasing. If enough people use a hashtag, it will show up under different trends that Twitter displays, and any individual's Twitter page will also show trends that may interest the user. As such, Twitter is a space where many topics can be discussed— hence, Twitter produces a hybrid space by bringing topics from the physical world into the digital and, likewise, topics from the digital into the physical so that conversations proceed iteratively.

In understanding Twitter as a hybrid space, it is important to recognize that the space is not homogeneous but rather splintered into communities through the organizing principle of the hashtag. Among these communities and important for this chapter is Black Twitter—a Twitter community often created around the hashtag #blacktwitter Although comprised not only of black individuals, Black Twitter users primarily discuss issues related to black cultural expression. Brock (2012) defines Black Twitter as "a user-generated source of culturally relevant online content, combining social network elements and broadcast principles to share information" (p. 530). Black Twitter is a unique community within Twitter because it is relevant for the study of black cultural expression. As Lu and Steele (2019) explain, the use of hashtags "among black users must be understood historically and culturally" (p. 827). As I argue, hashtags can be used to produce contemporary AAHHs—spaces where individuals can safely "go" to engage in cultural exchanges.

African American Hush Harbors

AAHHs have been part of Black experiences in the United States since Africans were brought to the country and enslaved. Hush Harbors have been described as secretive religious meetings conducted by slaves in remote locations (Nunley, 2005): "places where slaves gathered to participate in various aspects of public life, hidden, unnoticed, and especially inaudible to their white masters" (Byrne, 2008, p. 17), and "secluded, usually wooded, places near the slave quarters where the enslaved could congregate for religious services and social gatherings" (Smith, 2010, p. 25). These spaces were also known as Bush Arbors because they were located in open spaces within nature and caves. Hush Harbors were important because they were spaces where African Americans could meet in the absence of the oppressive white gaze and had, therefore, freedom to articulate their experience in front of others familiar with that experience.

The original AAHHs needed to be secret, or removed from the public, in order to preserve and protect the individuals in those spaces. Today, although American slavery is gone, AAHHs still exist in spaces (physical, digital, or hybrid) where black people feel free to express themselves. Over the years, AAHHs have remained central to the experiences of Black Americans in the United States. Walls (2017) suggests that "rhetorical forums such as secret schools, underground railroad meeting places, and barbershops are places that have functioned and are functioning as AAHHs" (p. 398). Hush Harbors can be created anywhere and anytime, but what makes them unique is understanding the importance of what is being said and where it is being stated. Walls' discussion encompasses the historical location-specific hush harbors (e.g. underground railroad meetings) and more contemporary iterations (e.g. barbershops).

Although many studies of contemporary Hush Harbors look for physical locales in which identity is performed, Kynard (2010) suggests that Hush Harbors can also be reinvented in digital spaces. In making this claim, she offered a case study of an email listserv, which functioned as a

Hush Harbor for black female college students. In her study, she demonstrates that young black women, feeling silenced and disenfranchised in other spaces (e.g. physical classrooms, University campus, etc.), used email accounts to create a space where they could feel comfortable to communicate (p. 34). Similarly, Bruce Campbell (2009) discusses Blackplanet.com as a Hush Harbor for black individuals to generate "a deeper appreciation of the experiences and perspectives of other members of their community" (p. 18). As Campbell (2009) argues, "the ability to express one's perspectives and beliefs in online discussions—particular discussions occurring within a community that is central to one's offline identity—constitutes an important social resource for some users of this site" (p. 18). Significantly, these examples demonstrate that Hush Harbors need not be fixed in physical space but can transpire in hybrid spaces. While Campbell (2009) distinguishes between the offline and online identities, the way he references these two spaces implies their co-constitutive nature. This perspective is furthered by Delaney (2002), who explains "there is no outside to a wholly racialized world" (p. 7) which means that race can be found embedded within processes or systems, whether it is explicitly mentioned or not. Importantly, this perspective offers an ethical imperative for understanding Twitter as a hybrid space: That is, by understanding that the digital is constituted in part from the biases and prejudices that permeate the physical world, we can understand how Twitter exists a space for cultural engagement (rather than a place somehow devoid of the "real"). Taken a step further, we can recognize that Hush Harbors, formed in hybrid spaces, arise out of the fundamentally racialized world; they also shape that racialized world, in turn, through the constitutive rhetorics practiced therein.

Hush Harbor rhetorics

Nunley (2011) defines the rhetorical work being done in contemporary AAHHs as AAHH rhetoric. According to Nunley, African American rhetorics exist outside of Hush Harbors, but at a high cost: "African American rhetorics and their affiliated epistemes (knowledges), politics, and subjectivities are hollowed out for more acceptable public consumption" (p. 1). In other words, African Americans often downplay important and crucial facets of themselves, their experiences, and their knowledges to be more acceptable to those who do not understand their culture. For example, I might be someone who uses a raised voice to express my excitement about something, but because black women are often viewed as loud or boisterous, I choose to quietly celebrate. A behavioral change like this is also a strategy that can be associated with what Jones and Shorter-Gooden (2009 [2004]) call "shifting." They explain shifting as "a sort of subterfuge that African Americans have long practiced to ensure their survival in our society" (p. 6). Shifting is what black women do to accommodate the needs of others or to counter expected assumptions or stereotypes—in other words, to pacify others. Shifting is not always done in public; black women often shift in their home spaces. For example, if a black woman wants to discuss her hard day at work but her partner comes home and wants to talk, she'll shift into a supportive or listening mode for them and push her own needs to the side. Shifting impacts black women's health and well-being (Jones & Shorter-Gooden, 2009 [2004]) which is why spaces like AAHHs are so important.

While shifting is a concept primarily defined and applied to the experiences of black women, the idea that one must present aspects of themselves one way in one space and another way in other spaces is not just an African American experience. Goffman (1973) discussed how a person presents or performs based on how they may be perceived or what is learned about them. This is important because it speaks to an awareness that people have of how they are received and how they can work to be seen more favorably. In Hush Harbors, people feel free to be themselves, express their thoughts, opinions, frustrations, and fears. While people understand that they can still offend others in a Hush Harbor with their sexist, offensive, or unpopular opinions, Hush Harbors are spaces that allow for inflammatory language and moments of offense—even more so they exist as a space where these instances can be uniquely negotiated or handled less harshly.

Nunley (2011) offers an important perspective about how this attitude of openness and expression takes form in AAHHs. Specifically, he offers three dimensions of AAHH rhetoric: nommo, parrhesia, and phronesis. He explains nommo as "the material and symbolic power of the spoken word" (p. 3). Nommo relates to an understanding that through "human utterance or through the spoken word, human beings can invoke a kind of spiritual power" (Alkebulan, 2003). Nommo is the spiritual or religious understandings of words, and the origins of nommo can be traced back to the Dogon people of Africa (Karenga, 2003). Part of the power of nommo is that the black rhetor speaks their experiences and is empowered. While enslaved Africans were silenced in public spaces, they could speak freely in Hush Harbors. They could encourage one another, pray, and speak powerfully over themselves.

Nunley (2011) further explains that parrhesia refers to "speaking frankly, or speaking truth to power" (p. 1). Accordingly, parrhesia requires that "the rhetor puts herself at risk in speaking truth to power, to the dominant rationality, or to a hegemony that could result in loss of status, influence, resources, legitimacy, or life" (Nunley, 2011, p. 46). If these truths are discussed or shared outside of the Hush Harbor, there is a risk but, in spite of the risk, the rhetor speaks anyway with the goal of being real and honest. Hush Harbors, therefore, cultivate a space of "safe risks" where criticism and outspokenness are valued rather than oppressed, particularly when compared to the norms of society. For example, if a congregation member were to publicly disagree with a Pastor, that person is exercising parrhesia. The Pastor holds the higher position of authority, but the congregant feels led to speak frankly anyway. This may lead to consequences for the speaker but, as a Hush Harbor, the Black church is a space where speaking frankly can, and is sometimes, encouraged to happen.

Finally, phronesis is concerned with speaking with wisdom or intellect. Phronesis can be traced to the work of Aristotle and refers to the sharing of practical wisdom informed by life experiences (Chiavaroli & Trumble, 2018). Nunley (2011) explains phronesis as "more than quaint wisdom because it coalesces theory within lived everyday experience and usefulness" (p. 47). For example, an elder in the church who imparts wisdom or a word to the congregation demonstrates phronesis. A person demonstrating phronesis shares wisdom with others, so they can judge for themselves what to do in a situation and learn from what the rhetor has shared. Through Nunley's emphasis on the practiced rhetorics of Hush Harbors, it becomes clear that these are important spaces for identity performance and negotiation, particularly given the recognition that rhetoric is constitutive of our identities (Charland, 1987). This is particularly important to this study because Black users "often perform their identities" online through text, images, and other indicators (Brock, 2009; Florini, 2014).

In what follows, I apply these concepts of nommo, parrhesia, and phronesis to understand how the affordances of hybrid spaces, like Twitter, allow the formation of AAHHs through which African Americans rhetorics can be practiced.

Methods

I used a mixed-method approach that is comprised of critical and qualitative content analysis methods. In compliance with the first step of Bock, Isermann, and Knieper's (2012) quantitative content analysis, I established my data to come from Twitter, with tweets containing the hashtag #sunkenplace and my unit of analysis to be tweets. I collected all tweets with the hashtag #sunkenplace from February 17, 2017 through June 2, 2017. This date range includes the week prior to the release of *Get Out* up until the end of the film's initial run in theaters. My search returned 28 pages of data, which is comprised of 102 tweets. I included 41 tweets as part of my final data—the remaining were duplicates or replies to other tweets. I then coded these 41 tweets applying Nunley's categories of nommo, parrhesia, and phronesis. I additionally coded for a fourth category, which I called "visuals" that included tweets with visual information, such as photos, memes, and GIFs. These categories are important because they define and operationalize AAHHR which are characteristics I use to identify a Hush Harbor. The tweets analyzed in this study were all publicly accessible and not privately tweeted.

To analyze the data, I paired qualitative directed content analysis (QCA) with textual analysis informed by theoretical underpinnings of Brock's (2009) Critical Technocultural Discourse Analysis (CTDA). QCA is an approach to content analysis where the researcher uses predetermined categories to define codes and guide the coding of the texts. Additionally, I used textual analysis to view and identity GIFs and memes on Twitter that may visually represent aspects of AAHH rhetoric. Textual analysis is useful for understanding how texts can be interpreted at different points in time and how they can make meaning culturally. I apply textual analysis with QCA to interpret, manage, and organize the tweets I coded. To code the data, I used a codebook adapted from Bock, Isermann, and Knieper's (2012) five-step process of quantitative content analysis combined with QCA (Hsieh & Shannon, 2005).

#sunkenplace as a response, criticism, and commentary to *Get Out*

I organized the coded tweets into three categories: response, critique, and commentary. The first category, #sunkenplace in response to the film, includes tweets I identified as specifically written in response to the film. In other words, the tweets in this category are about the film, its impact, or messages contained within the film. The second category, #sunkenplace as critique, includes tweets that used #sunkenplace as a criticism of the behavior or behaviors of specific public or visible figures. The tweets in this category call out specific individuals and use #sunkenplace as part of the point the person who tweeted is trying to make. The last category, #sunkenplace as commentary, comprised tweets that were more general in nature but still used #sunkenplace. The tweets in this category included broader statements/comments about black culture. In what follows, I offer examples of responses, critiques, and commentary.

> *#sunkenplace as a response to the film*
> *The powerful message of #getout. The slavery of our bodies has become the slavery of our minds. Society conditions us into the #sunkenplace.*

This tweet, which discusses a form of contemporary mental slavery, demonstrates the presence of parrhesia. This user tweeted about the powerful message to discuss their perception of the contemporary society. In addition, this tweet involves a certain amount of risk involved in talking about slavery and presenting it as still active. Nevertheless, this user balances the risk by exercising phronesis—their username, which does not include their name—indicates a desire for privacy or anonymity. Further, while the aforementioned person's account is not locked, the image on their homepage is a picture of a shoe. There is a certain phronesis demonstrated by these choices, since social media has become a place that can interfere with professional opportunities and create issues for users who speak openly against the dominant discourse (Smith, 2013; Walls, 2017). Hence, this user's choices may emphasize an awareness about the prominence and visibility of social media and, at a minimum, this user demonstrates how to use the affordances of Twitter to speak without readily identifying one's self.

Other response tweets demonstrated nommo—the power of putting truth into one's words. Take, for instance, the following two tweets by different users:

Tweet 1: *on the theological implications #sunkenplace. "How can we ignore the loss of the soul for the sake of gaining the whole world?"*
Tweet 2: *Saw #GetOut this weekend and am still a little freaked. Might need to reevaluate some life choices #SunkenPlace?*

Both of these tweets demonstrated nommo because the users, identified or identifying as black individuals, exercise the power of putting their responses into words. Further, these tweets demonstrated phronesis by suggesting how this film prompted critical reflection about society and their own life. Collectively, these three examples demonstrate the affordances of Twitter as a space for African Americans to engage in response and to demonstrate Hush Harbor rhetorics in doing so.

#sunkenplace as critique

In addition to using Twitter as a space of response, users additionally used it for performing critique. Notably, there were three tweets specifically criticizing Ben Carson, an African American politician, who previously made statements that enslaved Africans were also immigrants who worked long and hard for less (Jan & DelReal, 2017). He even defended his statements claiming that a person "can be an involuntary immigrant" (Stack, 2017). Tweets about Carson, using #sunkenplace, were coded as nommo, parrhesia, and visual. For example:

> *Ben Carson went from neurosurgeon to surgery victim a long time ago, ya'll...#sunkenplace.*

This tweet contains parrhesia because the user makes a strong claim about a very public figure and someone in a position of power. Further, this tweet was coded visual because it included an image of Logan, a character from *Get Out* who is trapped in the sunken place, in a playful reference which suggests that Ben Carson has lost his autonomy as a black man.

Beyond tweets about Ben Carson, there were also two tweets criticizing the choice of Betsy DeVos as a keynote speech for Bethune Cookman's College graduation, a Historically Black College. Devos is the current

U.S. Secretary of Education and has been criticized for her policies and past practices, and thus was an unpopular choice as a speaker. For example, two tweets demonstrate the discontent with the Bethune administration's choice:

Tweet 1: *How can an entire HBCU administration be in the #SunkenPlace?*
Tweet 2: *SINK![emoji] When you've gotten too comfortable in the #sunkenplace #bethunecookman*

In both of these tweets, the hashtag #sunkenplace further contextualizes the criticism because it relates specifically to a space where people are knowingly trapped but powerless. The implication is that faculty and administration are acting against their own interests because they are in the "sunken place," despite being in power positions. Significantly, the second tweet also includes a meaningful image: DeVos is presumably presenting her keynote to the audience with members of Cookman's faculty/administration seating behind her. One of the faculty members, however, has a photoshopped Michael Jordan's crying face over their faces. Michael Jordan's crying face is a well-known meme that has widely circulated on Twitter. The picture, taken by the associated press during Jordan's 2009 Hall of Fame induction ceremony speech, and has often been used to express disappointment about something (Wagner, 2016). Placing it over the face of the College's faculty members expresses the user's disappointment with the faculty's keynote speech choice, alluding that they are lost in the "sunken place." These tweets were coded as nommo, parrhesia, and visual because they were direct critiques of Bethune Cookman College's administration.

Through these tweets, we can see how via Twitter, people have found ways to link an African American rhetorical tradition with popular culture and real-life experiences. In these tweets, AAHHs are not only spaces for individuals to uplift one another but also for offering opportunities for people to speak truthfully and freely about one another. Black users tweeting to critique Bethune Cookman College is exactly what AAHHs are about—a venue for publicly and "safely" expressing discontent.

#sunkenplace as social commentary

Following *Get Out's* plot, a number of tweets offered commentary about the social issues raised by the film, such as interracial dating. These tweets displayed still shots from the film to express feelings about everyday interactions and observations. For example:

Tweet 1: *white boy just sent me a DM saying he crushing on a sista [emoji] he cute af but imma pass. Ain't bout to have my ass in the #Sunken-Place [emoji] #Nope.*

Tweet 2: *Any Black person still wearing colored contacts in 2017 is totally in a #SunkenPlace. #SunkenTeaCup #HustleAndSoul*

These tweets connect the "sunken place" to a commentary on their personal experience and an indictment about a Black person's appearance. They are both coded as nommo and parrhesia, because the people who tweeted speak openly and are creating space for their words. There is also an inherent risk to tweeting publicly, but they chose to tweet their thoughts anyway. There are black people who proudly wear colored contacts, implying that they are in the "sunken place" which could be offensive.

Discussion

The tweets presented offer productive interventions and insights about the contemporary black experience. While the "sunken place" was introduced in the context of a fictional movie, Twitter helped move this idea into the public discourse and mobilize it as a form of response, critique, and commentary. The tweets criticizing Bethune Cookman's College, for example, demonstrate bravery in sharing critiques, opinions, and thoughts even though this may come at a cost for the users who do so. Importantly, though, these tweets also suggest a possibility of enacting change by speaking out or, at a minimum, not being complicit through silence. From this perspective, Twitter's use for creating an AAHH counters the dangers of the sunken place.

Black Twitter has helped present "uniquely black concerns and perspectives into the national discourse" (Graham & Smith, 2016, p. 433) and people tweeting responses to films with uniquely black perspectives can do the same. In my analysis, I found out that the majority of these tweets could be coded as nomos, parrhesia, and phronesis alike. Any person who tweeted that appeared to be black was coded as nommo because I assumed, unless otherwise presented, that the person was coming from a centered black worldview. In coding them as nommo, I was also centering their worldview and "unhushing" the narrative (Kynard, 2010) in a way that explores different ways of expression. Twitter users referenced issues that are significant to members of the black community and members of that community felt the need to comment on them. Coding tweets as nommo and positioning Twitter as a participatory platform support the understanding that in joining a public dialogue, their words acquire power in themselves.

When Black people publicly tweet, they are choosing to present a perspective into an open space. To a degree, any publicly released tweet can be coded as parrhesia because there is always a risk in speaking publicly. There is an inherent risk in being black and speaking publicly, because of the history of surveillance and oppression this community experiences. The inclusion of #sunkenplace further increases this risk because this hashtag specifically relates to marginalized groups. People's [implied] understanding of the risks involved with public tweeting using creativity to demonstrate phronesis by, for example, using avatars and other images that might mask users' identities.

The American Civil Liberties Union (ACLU) reported that the #blacklivesmatter movement, a movement to protest violence against the black community, has been watched by the American government since 2015 (Choudhury, 2015). This further cements the notion that parrhesia—or speaking frankly despite the potential risk—is inevitable on Twitter because of the potential of being surveilled. As such, I found out that parrhesia is always present in these Tweets because since people are always surveilled online, the internet is a place where speaking freely can cost individuals greatly, particularly for disenfranchised or marginalized groups. Additionally, when users who are not black engage with hashtags being used primarily by black users, they can also become part of the overall dialogue and use parrhesia. There can be risk involved in being an ally for disenfranchised people. In 2017, a white woman was killed in Charlottesville while protesting a white supremacy rally. This, of course, is not to say that this will happen if someone who is not black uses a hashtag made popular by black users, but it is to suggest that the "risk" associated with speaking out is real.

Hush Harbors were and are still created out of recognition of these risks, but part of the power of contemporary Hush Harbors is how people choose to engage within those spaces. There are likely many people on Twitter who have no real understanding or desire to understand what the "sunken place" means and have never used the hashtag. This does not decrease the importance of the concept, but it does mean that some may not acknowledge it. Contemporary Hush Harbors are also sometimes ignored by people who do not personally see them as relevant spaces, but this does not negate their importance. Twitter, as an AAHH, offers a powerful example of connecting to a wider public audience—of engaging in difficult conversations, despite the risk. Further, Twitter encourages playful exchanges about life experiences, commentary, and critique through the use of GIFs and memes from anyone on the platform. It is also a fertile ground for users to creatively contribute to different discourses about being Black in America or commenting on black experiences in America. *Get Out* is a horror film about an interracial relationship but it is also a commentary on a contemporary understanding of race in America. Twitter as a contemporary Hush Harbor allows people to present their embodied experiences by connecting the real of their lives to the fictional experience performed in a narrative film. It is also a space where anyone can participate but much of the understanding of the interactions come from lived experiences or understanding.

Conclusion

This chapter analyzed tweets containing the hashtag #sunkenplace as a reference to the film *Get Out* and its relationship to African American rhetorics. As a hybrid and uniquely participatory space, Twitter is open to many playful forms of expression. *Get Out* itself was not always the focus of the tweets, but rather the idea of the "sunken place" was used, often in conjunction with GIFs and memes, to critique and comment on different happenings. Understanding Twitter as a Hush Harbor is significant because the performative aspect of the space leaves opportunities for people to engage in playful ways. Like barbershops and churches, Twitter is a space where people choose to perform aspects of Hush Harbor rhetoric. If a black user uses the hashtag #blacktwitter, they are purposely choosing to enact blackness within that space. Unlike previous studies that focused on private or locked Twitter accounts, Walls (2017) analyzed Twitter as a Hush Harbor space where people in the African American community feel free to speak their minds. Following Walls, I found AAHH rhetoric to be present in public tweets and learned that Hush Harbor rhetoric need not always be private or from someone who knows they're using it. In this chapter, I extended Walls (2017) discussion of Twitter as a Hush Harbor by analyzing the particular hashtag #sunkenplace. I conclude that using #sunkenplace in a tweet is an indication that people want to be considered part of a conversation where race matters.

People's ability to tweet also emboldens them because it gives them options for how they want to introduce their embodied experiences as African Americans. If they want to mask their identity but highlight their blackness, they can; if they want to share publicly with no desire to shield, they can. Twitter is an important contemporary Hush Harbor because it broadens who can participate in these conversations. As demonstrated, the use of #sunkenplace spawned tweets where users seemingly understood their words and/or position of using those words from the African American community. When people tweeted #sunkenplace, it was often using AAHH rhetoric from a place of knowing about black experiences and in response to others. This encouraged more use of AAHH rhetoric. Although the sunken place has been introduced by Jordan Peele in a fictional film, it has been later on used in multiple ways to relate to people's real-life experiences. The hybrid nature of Twitter, temporal and expansive, allows people to contribute in and out of conversations. AAHHs were created out of necessity and a space for enslaved Africans to speak and exist freely. Contemporary AAHHs are also necessary spaces and Twitter extends this tradition.

Note

1 In this chapter, I use black and African American interchangeably; however, black is viewed as less restrictive as it includes the diaspora.

References

About Twitter. (2019). Retrieved March 24, 2019, from about Twitter website: https://about.Twitter.com/en_us.html

Alkebulan, A. A. (2003). The spiritual essence of African American rhetoric. In R. L. Jackson II & E. B. Richardson (Eds.), *Understanding African American Rhetoric: Classical Origins to Contemporary Innovations* (pp. 23–39). New York: Routledge.

Blank, G., & Reisdorf, B. C. (2012). The Participatory Web: A user perspective on Web 2.0. *Information, Communication & Society*, 15(4), 537–554.

Blevins, J. L., Lee, J. J., McCabe, E. E., & Edgerton, E. (2019). Tweeting for social justice in #Ferguson: Affective discourse in Twitter hashtags. *New Media & Society*, 21(7), 1636–1653.

Blum, J. (Producer), & Peele, J. (Director). (2017). *Get Out* [Motion Picture]. United States: Universal Pictures.

Bock, A., Isermann, H., & Knieper, T. (2012). Quantitative content analysis of the visual. In E. Margolis & L. Pauwels (Eds.), *The SAGE Handbook of Visual Research Methods* (pp. 265–282). London: SAGE.

Bonilla, Y., & Rosa, J. (2015). #Ferguson: Digital protest, hashtag ethnography, and the racial politics of social media in the United States. *American Ethnologist*, 42(1), 4–17. Doi: 10.1111/amet.12112

Brock, A. (2009). Life on the wire. *Information, Communication & Society*, 12(3), 344–363. Doi: 10.1080/13691180802660628

Brock, A. (2012). From the Blackhand side: Twitter as a cultural conversation. *Journal of Broadcasting & Electronic Media*, 56(4), 529–549.

Byrne, D. C. (2008). The future of (the) 'Race': Identity, discourse, and the rise of computer-mediated public spheres. In A. Everett (Ed.), *Learning Race and Ethnicity: Youth and Digital Media* (pp. 15–38). Cambridge, MA: The MIT Press. Doi: 10.1162/dmal.9780262550673.015

Campbell, J.E. (2009, April). *From barbershop to blackplanet: The construction of hush harbors in cyberspace.* Paper presented at the Media in Transition 6 conference, MIT, Cambridge, Massachusetts.

Charland, M. (1987). Constitutive rhetoric: The case of the Peuple Quebecois. *Quarterly Journal of Speech*, 73(2), 133–150.

Chiavaroli, N., & Trumble, S. (2018). When I say... phronesis. *Medical Education*, 52, 1005–1007. Doi: 10.1111/medu.13611

Choudhury, N. (2015, August 4). The Government is watching #BlackLivesMatter, and it's not okay. *ACLU*. Retrieved from https://www.aclu.org/blog/racial-justice/government-watching-blacklivesmatter-and-its-not-okay

de Souza e Silva, A. (2006). From cyber to hybrid: Mobile technologies as interfaces of hybrid spaces. *Space and Culture*, 9(3), 261–278. Doi: 10.1177/1206331206289022

de Souza e Silva, A., & Sutko, D. (2008). Playing life and living play: How hybrid reality games reframe space, play, and the ordinary. *Critical Studies in Media Communication*, 25(5), 447–465.

Delaney, D. (2002). The space that race makes. *The Professional Geographer*, 54(1), 6–14.

Desta, Y. (2018, March 4). Oscars 2018: Jordan Peele Wins an Oscar and makes history. *Vanity Fair*. Retrieved from https://www.vanityfair.com/hollywood/2018/03/oscars-2018-jordan-peele-best-original-screenplay-get-out

Florini, S. (2014). Tweets, Tweeps, and Signifyin' communication and cultural performance on "Black Twitter". *Television & New Media*, 15(3), 223–237.

Goffman, E. (1973). *Presentation of Self in Everyday Life.* Woodstock, NY: Overlook Press.

Graham, R. & Smith, S. (2016). The content of our #characters: Black Twitter as counterpublic [abstract]. *Sociology of Race and Ethnicity,* 2(4), 433–449. Doi: 10.1177/2332649216639067

Hennig-Thurau, T., Wiertz, C., & Feldhaus, F. (2015). Does Twitter matter? The impact of microblogging word of mouth on consumers' adoption of new movies. *Journal of the Academy of Marketing Science,* 43(3), 375–394. Doi: 10.1007/s11747-014-0388-3

Hsieh, H.F., & Shannon, S.E. (2005). Three approaches to qualitative content analysis. *Qualitative Health Research,* 15(9), 1277–1288.

Jan, T., & DelReal, J. A. (2017, March 6). Carson compares slaves to immigrants coming to 'a land of dreams and opportunity.' *The Washington Post.* Retrieved from https://www.washingtonpost.com/news/wonk/wp/2017/03/06/carson-compares-slaves-to-immigrants-coming-to-a-land-of-dreams-and-opportunity/?noredirect=on&utm_term=.aea614965597

Jones, C., & Shorter-Gooden, K. (2009 [2004]). *Shifting: The Double Lives of Black Women in America.* [Kindle version]. Retrieved from https://www.amazon.com/Shifting-Double-Lives-Black-America-ebook/dp/B001P9O32G/ref=sr_1_1?keywords=shifting+the+double+lives+of+black+women+in+america&qid=1571266781&sr=8-1

Karenga, M. (2003). Nommo, Kawaida, and communicative practice: Bringing good into the World. In R. L. Jackson & E. B. Richardson (Eds.), *Understanding African American Rhetoric: Classical Origins to Contemporary Innovations* (pp. 3–22). Retrieved from https://ebookcentral.proquest.com/lib/ncsu/reader.action?docID=1694364&ppg=24

Kuo, R. (2018). Racial justice activist hashtags: Counterpublics and discourse circulation. *New Media & Society,* 20(2), 495–514.

Kynard, C. (2010). From candy girls to cyber sista-cipher: Narrating black females' color-consciousness and counterstories in and out of school. *Harvard Educational Review,* 80(1), 30–52.

Lu, J. H., & Steele, C. K. (2019). 'Joy is resistance': Cross-platform resilience and (re)invention of Black oral culture online. *Information, Communication & Society,* 22(6), 823–837. Doi: 10.1080/1369118X.2019.1575449

Manjoo, F. (2010, August 10). *How Black People use Twitter: The Latest Research on Race and Microblogging.* Retrieved from https://slate.com/technology/2010/08/how-black-people-use-twitter.html

Maragh, R. S. (2018). Authenticity on "black Twitter": Reading racial performance and social networking. *Television & New Media,* 19(7), 591–609.

Nakamura, L., & Chow-White, P. A. (eds.). (2011). Introduction—race and digital technology: Code, the color line, and the information society. *Race after the Internet* (pp. 1–19). New York: Routledge.

Nunley, V. L. (2005). Hush/Bush arbors. In A. Prahlad (Ed.), *The Greenwood Encyclopedia of Black Folklore* (Vol. 2, pp. 651–653). Westport, CT: Greenwood Publishing Group.

Nunley, V. L. (2011). *Keepin it Hushed: The Barbershop and African American Hush Harbor Rhetoric.* Detroit: Wayne State University Press.

Pink, S., Hjorth, L., Horst, H., Nettheim, J., & Genevieve, B. (2018). Digital work and play: Mobile technologies and new ways of feeling at home. *European Journal of Cultural Studies,* 28(1), 26–38.

Rayner, A. (2018, March 17). Trapped in the Sunken Place: How Get Out's purgatory engulfed pop culture. *The Guardian.* Retrieved from https://www.theguardian.com/film/2018/mar/17/trapped-in-the-sunken-place-how-get-outs-purgatory-engulfed-pop-culture

Saker, M., & Evans, L. (2016). Everyday life and locative play: An exploration of Foursquare and playful engagements with space and place. *Media, Culture, and Society,* 38(8), 1169–1183.

Serner, L. (2017, February 28). Twitter went nuts over Jordan Peele's 'Get Out'. *Inverse.* Retrieved from https://www.inverse.com/article/28344-twitter-reaction-jordan-peele-racial-get-out

Sims, D. (2017, December 5). What made that hypnosis scene in Get Out so terrifying. *The Atlantic.* Retrieved from https://www.theatlantic.com/entertainment/archive/2017/12/get-out-hypnosis-scene-sunken-place/547409/

Smith, J. (2013, April 16). How social media can help (or hurt) you in your job search. *Forbes.* Retrieved from https://www.forbes.com/sites/jacquelynsmith/2013/04/16/how-social-media-can-help-or-hurt-your-job-search/#561444227ae2

Smith, S. E. (2010). *To Serve the Living: Funeral Directors and the African American Way of Death.* Retrieved from https://ebookcentral.proquest.com/lib/ncsu/reader.action?docID=3300886

Stack, L. (2017, March 6). Ben Carson refers to slaves as 'Immigrants' in first remarks to HUD staff. *The New York Times.* Retrieved from https://www.nytimes.com/2017/03/06/us/politics/ben-carson-refers-to-slaves-as-immigrants-in-first-remarks-to-hud-staff.html

Wagner, L. (2016, March 31). The evolution of the Michael Jordan crying face meme. *NPR.* Retrieved from https://www.npr.org/sections/thetwo-way/2016/03/31/472330783/the-evolution-of-the-michael-jordan-crying-face-meme

Walls, D. (2017). The professional work of "unprofessional" tweets: Microblogging career situations in African American Hush Harbors. *Journal of Business and Technical Communication,* 31(4), 391–416. Doi: 10.1177/1050651917713195

12 "You broke *Minecraft*"

Hybrid play and the materialization of game spaces through mobile *Minecraft*

Joel Schneier

Purchased by Microsoft in 2014, over 154 million copies of *Minecraft* have been sold as of 2018, making it one of the highest-selling videogames in history (Gilbert, 2018). Much of *Minecraft*'s popularity derives from its simple open-endedness: Players are placed into a block-like "algorithmic ecology" (Phillips, 2014, p. 113) that seemingly extends *ad infinitum* a world in which they can alter and explore the digital landscape through mining resources, crafting structures, surviving environmental threats, and even creatively modifying the game itself. *Minecraft Pocket Edition* (henceforth mobile *Minecraft*), a mobile version of the wildly popular and more frequently researched PC- and console-based game, involves players interfacing directly with their touchscreens to play the game with ultimately the same in-game objectives. Due to the similarities between the PC and mobile versions of the game, it is possible to play mobile *Minecraft* as if it were the PC version of *Minecraft*.[1] As a consequence, mobile *Minecraft* may appear bereft of characteristics typically associated with play in hybrid-reality or location-based mobile gaming (de Souza e Silva & Hjorth, 2009). Indeed, individual gameplay events may be isolated to occurring in living rooms, bedrooms, basements, etc., rather than engaging players in seemingly more frenetic interactions with their extended networked urban spaces, as in games like *Pokémon Go* (Hjorth & Richardson, 2017).

This chapter examines *Minecraft* (Mojang, 2011) as a game through which players may engage in collaborative and locative play that extends across vast game spaces—both digital and physical—through interfacing with mobile devices. As such, I discuss how hybrid play is materialized through seemingly *immobile* games, such as mobile *Minecraft*, and also how distributed co-present relationships are entangled together and materialized in mobile gameplay. In doing so, I offer a case study of collaborative play (previously discussed in Schneier & Taylor, 2018) in which I examine how players hybridize digital and physical game spaces. When individuals play mobile *Minecraft* with separate mobile devices on the same WiFi network, they are able to play collaboratively within the same uniquely generated digital game spaces (called seeds). I understand this form of collaborative play as "location-based" in the sense that players' real-world proximity is a precondition in order to access a shared digital game space through a wireless network. Once engaged in these spaces, players materialize such idiosyncrasies of their social relationships, digital literacies, gaming expertise, and in-the-moment gameplay in a manner that demonstrates the "blurring of borders between physical and digital spaces" (de Souza e Silva, 2006, p. 274). I argue that while the materialization of these game spaces may appear limited to physical proximity, the "spontaneous gamic performances" (Schneier & Taylor, 2018, p. 3434) that occur in these spaces highlight how collaborative mobile *Minecraft* play entangles and even remediates unique social and technological relationships between the bodies engaged in hybrid play.

In presenting this argument, I first outline an analytical framework for hybrid play. I frame hybrid play as performative in order to attend to how various distributed bodies synchronize through spontaneous gameplay. This involves considering what Barad (2003, 2007) identifies as a "posthuman" account of performativity that frames human–machine interfacing as entangling various bodies. Read through Barad's performative framing, mobile gaming devices are agential "apparatuses" that discursively collaborate with other agents—human and nonhuman—through their performances, thus conceptualizing mobile technology as extensions of the body. Then, I review prior scholarly work that positions *Minecraft* as both a "sandbox" videogame and a digital "playground," in Seth Giddings' (2014) terms, which makes the game ripe for researching various digital, social, and gamic literacies (Bebbington & Vellino, 2015; Brand et al., 2014; Dezuanni et al., 2015; Fanning & Mir, 2014; Mavoa et al., 2018; Trček, 2014). While focusing exclusively on mobile *Minecraft*, I contribute to this reading of *Minecraft* as a "playground" since this metaphor implies a simultaneous and active presence of multiple realities, i.e. a hybrid space. Finally, I provide an analysis of three collaborative mobile *Minecraft* gameplay sessions. These sessions, previously reported in Schneier and Taylor's (2018) comparison of console/PC and mobile *Minecraft* play, involved a *microethological* (Giddings, 2009; Giddings & Kennedy, 2008) study of gameplay that documented multiple audio-visual data channels in order to synchronously map the coordination between digital and physical game spaces (Taylor, 2006; Taylor, Jenson, & de Castell, 2009). Unlike Schneier and Taylor (2018), however, I exclusively examine mobile *Minecraft* in order to attend to how game spaces are materialized through instantiations of play that hybridize various spaces. Furthermore, drawing upon Balmford and Davies' (2019) observations, I additionally attend to how various co-present bodies in the game space—even if those not directly interfacing with gameplay apparatuses—are enfolded into gameplay.

Framing performativity and hybrid play

Judith Butler (1999) defines the body as "a variable boundary, a surface whose permeability is politically regulated" (p. 177). Butler suggests that bodies do not exist as "beings" that were assigned *a priori* socio-political categories, such as gender, but as something highly variable and contingent that is always "becoming" through "incessant and repeated action of some sort" (p. 143). Butler calls this process of bodies continually becoming *performative*, because it "suggests a dramatic and contingent construction of meaning" (p. 177). In order to examine how mobile technology is entangled with how individuals are *performative*, Barad (2003) extends Butler's framing to argue that it is necessary to further collapse the boundaries between human and nonhuman bodies by examining the site of their intra-activity: The apparatus.

According to Barad (2003), apparatuses are "(re)configurings/discursive practices that produce material phenomena in their discursively differentiated becoming" (p. 820). Barad proposes that any apparatus—whether a scientific instrument or mobile gaming device—co-constructs phenomena along with human participants. Instruments of gameplay, therefore, co-configure the experiences of players, "materializing' the players" bodies and experiences through the distributed "intra-acting" components that are brought together through gameplay. Further, since mobile devices are always on, portable, collapse distances, and can serve multiple simultaneous uses, they allow individuals to collaboratively redefine what it means to intra-act in spaces that are simultaneously physical and digital (de Souza e Silva, 2006; de Souza e Silva & Hjorth, 2009; Hjorth, 2017; Humphreys, 2012). For example, since the flatness of a touchscreen interface on a mobile device collapses inputs and outputs, Parisi (2018) argues that touching the screen is "encountered simply as a homogenous and dedifferentiated tactual space" (p. 282). He argues that this flattening of an interface into a "unidirectional information channel" (p. 286) means that the touchscreen can be purposed for various forms of intra-activity. It is, therefore, possible to see mobile touchscreen devices as a malleable apparatus that allows for human and machinic components to spontaneously shift between different performances—i.e. "(re)configurings/discursive practices" (Barad, 2003, p. 820)—that materialize the intra-acting bodies in variable ways.

Butler's (1999) conceptualization of bodies as a permeable surface is, therefore, a curious phrasing, considering that touchscreen interfaces themselves appear quite literally as permeable interactive surfaces. Farman (2012) has argued that "ubiquitous or pervasive computing often seeks to create an environment in which the technologies remain invisible" (p. 7). In other words, mobile interfaces, which themselves appear simultaneously ever-shifting and invisible, may be seen as a machinic extension of organic bodies. Of course, as Farman emphasizes, these extensions and uses are nevertheless culturally, socially, and politically contingent. Mobile devices are themselves, therefore, anything but "natural" extensions of the body; however, as Butler argues, in particular socio-political contexts, individuals intra-acting with these interfaces may seize upon mobile technology and make it a material and contingent part of their performances. In this way, a child playing mobile *Minecraft* engages an embodied performance that is necessarily different from a child playing Nintendo Gameboy that is different from a child playing with a paddleball. In each case, the human and machinic bodies performatively intra-act, but each performance is contingent upon what these intra-acting bodies can do when brought together in a particular context.

In the case of mobile and locative technology, such as smartphones, Farman (2012) argues that because these devices allow individuals to access vastly distributed digital networks, they engage two simultaneous forms of bodily perceptions: that of "being-in-the-world" and "reading of the world and our place as an inscribed body in the world" (p. 33). Farman calls this the "sensory-inscribed body," as it "serves as a bridge between the body as sensory and body as sign system" in order to "work in conjunction to produce the embodied space of pervasive computing culture" (p. 33). This may be demonstrated through the classic example of using a GPS-enabled mobile application, such as Google Maps, to visualize one's physical location. In this example, this dual perception means simultaneously *feeling* physically present in a space, *seeing* one's signified location through the GPS application, and *coordinating* these perceptions in order to meaningfully move about both worlds in order to, for example, walk to a coffee shop. Read as a Baradian apparatus, the mobile locative device, therefore, serves as the site at which the sensory-inscribed body is continually materialized through intra-activity between interfacing bodies.

In addition to offering a conceptualization of bodies as continually "becoming," Butler's (1999) performative framework requires attending to time in relation to bodies. After all, if bodies are not "beings" but are "being," then what a thing *is* depends entirely upon the space and time in which it is performed. As with bodies, Barad (2007) argues that temporalities are materialized through the performative intra-action in a form of quantum entanglement, so that, for example, workdays are configured as a unit of time according to the relationship between labor at a factory. The ways time may be experienced, therefore, bear direct relationships to how bodies intra-act in time and space, and this may be particularly evident in the way mobile technology is used to maintain relationships across space and time, called *co-presence* (Hjorth, 2007; Urry, 2007). Farman (2012) has noted that, even when mobile technology is used for transmitting asynchronous messages in order to maintain social relationships, "simply by being tethered to the device, we are engaging in a sensory inscription of continual co-presence that does not require the modes of immediacy typically attached to the practices of synchronous communication" (p. 108). Hjorth (2007), in turn, argues that this is particularly "prevalent in the practices of mobile technologies and game spaces," as well as mobile applications that engage both social networking and gamic elements because such applications are continually in flux in real- and mediated-time (Frith, 2013; Hjorth, 2017; Humphreys, 2011).

Mobile *Minecraft* and momentary play

Part of what makes *Minecraft* play such a fascinating playground for researchers is its seeming malleability. The variations in play afforded in each block-like, procedurally generated game world (i.e. *seeds*), and the manner in which players are able to collaboratively or individually shape the game worlds effectively renders each gameplay event unique. Furthermore, *Minecraft's* game modes allow players to strategically alternate between styles of play that give players either restricted resources (Survival mode) or unrestricted resources (Creative mode). Players are additionally able— and, in some cases, institutionally encouraged in educational contexts[2]—to modify the game worlds in order to customize their experiences.[3] As stated previously, in thinking of *Minecraft* as both a digital and metaphorical playground, we may see *Minecraft* play as engendering a "two-way flow between environment and children" (Giddings, 2014, p. 124). As such, various researchers have investigated how *Minecraft* play has real-world developmental and educational impacts on children, with a predominant focus on play with console- or PC-based versions (Bebbington & Vellino, 2015; Brand et al., 2014; Dezuanni et al., 2015; Fanning & Mir, 2014; Mavoa et al., 2018; Trček, 2014). However, examining mobile *Minecraft*, which can be played across various relationally intimate spaces, in addition affords observations of how players may spontaneously engage co-present relationships and literacies through everyday play that may otherwise fall outside the purview of institutionalized educational spaces.

Mobile *Minecraft* is an incredibly popular platform, especially among young children. Mavoa et al. (2018) report that among a sample of Australian children between the ages of 3 and 12, a tablet or smartphone device is the primary platform for playing *Minecraft*. This is supported by Marsh et al.'s (2015) findings in the UK, in which *Minecraft* is among the most popular mobile applications for children under the age of 5. As such, mobile *Minecraft* offers opportunities to observe a "playground" space as the site of hybridized social, gamic, and digital literacies/realities. Indeed, a growing body of researchers have sought to examine such playgrounds, frequently through forms of observational ethnographic work that follow players across spaces and gaming platforms. For example, Dezuanni et al. (2015) observed pre-adolescent female *Minecraft* players in Australia, and Trček (2014) interviewed pre-adolescent male players in Slovenia, both in and out of school. By concentrating on various bodily configurations of play (i.e. where and how they played, and who they played with), Dezuanni et al. (2015) argue that the development of expertise was constantly "transient and contested" among various spaces and assemblages (p. 161). Trček (2014) similarly demonstrates that *Minecraft* players negotiate various nonhuman components and assemblages to build expertise. Participants in Trček's study detailed how they played *Minecraft* across a combination of gaming platforms (mobile and PC) and spaces (collaborative and solitary), engaged with local and distant social networks and paratexts (e.g. YouTube and various wikis) to discuss and develop gaming expertise, and even remediated *Minecraft* play and planning through LEGOs and ad hoc schematics. These studies demonstrate that *Minecraft* expertise may be developed through a complex array of spaces, performances, materials, and gaming devices that consider but do not center on mobile *Minecraft*.

As further noted in Balmford and Davies (2019), use of different plat-forms to play *Minecraft* is in part a negotiation of the particular social contexts and households of individual players. Since play may occur across and enfold various spaces, each space may index particular embod-ied performances. Again, invoking Barad's (2003) notion of the appara-tus, specific spaces intra-act with the players and their devices in order to co-configure the discursive becoming (i.e. gameplay) in that game space. Observing players within the context of a single space may, however, offer researchers a seemingly stable context in which to observe the two-way flow embodied within that space. For example, Hollett and Ehret's (2015) ethnographic observations of Parker, a 12-year-old oncology patient learn-ing to play *Minecraft* during a hospital stay, noted the numerous ways in which gameplay in a hospital room involved a two-way flow of intra-acting components. They centered their analysis around various "interruptions" in gameplay, from audible blips from medical machinery to the incursion of medical staff into Parker's field of vision. Throughout the details of such "interruptions," Hollet and Ehret (2014) examined how Parker maintained himself "as agentive and in control of his body and how others responded to it" (p. 1863). Interruptions, therefore, become highly meaningful mo-ments in gameplay, since sudden shifts in attention to other vectors in the game space—from ringing doorbells to flatlining heartrate monitors—serve as material evidence to players they are engaged in an intense "cy-bernetic feedback loop" with other material components in the game space (Giddings, 2009; Giddings & Kennedy, 2008).

In the examples described earlier, the game spaces and gameplay hard-ware (both of which are apparatuses) are primarily static. Schneier and Taylor (2018) observe that various *Minecraft* players playing on PC or con-sole versions more frequently engaged in what was termed *monumentary* play, which is identified as play concerned with establishing and maintaining seeds in order to manipulate the algorithmic landscape and erect complex structures. Such meticulously crafted structures may serve as meaningful symbols demonstrating gamic achievement and expertise, which Schneier and Taylor (2018) suggest may be fittingly engendered by sitting at a sta-tionary computer or console interface, which locks players into a cybernetic circuit so that players' eye-gaze can remain fixed on the screen rather than the input mechanisms.

Playing *Minecraft* on a mobile device, however, converges input and out-put components onto the touchscreen display so that eye-gaze and touch are competing for the touchscreen's relatively limited surface space (Parisi, 2018). Moving an avatar requires pressing a semi-transparent directional button-pad that is overlaid onto the bottom corner of the screen; manipu-lating the camera orientation requires swiping on the screen; and engaging in attack or dig actions with quick or long presses onto an onscreen object. These inputs may involve simultaneous discrete or continuous contact with the touchscreen, and, depending upon how a user engages in this input process, the screen may be obscured during inputting. Bodily movement and gesticulation while playing mobile *Minecraft* may appear quite frenetic since there is not necessarily a one-to-one input/output configuration, and the mobile gaming device can enfold multiple spaces into the game space itself. Indeed, Balmford and Davies (2019), as well as Schneier and Taylor (2018), observed what Giddings (2014) describes as unique "versions of reality" and "rule-bound artifices" that are generated through games and play (p. 7). These realities appeared to extend and reconfigure *a priori* performances (i.e. relationships between players, developing gamic expertise, etc.), but also involved "haptic and spontaneous gamic performances" (Schneier & Taylor, 2018, p. 3434). In Balmford and Davies' (2019) observation of mobile *Minecraft* play as situated within family spaces (and frequently on shared devices), familial rules regarding appropriate play were often spontaneously renegotiated as players explored new gamic affordances, such as blowing up sheep with blocks of TNT or having avatars "shake hands" (p. 12–13). Further, even if only one or two family members interfaced with the game through a single device, other family members were often enfolded into play (even if not directly touching the device) by moving in and out of the shifting game spaces (i.e. rooms within the family house, or even ad hoc spaces at the dentist office) or observing or imposing 'rules' on off- or on-screen play. Play would occur in such spaces as living rooms, bedrooms, kitchens with bodies seated on couches or even lying on floors, all while being coordinated around everyday events in and out of players' family's homes. Even in unfamiliar game spaces, players appeared to resume familiar rules for play (both digital and physical), even if they spontaneously discarded those very rules when it suited their own enjoyment.

While *momentary* play (Schneier & Taylor, 2018) may not be limited to mobile devices, the haptic-mobile affordances of the touchscreen interface, as well as the entanglement between *Minecraft* expertise and computational literacies, may indeed co-configure *Minecraft* play as performatively momentary. This does not only demonstrate Farman's (2012) argument that the sensory-inscribed body engages in continually synchronous performances through mobile interfacing, but also Gidding's (2014) argument that "[g]ames and play are at once material and imaginary" (p. 3), as continually co-present play may flow seamlessly between physical and digital spaces. In other words, children engaging in collaborative mobile *Minecraft* play may demonstrate the multi-directional flow of physical, social, developmental, digital, and gamic realities through hybrid play.

Charting spontaneous moments in hybrid play

Schneier and Taylor's (2018) participatory observations from collaborative gameplay sessions of mobile *Minecraft* play involved a *microethological* (Giddings, 2009; Giddings & Kennedy, 2008) study of mobile and console-/PC-based *Minecraft* gameplay with multiple audio-visual recordings to observe on- and off-screen game spaces, and used ELAN 4.9.1[4] to align the two audio-visual channels, as is demonstrated in Figure 12.1. Such simultaneous recordings have two benefits: First, coordinating both channels affords "view [of] events as they occurred on- and off-screen simultaneously rather than enforcing, via instrumentation, *a priori* distinctions between events happening" in the physical and digital game spaces (Schneier & Taylor, 2018, p. 3426); and second, it allows for what Barad (2007) calls a "diffractive reading" of different configurations of gameplay, which attends to how apparatuses—i.e. mobile, console, or PC videogame apparatuses—that agentially co-configure the entangled realities centered around gameplay (p. 146). Here, I focus exclusively on observations of mobile *Minecraft*, not to compare different digital gaming apparatuses, but to attend to how spatial realities are materialized through mobile gameplay. After all, following Balmford and Davies' (2019) observations that various co-present bodies may be enfolded into mobile *Minecraft* game spaces, I suggest that the simultaneous audio-visual observations from Schneier and Taylor (2018) are ripe for a new form of analysis that attends to this "blurring of borders between physical and digital spaces" (de Souza e Silva, 2006, p. 274). In doing so, I demonstrate how mobile *Minecraft* play is evocative of a particular kind of hybrid play that pulls in various distributed realities, literacies, relationships, etc., through collaborative performances within game spaces that are spontaneously configured by various human and nonhuman bodies.

I analyze three participant groups, A, B, and C. Participants ($N = 6$) all regularly played mobile *Minecraft* with other participants within their groups. The primary difference between gameplay observed for this study and these participants' everyday gameplay was that gameplay for this study took place in a formal research space on a university campus (which participants in this group opted for) and included the researcher as part of play. While participants S and O were previously familiar with this space (as well

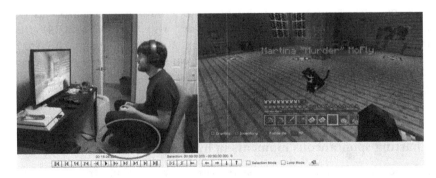

Figure 12.1 A screenshot from ELAN 4.31 coordinating multiple video files. Copyright: Joel Schneier 2019 (Left)/Mojang 2009–2019 (Right).

as familiar with the researchers), participants in Groups B and C had neither met the researchers nor been to the research space previously. Further, the parents of participants in Group B noted that while participants C and J commonly play various kinds of games together, including *Minecraft*, it is rare that they are continually present in the room with them throughout play as they were during the observation.

Group A: *"you broke* Minecraft*"*

Participants S and O's gameplay session occurred on a Saturday afternoon in March of 2016. The two brothers, along with their father, trundled into the research space with a paper grocery bag filled with healthy snacks, and their individual tablets in plain black cases (Figure 12.2). The research space was arranged with two couches facing one another with a small table in between (this is where the snacks were placed). A number of short stools were littered around the space, which O, the five-year-old, immediately seized. With S seated on a couch opposite to the researcher and their father (who put on headphones and began working on his own laptop), gameplay began by first debating which seed to go into. This tug-of-war was continual throughout the play session, with the researcher being the metaphorical rope in between. S wanted to play in his seeds in order to demonstrate his skills in Survival mode, and O wanted to remain in Creative mode. This perhaps was due to the fact that, at nine years old, S was becoming more skilled at more quintessential *Minecraft* tasks. For example, according to S's mother, S would commonly watch videos about *Minecraft* play, and would even draw plans for structures he would later attempt to make in the game. During the play session, he frequently rattled off information

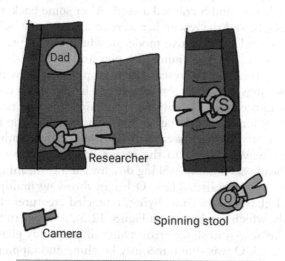

Figure 12.2 Group A gameplay arrangement. Copyright: Joel Schneier 2019.

about different kinds of weapons or structures to craft depending upon the resources available. Further, as observed in Balmford and Davies (2019), S was insistent on certain "rules" of play, for example, that playing in his seed in Survival mode meant that all players had to start with nothing in their inventory—otherwise, it was "cheating."

O, on the other hand, appeared to balk at any such predetermined rules. At the first mention of switching from Creative to Survival mode in his brother's seed, O opted to leave the seed entirely and open one of his own. "Do anything you want to in my world," O would say in an attempt to entice the researcher into his world. As detailed by their parents, S and O frequently played "together" through this sort of oscillation. While they were frequently on the same couch or in the same room playing together (due to how their parents structured screen time), they would typically remain in their own separate seeds, and only pop in-and-out of a shared seed in order to antagonize or, in some cases, aid one another. That S had more refined digital literacy skills, and was more familiar with popular *Minecraft* personalities on YouTube, suggested that S engaged more deliberate knowledge building about *Minecraft* play, perhaps yearning for more complex ways to play *Minecraft*.

O, on the other hand, appeared more interested in exploring the confines and limitations of *Minecraft* himself. External expectations of how to play *Minecraft*, i.e. "rules" that S appeared to enforce, were, therefore, anathema to O, which is why he insisted, "Do anything you want to in my world." In other words, in order to maintain his own sense of gamic expertise, O preferred to remain in his own seeds where his avatar could not be harmed, he could kick anyone out, and he could make and do anything he wanted to within the confines of the default inventory.

One particular moment appears to locate these converging realities— the moment when O and S crashed a seed. After some back and forth between seeds, O, S, and the researcher were in a seed made by O. This was an entirely flat world in Creative mode, in which O had previously made glass structures and spawned numerous pigs and sheep. S slouched on the couch, trying to convince the researcher to arm his avatar with a bow and arrow to shoot pigs. O sat on a stool next to his brother's couch, smiling and spinning himself occasionally on the chair. This was nearly an hour into the play session, and their father had begun glancing up to the brothers more frequently, perhaps weary of the time or that both were in the same seed. As S was talking to the researcher about bows and arrows, O's avatar's head was notably looking downward (i.e. meaning that O had pulled up his inventory list). Then, O began throwing multiple gray eggs that spawned ghasts (large gray, flying, tentacled creatures that mob and shoot fireballs, which can be seen in Figure 12.3). As S began tapping frantically upon his screen to shoot arrows and kill the many ghasts that were filling up the seed, O was simultaneously laughing and tapping maniacally on his own screen to spawn more and more ghasts. S exclaimed, "Whoa! Too many! Shoot the ghasts!" as the brothers kept tapping on their screens

Figure 12.3 Participant O spawning ghasts. Copyright: Mojang 2009–2019.

while laughing and wriggling in their seats as ghasts filled the researcher's screen. Within seconds, the researcher's screen was experiencing severe lag, and all three players exited the seed. S then told his brother to permanently delete that seed, which made O laugh even harder. "Nice work guys," one of the researchers said, "you broke *Minecraft*."

Group B: "I'm gonna ban you"

Participants C and J, both nine years old, considered each other best friends. Their mothers were friendly with one another and remarked that since they lived nearby, play dates were quite frequent as they had grown up together. The two would regularly play *Minecraft* as well as other games (digital and other). Once in the research space, the two boys sat down on the same couch with their mothers seated on the opposite-facing couches, and the researcher sat on a stool next to their couch, able to occasionally glance both of their tablets (Figure 12.4). Their mothers socialized quietly during much of the play session, although the two would frequently fall silent to observe their boys as well.

Like Participant S, C and J each claimed widespread knowledge about *Minecraft*, and that they both watched YouTube videos for *Minecraft* play. The two friends, again like S, also appeared eager to demonstrate their knowledge and skills with *Minecraft*, toward one another and to the re-searcher. As such, like S, both claimed various forms of "rules" for play, and violating these rules would result in the other threatening to "ban" the other. In the play session, though, once one of them made a claim to a spe-cific "rule," such as to not harm the avatar of the owner of the seed or look

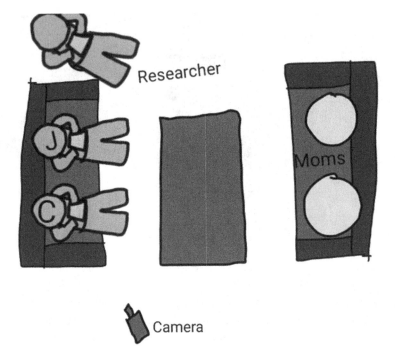

Figure 12.4 Group B gameplay setup. Copyright: Joel Schneier 2019.

at the other's screen, that "rule" was deliberately violated by the other. On two occasions, this resulted in J following through with his threat to "ban" C, by changing the seed settings to private, thereby automatically ejecting C and the researcher from the seed. While these rules appeared to primarily center around *Minecraft* "etiquette," perhaps specific to their own collaborative play, there was one instance early in the session when J reminded C of the "first rule of *Minecraft*," to not dig up soil directly beneath one's own avatar (the result being that the avatar could dig into a cave and fall to their avatar's death). Of course, C immediately began digging beneath his avatar's feet, and eventually became buried in sand and suffocated. In other words, the "rules" that both C and J laid competing claims to appeared to be at once specific to their friendship's competitive style of play (a norm, according to their mothers), as well as to their developing (and competing) expertise related to playing *Minecraft*.

This may be further demonstrated by one sequence of events toward the end of C and J's play session. Like Group A, C and J both preferred to play in their own seed so that they could enforce their own rules. After going back and forth, the researcher spawned a new seed of his own as a "neutral" ground to play in. Upon entering this new seed, C and J quickly surveyed the area around where they spawned. J spotted a procedurally generated village in the distance, and loudly exclaimed, "I claim black-smith!" C, on the other hand, spotted a temple in a desert-like terrain and claimed the temple as his. These "claims" allowed the two boys to tempo-rarily maintain some form of civility toward one another as they occupied distant digital spaces, while simultaneously being co-present in the same physical space on the couch.

Within a few minutes, though, C's avatar came into the village where J had claimed blacksmith. In that time, J had gathered many of the crops that the non-playable villagers had grown, as well as gleefully killed many of the villagers. As C's avatar came into the village and began similarly gathering crops, the two friends began what can only be described as a digital "slap-fight," which involved the two tapping the screen frantically to attack one another with their avatars' hands. This prompted multiple respawns from them both, with the "slap-fight" continuing unabated after each respawn, and each exclaiming, "Quit it!" In one case, J even exclaimed, "I'm gonna ban you!" having forgotten that he was not the owner of the seed. While the researcher expressed amusement to their mothers, both boys remained in the same seated position on the couch, occasionally glancing at one an-other's screen (again, another "rule" violation) while they continued to tap frantically upon their screens. Eventually, both mothers interceded and sug-gested that it was time to end the session, as both mothers appeared dis-proving of this behavior. Nevertheless, as C and J packed up their tablets, both began talking about a future play date and said that they appreciated playing with the researcher because he "respected the rules."

Group C: father and son

Unlike Groups A and B, participants in Group C played together on the same tablet device rather than on their own. Participant BB was eight years old and played *Minecraft* with his 30-something-year-old father, partici-pant P. Despite the researcher having multiple mobile devices available for them to play on, BB and P insisted that they normally play on the same tablet device and as the same avatar made by BB. They had also played in the same seed, set to Creative mode, in which they had been constructing multiple structures together for some time. Within the research space, both sat on the same couch, with P seated just behind his son. Their tablet rested on the table, and during multiple moments in their play session, P's arms would come from behind his son to gesticulate on the touchscreen, while BB's hands would "unlock" from the screen (Figure 12.5).

Throughout their gameplay, BB and P primarily focused upon build-ing structures that BB had observed from other media, such as Hagrid's hut from the *Harry Potter* movies. Within the seed, BB also showed the researcher a tower with a throne room and dungeon they had previously made. During construction of Hagrid's hut, BB and P would often deliberate about what materials to use, and B would often hand off the construction

Figure 12.5 Group C arrangement. Copyright: Joel Schneier 2019.

process to his father when more repetitive tasks were required. Unlike participants in Groups A and B, BB was primarily concerned with building structures to save in this seed, and often referenced other media as well as other YouTubers he had watched that demoed how to make complex structures in *Minecraft*. Despite his interest in erecting structures, i.e. a bias toward *monumentary* play, BB nevertheless demonstrated a willingness to spontaneously shift directions. Whether it was changing the designs for Hagrid's hut so that it lacked a door (so that a villager designated "Hagrid" couldn't walk out), or renaming an underground spider trap the "Chamber of Secrets" (again, in reference to the *Harry Potter* series), BB was all-too-willing to reconfigure the digital space's relation to other imagined spaces at a moment's notice.

While BB and P, therefore, appeared to invoke what may be the expected form of gameplay they may engage in at home, there were moments when BB's spatial experiences within this observed game space were noticeably interrupted. For example, as mentioned, BB and P played on the same device, using the same avatar. However, in being invited into this observed game space by the conditions of a formal research project, and thereby inviting the researcher into their seed, an atypical element was introduced in the game space: the researcher's avatar. Indeed, as part of documenting their in-game play, the researcher's avatar followed around BB and P's avatar, and even was tasked with contributing to constructing Hagrid's hut at one point. However, this led to three moments when BB moved his avatar's first-person perspective to suddenly reveal another avatar on his screen.

Each of these moments resulted in BB exclaiming, "Ahh! You scared me!" In these moments, BB's exclamation and gaze shifted quickly between the tablet and the researcher, thereby acknowledging the simultaneous unexpected presence of the research in digital space and expected presence in physical space.

Conclusion: on hybridized, entangled realities

In each of the aforementioned spontaneous moments in gameplay, I have demonstrated how various realities were entangled together within the game space. When locating *Minecraft* play through both the mobile device and the game space itself as an apparatus, it is possible to observe players bringing together their gamic expertise, developing digital literacies, and interpersonal relationships into the already synchronously present physical and digital worlds. In engaging in collaborative mobile *Minecraft* play, participants synchronously coordinated their physical and digital bodies within the game space, resulting in spontaneous events that were both wholly unique (and conditioned upon) to the physical location in which they played, as well as yet another performative instantiation of their play. Whether it was S and O giddily crashing a seed with ghasts, C and J constantly vying for the upper hand, or BB's surprise at the presence of the researcher's avatar, these participants all brought their lived experiences into the game space. Play was both physically and digitally embodied, as well as co-present with various relationships, knowledges, and sense of selfhood. Based on these conceptualizations of bodies and time, we can examine hybrid play through Butler's (1999) and Barad's (2003) performative frameworks, as well as how these performances maintain co-presence within and through these spaces (Balmford & Davies, 2019; Farman, 2012; Hjorth, 2007).

First, conceptualizing mobile gaming devices as a body (Butler, 1999) positions these apparatuses as agential apparatuses (Barad, 2003, 2007) that performatively intra-act with the players in particular game spaces in a manner that extends and co-configures the body. This may be seen through attention to the micro-coordination between hybrid spaces through spontaneous moments that demonstrate the "blurring of borders between physical and digital spaces" (de Souza e Silva, 2006, p. 274). For example, in Group A, participant O crashing his own seed demonstrated his effort to impose his own threshold of control upon gameplay through disregard of his older brother's "rules." This act rendered both the digital and physical game spaces O's domain, as his brother desperately attempted to kill the ghasts through despite the lag while O laughed gleefully. In other words, through embodied entanglement with the mobile *Minecraft* apparatus O imposed his own sense of "order" on both digital and physical spaces simultaneously. This may be similarly observed from the slap-fight and claims to digital spaces between C and J in Group B, or even BB exclaiming in fright at the sight of the researcher's avatar. Each moment demonstrates a "two-way flow between environment and children" (Giddings, 2014, p. 124), an intimate entanglement of players, co-present bodies, mobile apparatuses, as well as digital and physical game spaces. In thinking of these spontaneous evocations of hybrid spaces as bodily entanglements, it is possible to see each moment as part of player's continual becoming that is conditioned and exerts control upon the multiple overlaid game spaces. Researchers who seek to use mobile *Minecraft* as a vehicle for educational and developmental outcomes would, therefore, do well to attend to how the complex entanglements of spaces and bodies are part and parcel to *Minecraft* play.

Second, following Hjorth (2007) and Farman (2012), observations of *Minecraft* play through mobile interfacing additionally demonstrate that as bodies are performatively entangled through new coordinated senses, what Farman (2012) calls the "sensory-inscribed body," various co-present bodies and relations are reinforced and reperformed. Balmford and Davies (2019) argued that as mobile *Minecraft* is played in various familiar and unfamiliar spaces both physically and digitally co-present bodies are pulled into gameplay. A parent walking through a living room, friends from school, siblings, or even the family dog can become accessories to play. In observations from this current study, these co-present relationships were reperformed and in a continual state of becoming. This was demonstrated by the reperformance of familiar relational dynamics, particularly S and O's as well as C and J's constant vying for control of the seed, a reperformance of ongoing dynamics of their relationships. Furthermore, BB's attempts to recreate elements from *Harry Potter* media or YouTube videos demonstrate how distant or imagined relations can simultaneously be made co-present through the game spaces. Through this lens, mobile *Minecraft* play can be seen as another mode through which individuals use mobile interfacing and technology to iteratively manage and construct co-presence through the digital and physical game spaces. Mobile communication researchers who study the communicative construction and coordination of physical and digital spaces would therefore benefit from additional attention to mobile games, such as *Minecraft*, that afford vast hybrid spaces in which individuals can manage co-presence, in spite of mobile *Minecraft*'s seemingly immobile and non-communicative appearance.

Individuals engaging with mobile technology, whether for play, communication, or various other forms of intra-activity, necessarily materialize an extended and always-in-flux reality that collapses spacetime, and this may be observed through attention to interfacing as the site of the apparatus. Read this way, hybrid play is a performance that enfolds digital and physical realities as well as various other layers of bodily- and temporally contingent meanings and realities. As I suggested through an examination of spontaneous moments in collaborative play of mobile *Minecraft*, the social, relational, developmental, and gamic realities of players are pulled into the game spaces that hybridize the digital and physical realities.

Notes

1 In September 2017, the "Better Together Update" effectively rendered all versions of *Minecraft* (regardless of platform or device) the same game (Davies, 2017). Prior to this, *Minecraft Pocket Edition* was the version of *Minecraft* exclusively for mobile Android and iOS devices.
2 See Microsoft's Minecraft Education Edition website, which includes various institutionalized examples of Minecraft's use in educational settings https://education.minecraft.net/
3 See "mods" entry on the *Minecraft* wiki https://minecraft.gamepedia.com/Mods for links to various examples.
4 ELAN is software developed by Lausberg and Sloetjes (2009) to annotate audio and video data channels simultaneously. This allowed the author to annotate two video sources from the gameplay sessions simultaneously.

References

Balmford, W., & Davies, H. (2019). Mobile Minecraft: Negotiated space and perceptions of play in Australian families. *Mobile Media & Communication*. Advanced online publication: https://doi.org/10.1177/2050157918819614.

Barad, K. (2003). Posthumanist performativity: Toward an understanding of how matter comes to matter. *Journal of Women in Culture and Society*, 28(3), 801–831.

Barad, K. (2007). *Meeting the universe halfway: Quantum physics and the entanglement of matter and meaning.* Durham, NC: Duke University Press.

Bebbington, S, & Vellino, A. (2015). Can playing minecraft improve teenagers' information literacy? *Journal of Information Literacy*, 9(2), 6–26.

Brand, J., de Byl, P., Knight, S.J., & Hooper, J. (2014). Mining constructivism in the university: The case of creative mode. In: Garrelts, N. (ed.) *Understanding Minecraft: Essays on play, community, and possibilities.* Jefferson, NC: McFarland, 57–75

Butler, J. (1999). *Gender trouble: Tenth anniversary edition.* New York: Routledge.

Davies, M. (2017, September 20). The Better Together Update is here! [Web log message]. Retrieved from https://minecraft.net/en-us/article/better-together-update-here

de Souza e Silva, A. (2006). From cyber to hybrid: Mobile technologies of interfaces of hybrid spaces. *Space and Culture*, 9(3), 261–278.

de Souza e Silva, A., & Hjorth, L. (2009). Playful urban spaces: A historical approach to mobile games. *Simulation & Gaming*, 40(5), 602–625.

Dezuanni, M., O'Mara, J., & Beavis, C. (2015). 'Redstone is like electricity': Children's performative representations in and around Minecraft. *E-Learning and Digital Media*, 12(2), 147–163.

Fanning, C., & Mir, R. (2014). Teaching tools: Progressive pedagogy and the history of construction play. In: Garrelts N (ed.) *Understanding Minecraft: Essays on play, community, and possibilities.* Jefferson, NC: McFarland, 38–56.

Farman, J. (2012). *Mobile interface theory: Embodied space and locative media.* New York, NY: Routledge.

Frith, J. (2013). Turning life into a game: Foursquare, gamification, and personal mobility. *Mobile Media & Communication*, 1(2), 248–262.

Giddings, S. (2009). Events and collusions: A glossary for the microethnography of video game play. *Games and Culture*, 4(2), 144–157.

Giddings, S. (2014). *Gameworlds: Virtual media and children's everyday play.* New York: Bloomsbury.

Giddings, S., & Kennedy, H. W. (2008). Little Jesuses and fuck-off robots: On aesthetics, cybernetics, and not being very good at Lego Star Wars. In: Swalwell, M. and Wilson, J. (eds.) *The pleasures of computer gaming: Essays on cultural history, theory, and aesthetics.* Jefferson, NC: McFarland, 13–32.

Gilbert, B. (2018, October 1). 'Minecraft' is still one of the biggest games in the world, with over 91 million people playing monthly. *Business Insider.* Retrieved from https://www.businessinsider.com/minecraft-has-74-million-monthly-players-2018-1.

Hollett, T., & Ehret, C. (2015). "Bean's world": (Mine) crafting affective atmospheres of gameplay, learning, and care in a children's hospital. *New Media & Society,* 17(11), 1849–1866.

Hjorth, L. (2007). The game of being mobile: One media history of gaming and mobile technologies in Asia-Pacific. *Convergence,* 13(4), 369–381.

Hjorth, L. (2017). Visualizing play: A case study of a camera phone game for playful re-imaginings of place. *Television & New Media,* 18(4), 336–350.

Hjorth, L., & Richardson, I. (2017). Pokémon GO: Mobile media play, place-making, and the digital wayfarer. *Mobile Media & Communication,* 5(1), 3–14.

Humphreys, L. (2011). Who's watching whom? A study of interactive technology and surveillance. *Journal of Communication,* 61(4), 575–595.

Humphreys, L. (2012). Connecting, coordinating, cataloguing: Communicative practices on mobile social networks. *Journal of Broadcasting & Electronic Media,* 56(4), 494.

Lausberg, H., & Sloetjes, H. (2009). Coding gestural behavior with the NEUROGES-ELAN system. *Behavior Research Methods, Instruments, & Computers,* 41, 841–849.

Marsh, J., Plowman, L., Yamada-Rice, D., Bishop, J. C., Lahmar, J., Scott, F., Davenport, A., Davis, S., French, K., Piras, M., Thornhill, S., Robinson, P., & Winter, P. (2015). *Exploring Play and Creativity in Pre-Schoolers' Use of Apps: Final Project Report.* Retrieved from www.techandplay.org.

Mavoa, J., Carter, M., & Gibbs, M. (2018). Children and Minecraft: A survey of children's digital play. *New Media & Society,* 20(9), 3283–3303. doi:10.1177/1461444817745320

Mojang. (2011). *Minecraft* [PC game]. Stockholm: Mojang.

Parisi, D. (2018). *Archaeologies of touch: Interfacing with haptics from electricity to computing.* Minneapolis: University of Minnesota Press.

Phillips, A. (2014). (Queer) algorithmic ecology: The great opening up of nature to all mobs. In: Garrelts, N. (ed.) *Understanding Minecraft: Essays on play, community, and possibilities.* Jefferson, NC: McFarland, 106–120.

Schneier, J., & Taylor, N. (2018). Handcrafted gameworlds: Space-time biases in mobile Minecraft play. *New Media & Society,* 20(9), 3420–3436.

Taylor, N. (2006). Mapping Gendered Play. Loading... *Journal of the Canadian Games Studies Association,* 1(1).

Taylor, N., Jenson, J. & de Castell, S. (2009). Cheerleaders, booth babes, Halo hoes: pro-gaming, gender and jobs for the boys. *Digital Creativity,* 20(4), 239–252.

Trček, F. (2014). "The world of Minecraft is cubic": Lego blocks for e-kids? *Teorija in Praksa,* 51(1), 162–190.

Urry, J. (2007). *Mobilities.* Cambridge: Polity.

Index

Note: *Italic* page numbers refer to figures and page numbers followed by "n" denote endnotes.

Printed in the United States
by Baker & Taylor Publisher Services

Printed in the United States
by Baker & Taylor Publisher Services